The six-foot Hinged Man
poses with **Chief Henry, the
world's most photographed
Indian,** in Cherokee, NC.

A Fireside Book

Published by Simon & Schuster

New York   London   Toronto

Sydney   Tokyo   Singapore

the NEW ROADSIDE *America*

The Modern Traveler's Guide to the Wild and Wonderful World of America's Tourist Attractions

doug KIRBY

ken SMITH

mike WILKINS

FOR SUSIE, SHEILA, AND KEN'S "HONEY GIRLS"

FIRESIDE
Simon & Schuster Building
Rockefeller Center,
1230 Avenue of the Americas
New York, New York 10020

First Fireside Edition 1992

FIRESIDE and colophon are registered trademarks of Simon & Schuster Inc.

Manufactured in the United States of America

10   9   8   7   6   5   4   3   2   1

Library of Congress Cataloging in Publication Data
Kirby, Doug.
    The new roadside America : the modern traveler's guide to the wild and wonderful world
of America's tourist attractions / Doug Kirby, Ken Smith, Mike Wilkins.—Rev. ed., 1st
Fireside ed.
    p.   cm.
    Rev. ed. of: Roadside America. 1986.
    "A Fireside book."
    Includes index.
    1. United States—Guidebooks. 2. Automobile travel—United States—Guidebooks.
I. Smith, Ken, date-   . II. Wilkins, Mike. III. Roadside America. IV. Title.
E158.K56 1992
917.304'928—dc20   92-4064
                                                                                CIP
ISBN: 0-671-76931-6

Drawings and maps by Doug Kirby
Body Eclectic medical drawing by Phoebe Gloeckner
New Souvenir photography by Brigitta Hanggi
Original Souvenir photography by Dina Ferrante-Smyth

PHOTO CREDITS

Cover: Carter Peanut (Plains, GA); Weeki Wachi Mermaids (Weeki Wachi, FL); World's Largest Muskie
(Hayward, WI); Talking Paul Bunyan (Brainerd, MN); Carhenge (Alliance, NE) by Doug Kirby, Ken
Smith, Mike Wilkins.

Back Cover: Dixie Evans, Exotic World (Helendale, CA); World's Largest Uncle Sam (Lake George,
NY) by Doug Kirby, Ken Smith, Mike Wilkins. Wendell Hansen and Macaw (Noblesville, IN) by Susan
King Kirby. Prabhupada's Throne is courtesy of the Palace of Gold.

Attraction photos courtesy of:

Page

12—Moccasin Bar
14—Gatorland Zoo
16—Clyde Peeling's Reptiland
20—Marineland of Florida
21—Noah's Ark
26—Brigitta Hanggi
29—Dinosaur Land

32—Prehistoric Gardens
41—Liberace Foundations for the Performing
      and Creative Arts/Liberace Museum
45—Lawrence Welk Resort Village
48—Flintstone Bedrock City
48—The Ralph Foster Museum
55   (center)—Greg Peretti

(Photo credits continued on page 287)

Acknowledgments

Thanks to Stuart Gottesman—the relentless professional (and the only editor at Simon & Schuster recognized as a third class relic by the Catholic Church). Thanks also to Jeff Neuman, our man in the Corridors of Power.

We salute the Chambers of Commerce for providing information and help, even when they couldn't figure out what the hell we were up to. We genuflect, as always, to those heroes of tourism—the attraction owners—and the thousands of men and women that continue to keep our eyes a-poppin.

For leads, theories, encouragement, and cameras, special thanks to: Christine Agnelli; Gail and Scott Archibald; Jack Barth; John Crouch; Rob and Darilyn Dinsmoor; the Doherty family; Erwin Dugasz; Kevin Dzuban; Scott Fischler; Richard Grigonis; Ward Halligan; Ollie Hallowell; Brigitta Hanggi; Celeste Hoffner; Eli Hull; Michael Kaplan; Steve Kessler; Fred, Carolyn, and Julie King; Jack and Marlene Kirby; Jay and Denise Kirby; Dan Lieb; Fred Malley; Wayne and Cheryl Mason; Paul "Montana" McLeod; Jacquie Mraz; Donnalynne Pompper; Margaret Pultz; Carol Riley; Paul Rother; Mark Sarto; Herbert and Anita Smith; Sean Smith; Ron Spooner; Steve Szubak; Linda and Wayne Torbett; Joe Valeriani; Perry Vasquez; Betsy Wilkins; Jeff Wilkins; Robert and Gloria Wilkins; Dottie Wilson; and the late Curtis J. Frick.

Contents

ve seen, digested, written too many notes, and tried to strike a
. In these pages you'll find the eccentric and the stupid, the rock
nd the ultraweird. We give an oxen statue that pees a fair shake
any celebrated "folk art environment." And maybe we like the
more.

ways, our findings are authenticated with impeccable field instru-
such as the six-foot-tall Hinged Man (a scientifically calibrated
of measuring claims of largeness) or the Mystery Spot Test Kit™.
nputer database spits out weird maps, sorts readers' tips, and
s at the speed of light.

*time, and Road Hypnosis. Ideas crackle, defective neon in the
stance. Photo opportunities hop into our headlights—and are
verything is vacation grist. Grain silos blur into sacred Madonna
windmills ape Don Quixotic theme parks. Familiar phantasms
peek through our bug-congealed windshield—our old publicist,
"AM Des Moines! I got you on AM Des Moines!" through rotted
d the relentless Lady Bird Johnson smashing billboards with
n fists.*

w Roadside America is our baby—a two-headed, psychoactive
baby. One is the benevolent head of hearty appreciation and fair
other is the wrathful head of judgment, brought down on those
oze our favorite attractions, turn old Stuckeys into notions
and charge $17.99 to watch glass get blown.
face us at every interchange. Unclean vandals spirit away mon-
d gravestones. Moralists demand that attractions give back
bones, yet cozy up to the superrich who stole Geronimo's head.
urs and readers nag us about sites they couldn't find in our first
understanding that if it wasn't in *Roadside*, it just wasn't
h. Unless, of course, it happens to appear in the *New Roadside*.

*! A horrifying head-on collision! Your foot finally finds the
amid a shifting dune of loose-pack brochures and maps. Snow
edar trinkets tumble across the rear window ledge as you veer
e of the living. A 'Bago with out-of-state plates burns along
! Catch it on camcorder and keep moving! Keep moving!!!*

precious days of leisure end in another excursion to the dull
of Six Flags, Busch Gardens, and Disney? Or has the restless
tourism gotten hold of you?

New Roadside America show you the way. We're in your
ow what you're thinking. You'll never get us out.

—Doug, Ken, Mike

Roadside De[...]

Highway string cheese stretches ahead—
rear up out of the shimmering expanse[...]
eyes like a deck of thumbed playing ca[...]
to-go, a leaky cooler . . . keep moving![...]
lit at night? Drive 200 miles and find o[...]

"Let us be your travel brain." That[...]
edition of *Roadside America* was publ[...]
allowed us to burrow into the soft spo[...]
assume command, at least for a week[...]
laughed with abandon.

Roadside America was a starting p[...]
pack better. Compression is the code[...]
This edition is crammed with new [...]
forgotten places, barely remembered p[...]
breaking research down to a sentence[...]

The first things we jettison are ph[...]
admissions, and directions. You wa[...]
road and look yourself! Does your he[...]
another 500 miles! Maybe you didn'[...]

Will that bologna factory tour cl[...]
Drive faster! Interstate constructio[...]
it down, get on those back roads! M[...]
outlet stores in loser destinations[...]
the horizon. Ancient, doddering B[...]
talizingly across the road ahead[...]
horror. Not today! Bullet past ar[...]

Tourism does not sit still. Wil[...]
provising, bending with the mag[...]
attractions appear, established [...]
parking lots. Small towns desper[...]
They'll do almost anything to g[...]
zoo, they *know* you have corn.

We'[...]
balanc[...]
solid a[...]
against[...]
ox ever[...]

As a[...]
ments,[...]
method[...]

Our co[...]
loses fil[...]

Night[...]
dark di[...]
gone! E[...]
mirages[...]
race up t[...]
cackling[...]
teeth; an[...]
her ten-t[...]

The Ne[...]
monster [...]
play. The[...]
who bull[...]
boutiques[...]

Battles[...]
uments a[...]
their India[...]
Entrepre[...]
book, neve[...]
good enoug[...]

Look ou[...]
brake peda[...]
globes and [...]
into the la[...]
the shoulde[...]

Will your[...]
wastelands[...]
spirit of tru[...]

Let *The [...]*
head. We kn[...]

Animals

All are welcome to hoist a few
*at the **Texaco-a-Day gas station**, Wildwood, FL.*

*I*n the final analysis, we are all animals.

Beasts of burden, monsters of the id, sheep with a herd mentality. Anyone who's been caught in a mad scramble for the last seat on a bus (or a tram ride at Disney World) knows the clichés are accurate. We are animals! Hairy humanoids, scant generations from the jungle, still beating our breasts as we emerge from the shadows of gas rationing and the 55 MPH speed limit into the sunshine of a New World Order. Is it any wonder that we seek the company of other animals when we go on vacation?

Happily, we have the guiding hand of tourist attractions to transform our animals into magical beasts that will entertain us, rather than rip us apart for dinner. Many of these talented brutes are the best their evolutionary branch has to offer and have a greater range of skills than most of the humans you know. When was the last time your dumb brother-in-law could leap twenty feet out of a pool or ride a bicycle teetering on a high wire? And how many times have you felt, in your heart of hearts, that your boss could be successfully replaced by a chimpanzee?

We stand in awe before the concrete dinosaur. We bravely hurl insults at the indifferent alligator. We silently ponder the stuffed bear head that snarls from behind our motel Tiki bar. The animals are all around, eager for us to let down our hair and pay a visit, and we should. As one attraction owner put it, "All you need to make money in the tourist business is clean rest rooms and animals."

Chipmunks and ferrets are frozen in eternal frolic in animal heaven at the **Moccasin Bar,** *Hayward, WI.*

Gators

Nothing beats an alligator. They're big, ugly, smelly throwbacks to a dark time before Home Shopping Club, and they have the ability to swallow small children or the annoying dog next door without apology or even very much effort. Despite this admirable potential, alligators also have a serious problem. They don't do anything.

"Come on, alligators!" pleaded one frustrated tyke, hurling a sugar cookie into a pit filled with the dopey beasts. "Do something!" Alligator attractions know that gators can be, well, dull, and are constantly devising new gimmicks to make their scaly meal tickets seem exciting and dynamic.

Probably the easiest thing a gator farm can do is to throw a whole bunch of gators together in a pit. This increases the odds that at least one of them will be moving around when you come to visit. Attractions such as **Kliebert's Alligator Farm** in Hammond, LA, **Gatorama** in Palmdale, FL, and **Arkansas Alligator Farm** in Hot Springs, AR, rarely go beyond this simple device, though Gatorama does plan to begin regular feeding shows and AAF posts helpful signs near its pits ("These 10- to 12-year-olds are best for purses, billfolds and shoes").

Alligator wrestling shows are tried and true. Perfected by the Seminole Indians in the Everglades, it's still demonstrated by them at the **Miccousukee Indian Village.** But the politically correct Seminoles now insist that what they do isn't wrestling but "hunting without killing." Who wants to see an alligator wrestler who won't even spice up his act with gruesome anecdotes and bloody morality tales?

Our show of choice therefore belongs to **Gatorland** in Kissimmee, FL; their new 800-seat alligator wrestling arena is just part of a multimillion-dollar expansion plan. At Gatorland, tourists get to choose which alligator (from over a dozen) will go into the arena. This random alternation makes the gators "fresher"—and also more unpredictable. We advise screaming for Lefty when you visit; he's the most ornery and feisty and the wrestlers always get a little nervous when he's picked.

Gatorland is still famous for its Gator Jumparoo show. In this saurian spectacle, chicken carcasses are hung on a wire clothesline and pulled out over a swampy marsh filled with hungry fifteen-footers. Within moments of the chicken's appearance, a future handbag rises to the surface, eyeballs the tasty prize, then rockets five or six feet into the air! Clamping his jaws around the meal-to-be, he drags it back beneath the surface with a mighty splash. Camcorder-wielding dads *love* this one.

Perhaps the best alligator show we've seen isn't at an alligator attraction at all, but at **Snake-A-Torium** in Panama City Beach, FL. Scenes from the movie *Frogs* were filmed in this murky, moist assemblage of pits and cages, overgrown by years of uncontrollable Florida Gulf foliage. It's here that Willie "Clyde" Eiland and his gator sidekick, Tiny, put on a performance worthy of any Hollywood production.

The Clyde and Tiny show is simple; Clyde talks to visitors about snakes and gators while Tiny tries to kill him. "Me and Tiny, we have an understanding," Clyde explains as the sixteen-foot reptilian horror makes a lunge for his left leg. Clyde deftly deflects Tiny's jaws with a kick as Tiny lets out a threatening hiss and slides back into his pool to sulk. "I respect Tiny but he don't respect no one."

The smart Florida gator knows that good eats come from the sky.

Snake-A-Torium is currently undergoing a management change, but Clyde feels confident that he and Tiny will be retained by the new owners. We have to agree, as there seems to be no way to get Tiny out the door.

Tiny and Clyde, the dynamic duo of Snake-A-Torium in Panama City Beach, FL.

Reptiles

Reptile Gardens in Rapid City, SD, is chock full of gruesome exhibits that take pleasure in pointing out the "highly developed delivery system" of venomous snakes. One large photo on the wall shows a local man covered with huge blisters and swelling. "It's an ugly bite," you read, but not as dangerous as a neurotoxic one. Visitors are left to decide for themselves which fate is more desirable.

The **Snake Farm** in New Braunfels, TX, is a Johnson-era relic, built for the 1967 San Antonio World's Fair and never taken down. It still has its original paint, boasts the owner. The Farm used to have a live buffalo on display, but now it's dead. Then fire ants invaded its Prairie Dog Town and killed the prairie dogs. Thankfully, the Snake Farm still has its indoor display of hundreds of snakes, each meticulously identified with label gun strips. Its open-topped rattler pit is conveniently located next to a heart rate monitoring machine.

Even though Clyde Peeling insists that he's not "out to make another McDonald's," his **Reptiland** is the only franchised reptile attraction. At its new location in Kingston, NY, Peeling tried to get away without his lizard, frog, and snake touchy-feely shows, but he quickly learned what the public wants in reptile attractions and reinstated them. The shows have always been a mainstay at his Allenwood, PA, location, as are his "Feed Us A Live Insect" machines, which he also markets to mall pet shops. Drop a quarter into the machine and a lone cricket drops into a lower, glass-enclosed chamber filled with hungry frogs and salamanders! Clyde claims people pump money into these machines "to watch behavioral methods," but we know better.

Clyde Peeling (third from left) and friends pose with a reticular python at Allenwood, PA's Reptiland.

One of the Seven Wonders of The New Roadside America

AQUARENA SPRINGS
—SAN MARCOS, TX

An excited, sweaty crowd escapes the Texas heat and settles into the cool bleachers of the crescent-shaped "submarine theater"—the world's only. Thick glass windows separate the seats from the waters of **Aquarena Springs,** and face a runny cement mound with a dark cave entrance. Canned narration begins an addled account of the "Legend of Many-Springs."

Suddenly, a shirtless college-age guy in a mop wig and loincloth appears in the cave mouth. He methodically spritzes the cave entrance with a hose, then starts to erratically gesture at the theater. Part of the grounds crew? Or Indian sign language, perhaps? The crowd shifts uneasily: Is something wrong?

Where are the mermaids . . . and more important, where is Ralph, the Diving Pig?

Fear not, fellow spectators. It's just the latest confusing plot knot in a procession of psychedelic show themes at Aquarena Springs. This time, it's "Local Indian Folklore." The runny mound is what's

Aquarena's star performer Ralph, the Diving Pig, executes another perfect "swine dive."

ANIMALS

left of the volcano from last decade's show, "The Magic of Atlantis." But all the legendary Aquarena touchstones are here! Since Ralph and his Aquamaids first dove into the usually clear spring in 1950, the owners have been giving new names to old tricks!

The hose boy is Singing Wolf, in search of the beautiful Indian maiden She Blushes. "Help us call out the evil old Indian medicine man, He Smells!" the recorded narrator rallies. Another college kid with loincloth and beer gut saunters out and pitches into the greenish spring waters. "Now, let's call out She Blushes!"

Hot on the medicine man's heels is Ralph, the Diving Pig!

Ralph hits the end of the ramp and catapults into space. "Oh no! That's not a beautiful Indian maiden, that's Ralph!" Our pinkish-white hero hits the water and swims toward He Smells and his squeeze bottle of addictive "Pig Elixir." Water slowly rises over the windows of the self-contained submarine theater as it submerges into the spring. What's happening?

"He Smells secretly loves She Blushes. He has cursed the Indian maidens to spend their lives in the spring—with fish tales!" Now the theater is fully submerged. Three blond Aquamaids appear. "Looks like the Aquamaids are having an underwater picnic." As their fish tales beat gracefully, they dutifully swallow pickles and glug Pepsi by the bottle.

Suddenly, three mermen lunge from the shadows. The mermaids wiggle from their grasp and duck out through a submerged tunnel, leaving the audience at the mercy of these watery wags. The mermen "do windows"—swim right up to the glass to alternately kiss or wave their hindquarters at audience members. "Oh my . . . Singing Wolf isn't very subtle!" the narrator frets.

"Maybe if they smoke the Peace Pipe they can get the lovely maidens to return!" The narrator grasps for an excuse to introduce the air-ring-blowing portion of the show. "Women love gifts! Could you Indian braves make some jewelry for the Indian maidens? Look at those beautiful silver rings! . . . guess what? They're ready for a double ring ceremony!"

The Aquamaids are finally wooed out of the tunnel—"What red-blooded Indian could resist such charm and grace?"—and now, they have legs! After some underwater push-ups and the Indian Courting Ritual, the braves finally win over their maidens. As the show ends, Singing Wolf embraces the beautiful She Blushes and gooses her with his oxygen hose.

Aquarena's lovely Aquamaids slurp some liquid refreshment between shows. The mermen feed Ralph his rejuvenating pig elixir.

After the show is over and the crowd moves on, the Aquamaids recline on the volcano while a merman rustles up a fresh Ralph for a photo. But the midday Texas sun bakes the volcano's surface. The cryptic spritzing ritual that started the "Legend of Many-Springs" is at last deciphered.

"Get the hose! THE HOSE!" these sirens wail to the nearest merman. "It's HOT OVER HERE! Get the HOSE or we're goin' in!" Sweet relief arrives—the Aquamaids are rehydrated.

The Ralphs act as if they know that they have only a limited number of dives before they're a year old and played out—the age that even trained pigs generally cease to dive. Handpicked when only two or three days old, for whitish color, friendly personality, and curliness of tail, the Ralphs have nowhere to run, so they learn to dive and swim, dive and swim—and drown their sorrows in Pig Elixir. Ex-Ralphs number in the hundreds now, with a lot of break-fast skillets, but no Porker Retirement Home, in sight.

The submarine theater has surfaced for another performance, and the sizzling beat of belly-floppin' bacon continues. . . .

Performing Animals

Have performing animals taken their final bow? Scary as it may sound, a small group of wide-eyed nature nuts have succeeded in removing almost every trace of animal fun in this country, despite what you and every other normal American wants.

Happily, performing animals can still be found—but you have to look. Like science and literacy during the Middle Ages, performing animal shows are a candle that flickers dimly. We must vote with our vacation dollars if we want to keep from being left completely in the dark.

⭐ Some Selected Stars

For those of you who can't bear the thought of never having seen a diving horse, head north to Lake George, NY, and visit **Magic Forest.** Here Rex, the world-famous diving horse, performs daily. Rex marches up a ramp to a platform overhanging a pool. After several moments of silent mental preparation, Rex tucks his front legs and dives into the water. He's been doing this since 1977, which makes Rex, among other things, probably the cleanest horse in America.

Marineland of Florida, America's oldest marine park, is the home of Static, America's premier performing electric eel. Static sits sullenly in his display tank until show time, when a rubber-gloved Marineland employee starts poking him with a metal rod. Static responds with a burst of high-voltage electricity, illuminating a large dial and setting off a buzzer at the same time. "Six hundred volts!" cries Static's trainer with obvious pride. "That's enough current to stun a full-grown horse!"

Noah's Ark in Locust Grove, GA, is indistinguishable from hundreds of other, similar, laudable animal orphanages—except that it's the home of Snowball the Killer Goat. Snowball's original owner wanted him to be

Snowball the Killer Goat can't hide the gleam in his eyes at Noah's Ark, Locust Grove, GA.

Spiffy and Lesly Torgerson pose between shows at the Wonderful World of Tiny Horses, Eureka Springs, AR.

a "watchgoat," so he beat the animal with a stick to make him mean. One day, Snowball decided that he didn't want to be beaten with a stick anymore. He chased his owner around the yard, then knocked him off his back porch. The man died of a ruptured stomach and Snowball was condemned to death. But the animal activists—on the correct side for a change—raised such hell that when Noah's Ark offered to take Snowball, the offer was gladly accepted.

The Ark's management doesn't intend to promote Snowball as anything other than a normal goat. "He's a neat little guy," the Ark's manager told us. "He didn't mean to do what he did." While we appreciate this concern for Snowball's privacy, if you had a gold mine like a Killer Goat fall into your lap, what would you do? We know what *we'd* do. Set up regular battles between Snowball and foolhardy visitors: "Can you last five minutes with the Killer Goat?" Give 'em a stick, set 'em loose in a field, and watch the fun!

Animals en Masse

The **Wonderful World of Tiny Horses** in Eureka Springs, AR, pays its bills with the most recent additions to the performing animal stable—shaggy, two-foot-tall horses. The horses prance around a suitably tiny ring to the accompaniment of prerecorded pop hits, each displaying his or her special talents. Shazam appears dressed as Abraham Lincoln. Koko rides with a stuffed monkey. Chaparral plays the piano with his tongue. Spiffy is the star of the show; at only twenty inches, he's the smallest horse in America. Tiny Horses has been in Eureka Springs since 1988, fending off competition from **Land of Little Horses** in West Gettysburg, PA. Tiny Horses claims Little Horses' horses aren't really miniatures.

The roly-poly black bears at **Clark's Trading Post** in Lincoln, NH, have balanced on barrels and eaten ice cream for the entertainment of New Englanders since 1949. Tombstones outside the arena mark the final resting places of favorite bears from decades past. After you've taken in the show, hop aboard the Clark's steam railroad. Your train will be attacked by a bearskin-wearing maniac named Wolfman, who isn't really an animal but who might qualify as a missing link.

Venerable **Parrot Jungle** of Miami, FL, still stages daily shows in its Parrot Bowl Amphitheater. But even this timeless refuge of Golden Age tourism can't escape the relentless tick of time. Zeke, the shamrock

"Double down, Pancho, and let it ride!" Scarlet macaws at ***Weeki Wachee,*** *FL, have a keen sense of gamesmanship.*

macaw, no longer plays his organ or says his daily prayers. Cookie has retired from her job as the Parrot Show telephone operator. But don't despair. Parrot Jungle certainly has enough talented, ambitious birds to fill these vacancies. These up-and-comers are climbing the power ladder with a vengeance, pedaling their tiny bicycles and pulling their tiny chariots feverishly, eager to become the superstars of tomorrow. We can only benefit.

Does **Monkey Jungle** in Miami, FL, still feature a performing chimp show? We can't say, since the management here is terrified of (surprise) animal activists. We wanted to reprint a great old Monkey Jungle postcard of a chimp in a space suit standing next to its garbage can/space capsule, but Monkey Jungle said no way. You show a Monkey Jungle monkey in human clothing, they told us, and Monkey Jungle will get bomb threats. Must our love for animals turn us into animals? Who's making a monkey out of whom?

Perhaps *the* strangest performing animals in America can be found at **Dot & Lin's Exotic Animal Ranch** in Plentywood, MT. Sisters Dorothy Brockmier and Linda Halland raise rare "fainting goats" on their farm, which they cheerfully refer to as "the fun model of the goat world." Fainting goats are easily startled—like when you yell, "Hey, goat!"—and when that happens they immediately become stiff and keel over as if they were dead. Premium fainting goats can do this over and over again, all day long. "Weekends are just a rat race around here," explained Linda. "We have so many people coming to see them, they faint all the time."

 Bookworms and Eggheads

When most people come across a live, tic-tac-toe-playing chicken or smooching duck in a vending machine, they think they've stumbled onto something really weird. What they don't realize is that these brainy beasts in boxes can be found all over the country, and are the end result of supersecret WW II research conducted by Kellar Breland, the father of animal behaviorists. Breland had a chess-playing dog and lived in Hot Springs, AR, where his students' students keep his legacy alive at **Educated Animals,** the place that trains all those barnyard Einsteins.

Educated Animals puts on an elaborate show starring its most successful students. Sam is a chicken who won't jump through a hoop until "chicken and dumplings" are mentioned. Another chicken walks a tight-

The popular and populist "Pig Driving a Cadillac" at Educated Animals, Hot Springs, AR.

rope to turn on a fire alarm, while a goat jumps on a fire truck and rings the bell, and fleeing ducks slide into water. The showstopper here is the "original feather dancer" chicken, who scratches and struts amid flashing lights to "Manic Monday" in the Chick A Go-Go discotheque. The shows are continuous, like a grind house, to carry the metaphor further.

The most elaborate staging for Skinnerist stunts can be found at **Reptile Gardens** in Rapid City, SD. The same basic tricks and gags are woven into a complex tale of animal intrigue in the Old West. Billy (goat) the Kid busts out of jail, while dance hall chickens entertain at the saloon. Rabbits sound the alarm while a pig mines for gold. Is his loot safe with Billy on the loose? Meanwhile, a calf rings a school bell and school chicks are herded home for the day. Could this happy town be the real Walden Two?

Animal
Evacuations

Animal turds have always made popular gifts for the hard to please, and the past few years have seen an explosion in these souvenir shop items. The Turd Bird is from Kentucky, the cow patty sculptures from Arkansas, the gator crap and candy road apples from Florida. The moose nugget key chain from Maine seems suspiciously compact, but we're not *too* interested in investigating. Some people shy away from these fecal baubles, fearful of what might happen if the protective shellac coating gets wet or is left in a pants pocket for too long.

Behn's Game Farm
—Aniwa, WI

Wilbert Behn once carved a larger-than-life wooden version of himself with a chainsaw. The figure stood on a pedestal overlooking Wilbert's indoor lion and tiger arena. During a show, a whip he was cracking to hold an ornery tiger at bay wrapped around the statue arm. The statue fell and narrowly missed crushing Wilbert. "I almost killed myself," he cackles.

The broken statue's head now rests in an alcove off the entrance/office of **Behn's Game Farm,** home of an exciting life-or-death animal show, nestled among placid dairy farms. Wilbert's wife Martha shows off his other chainsaw sculptures, and his woodburning art. "We had to get a faster woodburner to keep up with his fast mind." A woman hooked to an oxygen tank and several children look on silently from an assortment of stuffed chairs crowding the office.

Wilbert is off preparing for his lion training show, so Martha issues us cans of corn and guides us through the attraction's farm. "That's Meg." Martha points out a little dog mooching corn kernels we've been instructed to feed to the goats. "She's a real corn dog." Martha has all the ad libs down pat. "That's Nuisance the little goat," she offers as we are butted in the shins by another farm friend.

Wilbert Behn nearly killed himself with his own head.

"Wilbert had a triple bypass in March, and was back up performing in five days." The noise and smells of animals permeate the air—ducks, geese, goats, dogs—and an occasional low-throated lion roars from some unseen cage. They all know we have corn. We meet Ringo the untamed wolf, Sandy the child-hating dog, Vietnamese Pot Bellied Pigs ("The latest craze in pets"), and Zimbro the Brahma bull. When Zimbro lies down, Nuisance dances on his stomach.

Wilbert Behn appears in his best tamer-of-wild-beasts garb. He's seventy-two years old, has been training and performing with animals for thirty-three years—bears, lions, tigers—yet has never worked in a circus. He's completely self-taught. He warms up with a hectic outdoor show of leaping, barking canines. But the real spectacle is in the indoor arena.

A "Not responsible for injuries" sign hangs outside.

Wilbert kicks off the arena show by eating fire three times—"Breakfast, Lunch, and Dinner." Breezy Tijuana Brass music creaks from a worn tape player as a lion races from its pen and jumps up on barrels. Behn cracks the whip and barks his commands. The audience is safe behind floor-to-ceiling hurricane fence. But how safe is Wilbert?

Tanya the tiger walks a high wire. Behn knows of only one other cat that has ever done this, and he trained his in two and a half months.

The "Theme from 'S.W.A.T.' " inspires Clyde, an eight-year-old lion that Behn has trained to perform *in slow motion*. He rolls over in slo-mo, walks up ladders, and jumps between blocks. A big cat leaps through a flaming hoop, but not without snarling menacingly. Wilbert fires a pistol at another tiger—it falls "dead" on the spot. He jams his head into a lion's mouth, and smiles defiantly.

The performance ends with enthusiastic applause and visible relief on the faces of the audience. "Why do you risk your life every day?" people ask. "Hell," snaps Wilbert, "I'm seventy-two years old. I lived most of it, I think."

Dinosaurs

Dinosaurs are the most American animals that have ever lived. They were big, strong, he-man animals who ruled the earth during a time of free-market ecology, and they didn't take flak from anyone. Every patriot loves and identifies with dinosaurs, and helps to ensure the continued, steady success of a dinosaur park long after its bumper boat and video arcade neighbors have become extinct.

At **Dinosaur Land** in White Post, VA, many of the prehistoric animals have had their toes, tongues, and tusks ripped off by derelict youngsters who wouldn't be so cocky if they'd lived during the Cretaceous period. This place also features a twenty-foot-tall King Kong and a monster shark, and humbly bills itself as "spectacular and colossal, out of this world, unbelievable but true."

Love means never having to say you're saurian at Dinosaur Land, White Post, VA.

Dinosaur World in Beaver, AR, used to be known as John Agar's Land of Kong, and thus is the only dinosaur park to have once been owned by a star of *Zontar, The Thing From Venus.* Dinosaur World's first owner, Ola Farwell, had originally intended its grounds for a giant statue of Douglas MacArthur, but nervous local authorities nixed the idea. Ola built the world's tallest (forty feet) King Kong instead and this, happily, is still standing. Even though Ola and Mr. Agar are gone, Dinosaur World still gives vent to its political leanings, as among its more interesting (and timeless) displays is a caveman Ronald Reagan slapping a caveman Tip O'Neill's butt with a spear that says "MX Missile."

We also heartily recommend **Prehistoric Gardens** in Port Orford, OR, for both its authentic jungle atmosphere and its creatively colored inhabitants. Owner E. V. Nelson, a crusty eighty-five-year-old, has been building dinosaurs since 1953 and shows no signs of slowing down. "Once you get in, you can never get out," he explains. "If my mother hadn't raised such an idiot, I never would've gone into this business in the first place." Mr. Nelson, despite his feisty words, obviously enjoys what he's doing; he completed his twenty-third dinosaur in 1991. What, we asked, would be his advice to others who want to build dinosaurs? "Don't."

One man who never would've heeded such talk was Claude Bell, who ran **The Wheel Inn** on I-10 near Cabazon, CA. Claude took a generation to build Dinny, a giant apatosaurus and arguably the largest dinosaur in America. A small museum in Dinny's belly still sells souvenirs. Claude's next project, a giant tyrannosaurus with a slide down its tail, was nearing completion when Claude's dinosaurs suddenly became the media darlings of the prehistoric world, appearing in everything from Coke commercials to rock videos to *Pee-wee's Big Adventure*. Claude died in 1989, the tyrannosaurus was never completed, and according to the museum manager in Dinny's belly, "it never will be."

Vernal, UT, bills itself as the "Dinosaur Capital of the World." A number of the older motels along U.S. 40 still have gaudy dinosaur signs, and you can still buy petrified dinosaur feces at most of the rock shops in town. Unfortunately, Vernal seems to be a town embarrassed by its boisterous boosterism of years past. **Dinosaur National Monument,** just outside of town, positions itself as a scientific and educational attraction. **The Dinosaur Museum of Natural History** gives lots of space to exhibits such as "The Story of Sedimentary Rocks," but scant attention to the bellowing, bulky behemoths that caused it to be built in the first place. **Dinosaur Gardens,** out in back of the museum, has about a dozen moderately well made dinosaurs, but they're too realistic and understated to be much fun.

Petrified Creatures Museum in Richfield Springs, NY, suffers from too much public awareness. "I had to get an unlisted phone number," gripes John Mlecz, its crabby owner. "All those crank calls when the bars let out." John is proud of the fact that most of the fossils exhibited at Petrified Creatures were dug out of a pit on this site. "Nature doesn't have to be spectacular to be interesting," he insists. The five primary-colored, life-sized dinosaurs out back, however, bear no relationship to the tiny crinoids and trilobites you're going to find in the Petrified Creatures diggings. "They're just for entertainment," Mlecz snorts.

Ossineke Dinosaur World in Ossineke, MI, is unique in that it mixes its dinosaurs and cavemen with a weird kind of Christianity. At the entrance, a homemade statue of Christ holds the earth in his hand. Once inside the park, the big apatosaurus has a ladder so that you can climb

U.S. 40 in Vernal, UT, takes you back to the time when dinosaurs ruled the lodging industry.

up into his belly. Inside, among the red and white simulated dino guts, you'll find a heart-shaped Jesus—"The Greatest Heart." The park was built, appropriately, in a swamp and the sculptures were created by somebody named Mr. Domke, who also constructed a nearby Paul Bunyan. The guy who runs Bunyan gave us a knowing smile when we asked about the sculptor. "When that guy made cavewomen, he made cave-*women*," he said, winking.

"Did you see those cavewomen at Ossineke Dinosaur World? Hubba hubba!" this elasmosaurus seems to be saying.

Without question, the best dinosaur attractions are the two **Prehistoric Forest** parks, one in Marblehead, OH, and the other in Irish Hills, MI. Both were the brainchildren of the late James Q. Sidwell, who designed his dinosaurs in conjunction with the Chicago Museum of Natural History and the Smithsonian. At least, that's what the tour guide tells you at the park in Irish Hills. At both parks a Jeep tram takes visitors past a variety of crudely animated dinosaurs that are almost identical in appearance, but here the similarities end.

At the Irish Hills park, a live tour guide informs you as you travel through a corrugated steel tube under a papier-mâché mountain that you are also traveling back in time. Once on the other side of the tunnel, the guide flips a switch and the dinosaurs come to life. "Quaaaaaa! Quaaaaaa!" they scream over and over, like prehistoric ducks, as you slowly wind your way toward the back of the park. "Watch out," the tour guide cautions, "the tyrannosaurus on your right has been known to leap into the tram and tear off arms and legs!"

At the Prehistoric Forest park in Marblehead all pretense of history and education are abandoned. Tram riders are issued miniature M-16 rifles and are instructed to "kill the monsters." A prerecorded tour guide panics repeatedly and screams, "To the left! To the right! Shoot! Shoot!!!" whenever one of the feebly nodding dinosaurs comes into view. The forest echoes with the chatter of toy M-16 fire spraying in all directions. The tram driver remains unaffected by the mayhem, smoking cigarettes and sipping coffee as the tram slowly chugs along. Management's biggest concern? The raccoons that infest Prehistoric Forest's papier-mâché mountain and rip out its polyurethane insulation for nesting material. Maybe they should send in a squad of battle-hardened tourist commandoes to finish the job.

Bugs

The **World's Largest Bug,** a shocking blue, fifty-foot-long termite, sits on the roof of the New England Pest Control building and overlooks I-95 just south of Providence, RI. It was nearly torn down a couple of years ago, but a cry went up from the local populace and the Big Blue Bug was saved. It was even christened with a new name, Nibbles Woodaway. Among its many claims to fame, Nibbles is the only hurricane-proof giant bug in the world and the only blue one. All termites look blue under a microscope.

The **World's Largest Hercules Beetle** stands next to U.S. 115, south of Colorado Springs, CO, adjacent to the sign that says "Come see the exotic world of giant tropical insects!" It was built by John May, now in his seventies, who uses it to advertise his museum of bugs. Mr. May moved the bug and his collection from Florida to Colorado, where the dry, mountain air helps preserve it. The twenty-five-foot-long beetle, unfortunately, has its legs regularly ripped off by local college students.

David Pontes, president of New England Pest Control, stands before his beloved termite, the world's largest, in Providence, RI.

The **World's Largest Bee** originally stood outside the Honey Museum in Wilmington, VT. The museum went under in 1989, and the bee was bought by a local building supply company that planned to sell it for scrap. A restaurant owner in neighboring West Dover named Jerry Costello heard about the impending destruction of the 800-pound big bee, bought it, and now proudly displays it in his back yard. Jerry Costello, we salute you!

The world's largest bee is happy and Jerry Costello (far right) is the reason why.

National Freshwater Fishing Hall of Fame

—Hayward, WI

The largest fiberglass structure in the world is also the world's largest fish, a leaping muskie, and the centerpiece of the **National Freshwater Fishing Hall of Fame.** Freshwater fishing is something we hold dear, an inalienable right somewhere between freedom of assembly and Sat-

urday mail delivery, and so every summer season some 100,000 vacationers visit here. The muskie is four and a half stories high, half a city block long, and has an observation deck in its toothy, open mouth. Visitors enter through the door in the back and climb up inside the angry "hog" to its maw.

From this perch, tourists can get a good view of the other fiberglass fish sculptures that seem to splash with happy abandon in the garden below. The rainbow trout comes complete with pole and line for the novelty photo buff. All of these fish are larger than the average angler, but none compare to the muskie, which has been immortalized as a Jim Beam decanter.

At one end of the garden is the entrance to the main museum. Inside, you're treated to the minnow bucket exhibit and the tackle box panorama. Walk through the Hall of Outboard Motors. In one room, two hairy bigfoot dummies are tagged "The Primitive Fisherman" and "The Primitive Fisherman's Son." And here's the "Examples of Poor Taxidermy" wall. Rest assured, hundreds of properly mounted fish are everywhere else.

Bob Kutz is the visionary who founded the hall in 1970. Kutz was a professional fundraiser, and has built his hall accordingly. All the big fish in the sculpture garden are sponsored. A fiberglass bass eating a fiberglass frog exists "In Loving Memory of Marjorie Anne Pazik Herrewig 1948–1983. 'The smallmouth was her favorite fish.' " Plaques are everywhere. Even the water fountain has been donated by a group "For Your Refreshing Pleasure." And anyone can remember a late beloved fisherman by baking his name into a ceramic brick and having it masoned into the memorial wall.

Still, what will stand out most in your memory is the big muskie. Its angry, merciless eyes. Its greenish sleek skin against a blue Wisconsin sky puffed with clouds. And its open mouth full of unsuspecting tourists, on the short end of the food chain for a change.

Bob Kutz, founder of the National Freshwater Fishing Hall of Fame, hooks another big one.

Dead Animals

Dead animals are worth your valuable time. People don't go to the trouble of stuffing a horse or burying a pig unless the animal was important. Dead animals are convenient. They're usually found in air-conditioned museums or in pleasant graveyards, and never off in some hellish, bug-infested forest or jungle. Dead animals are photogenic. Their gravestones have interesting inscriptions. If they're stuffed, they always hold exactly the right pose. And they never run and hide in some corner of a cage so that you end up with photos of a big, furry blob.

One fun destination for dead animal lovers is the **La Brea Tar Pits Museum** in Los Angeles, still bubbling away after all these centuries on Wilshire Boulevard. The museum has gone to great lengths to improve your understanding of the tar pits' power by sinking life-sized plaster replicas of dying mastodons into the ooze. A tape loop of animals howling in terror blares from speakers hidden in surrounding trees, thus creating a suitable atmosphere for metro L.A.'s patch o' paleogeography. Don't miss the "Discover What It's Like to Be Trapped in Tar" exhibit.

"Wildlife" museums gather together many dead animals and nail them up on the wall where we can see them better. **The Morse Museum** is a good example. Ira and Lillian Morse traveled around the world killing animals and bringing them back to the tiny town of Warren, NH, where their friends and neighbors could appreciate them. Mr. Morse seems to have had an affinity for hollowing out the feet of the larger animals he killed and using them as umbrella stands, garbage cans, and cigar humidors. The walls here are dripping with animal legs, ears, and other body parts. Also on view are flea chasers used by the Fuzzy Wuzzy tribe, a blanket from Hermann Goering's private train, and a certificate of thanks presented to the Morses by Pan American Airways.

Call of the Wild in Gaylord, MI, is a massive collection of stuffed animals dating back to the 1940s, housed in a building resembling a huge rock. Once inside, visitors can follow the bear tracks painted on the floor and find Pokey, the "sleeping" bear cub. Call of the Wild specializes in the unusual; one exhibit features an owl whose head is motorized, and continually turns in a 360-degree circle. Another display has a shepherd boy in springtime, kneeling among stuffed fawns and sheep. There's a spot where children can pet a stuffed deer and bear. You can even push a button to hear the cow and bull moose mating calls—through receivers made of dead animal horns, of course.

"Sportsmen's record clean . . . preservationists' suspect!" reads one of the readily available handouts at the **Fin, Fur & Feather Museum** in Haneyville, PA. "Who is really the best friend of our wildlife?" questions another. The answer, obviously, is the hunter—specifically, the license and permit fees that hunters pay. The FF&F Museum points out that these monies help animals that don't get shot. And the museum is an extension of this reasoning—displaying dead animals so that you can better appreciate the animals that are still alive. "It was created," says a sign at the entrance, "so that all could see the splendor and beauty of nature in leisure and comfort."

The **Buckhorn Hall of Horns** at the Lone Star Brewery in San Antonio, TX, is a must-see for those who get excited looking at antlers. Here are elk and deer head wall lamps with lightbulbs sticking out of their horns, a 4,000-pound chandelier made out of 4,000 deer horns, and a chair made for Teddy Roosevelt out of sixty-two sets of buffalo horns.

*Carol Conway poses with the head of Buck, the world's largest dead dog, at the **Shooting Star Saloon** in Huntsville, UT.*

Buckhorn caters to rattlesnake fanciers as well. The late Mrs. Friedrich, wife of the original owner, specialized in making signs and "pictures" out of rattlesnake rattles. Her 637-rattle whitetail deer portrait still holds the world record.

For the quintessential dead animal experience, it's hard to top a dead animal restaurant—a place where you can eat body parts while you look at all the body parts you can't eat. Travelers have their pick of such notable establishments as **Barkley's Tavern & Menagerie** in Phoenix, OR, **The Safari South Restaurant** in Spicer, MN, and **Ole's Big Game Lounge** in Paxton, NE.

A ten-point dining experience can be had at **Foster's Big Horn** in Rio Vista, CA. Bill Foster started displaying his trophy collection in his restaurant in 1931, and it grew until he died in 1963. Now the place is an institution. Here you can see the mounted head of a full-grown African elephant; at thirteen feet from top of head to trunk tip, it's the largest mammal trophy in any collection in existence. Also on display is a mounted giraffe head (one of only a dozen in the world) and a moose head with the largest antler spread in the world (seventy-six inches). You don't have to be psychic to predict that one day Humphrey the Humpback Whale—dizzy darling of the Rio Vista New Age nature nuts—will wind up in Foster's as its new largest mammal trophy.

Pet Cemetery of the Star Pets

Smokey the Bear is buried in the Capitan, NM, National Forest. A tree planted next to the spot is nourished, as in some way are all trees, by the great bear himself. **Smokey II,** like his predecessor, was a cub rescued from a forest fire. When Smokey II died, the Park Service didn't know what to do with his body, so they burned it.

Little Niggy was born on the Hoover Dam, AZ, work site and was the beloved pooch of the construction crews. After a truck backed over him, a memorial plaque marked the spot. It was later removed by the government, which ruled that the dam dog's name was offensive. Today, a concrete slab with the single word "Nig" honors him.

Elsie the Cow, mascot of the Borden milk company, was on her way to an appearance in Chicago when her custom-built trailer crashed. She was critically wounded and brought back to her home farm in Plainsboro, NJ, where she died. Elsie's real, prefame name is inscribed on her simple tombstone, "You'll Do Lobelia."

Herman the Mouse lived behind the fiberboard walls of a trailer outside Manhattan, NV. When the trailer was torn down, Herman was discovered. He had gnawed his way through an extension cord and electrocuted himself. Herman is currently on exhibit in the Manhattan Bar. He still has the wires clutched in his mouth.

Old Rip, a horned toad, was accidentally sealed into the cornerstone of the Eastland, TX, courthouse. When the cornerstone was opened thirty-one years later, Old Rip was found—still alive! He became an instant celebrity. When he died, his body was embalmed and is still on display in a tiny open casket in the new courthouse.

Ham was the world's first astrochimp and the first free creature in space. He died of old age in 1983, and is buried in the front lawn of the International Space Hall of Fame in Alamogordo, NM, under the first slab of natural-tone concrete poured in Otero County.

Chimp Farm

—Tarpon Springs, FL:
Animal Activist Waterloo?

"We're all paranoid here," says feisty Mae Noell, co-owner of the **Chimp Farm** in sunny Tarpon Springs, FL. Mae, who is seventy-seven, claims that the farm is under attack by "evil people" and "do-gooder" animal activists who want to take her chimps away and shut her down. "I think the whole damn thing is a conspiracy," she says. "They're trying to make criminals out of us."

The Chimp Farm is a fitting spot for the final showdown between the forces of Fun and the wet blanket animal activists. A big alligator sleeps out back in a swampy pit. A sign reads: "Caution: Dung-throwers." The chimps scratch themselves in their cages and have the disturbing habit of spitting water at passersby. Mae defends their antics like a doting mother defending her children. "Chimps only repeat what they've seen people do," she scowls.

The irony here is palpable. For thirty-one years, Mae and Bob Noell traveled the show circuit in what they called Noell's Ark, staging performances with their "athletic apes" in small towns throughout the Southeast. Their chimps would box or wrestle (and inevitably pummel) anyone who would get in the cage and fight them. It was a terrific show, but that was twenty years ago when you could still have fun with an ape. Now, Mae and Bob's chimps sit dully in their cages, bothering and being bothered by no one, and yet the Noells have to fight harder than ever just to keep them around.

Who are these people who are trying to sweep the Chimp Farm—and America's monkey legacy—under the rug? We say it's the religious fundamentalists. After all, if apes can ride bicycles and play the drums and run around in space suits, evolution becomes a whole lot easier to accept.

"I stood right here in the doorway," Mae remembers, pointing to a line etched into the cement. "Those animal rights people said, 'Oh, don't worry. We'll pay to get in.' I said, 'Not for ten thousand dollars will you set one foot in my place!' " Mae crosses her arms and stares defiantly out at U.S. 19. "They'll never get my chimps."

With all that pugilistic talent aching for a scrap, Mae, why not let them *try* to take your chimps away? And charge admission, of course.

Celebrities

Celebrity transcends mortality at
The Liberace Museum, *Las Vegas, NV.*

*W*hat makes a celebrity or folk hero? Are they the personification of some special part of the restless American spirit, or do they just make movies we like? Does the mighty forefinger of God reach down from the heavens and tickle them under the chin when they are but beswaddled toddlers? Or is their fame simply the drunken musing of unknowable Fate?

What makes celebrities special to us? Some are clearly made famous by the mere force of personality or genius. Others need the help of some media. Still other heroes spring, fully formed, from the fevered brow of the public imagination. Finally, there are those who do one shining thing that forever endears them to their countrymen.

Why visit the home, car, birthplace, or grave of a celebrity? When we stand on Graceland's front porch, we are only one dimension out of four from being Elvis himself! You see how similar the beginnings of heroes are to your own, and wonder why they are so famous and you are so not. Perhaps, as the parascientists tell us, fame seeps out in the sweat. If that is so, and you touch celebrity furniture, maybe some dried fame will stick to your skin, and get you that promotion you want when you return from vacation. Is there some "celebrity gland" in humans that dumps sticky addictive hormones into our bloodstream when we visit a famous man's restaurant or museum?

Why take chances? Instead, take a trip and meet some celebrities and folk heroes through their artifacts and artifallacies. Bring your camera in case you see one!

*T*he *Giant Fist of Joe Louis,*
Detroit, MI. A popular spot for
locals to put the arm on spare
change-pregnant visitors.

Celebrity Museums

A star knows that he or she has staying power when they can open a museum of themselves. It also takes a rare type of inner strength. If these museums are truly an indication of popularity, our most enduring personalities are Roy Rogers, Liberace, and Lawrence Welk.

The Roy Rogers Museum in the small California town of Victorville is a large monument to Roy and his wife, Dale Evans. The outside is shaped like an old cavalry fort, with a twenty-four-foot statue of Trigger

*T*he *mounted carcass of Trigger, Roy*
Rogers's famous horse, at The Roy Rogers
Museum, Victorville, CA.

on his hind legs at the entrance. Above the door to the museum is a sign reading "This is our life—Roy and Dale." And what a life! Inside are all sorts of things that give you the impression that Roy and Dale are the kind of people you'd like as neighbors. Along with their famous saddles are wedding pictures, hunting and fishing trophies, and Roy's favorite T-Bird and powerboat.

The best exhibit is that of Roy's bowling trophies (he rolls for the museum team) and of his clear acrylic bowling ball with Trigger's photo in the center. The museum is a favorite attraction of bikers, who dig the chivalry Roy laid down in his films.

Since Liberace's death, **The Liberace Museum** has grown in size and shrunk in tourist value. Set up in Las Vegas, in a shopping center Libbo once owned, the museum is now run by a foundation. There is still a lot to see, but it lacks a certain flair and panache that the maestro imparted to it. And you can't take photos anymore!

In the main building, pianos and cars are on display, including the fabulous red, white, and blue bicentennial Rolls. But the fan tributes (like the miniature Liberace made of bread dough and glue) and odd personal nicknacks have been removed. The effect seems to be one of (too late) sterilizing the things that Liberace touched.

Two other rooms of Liberace material are a walk across the parking lot. In the first is a gold casting exact replica of Liberace's hands, and a funeral wreath with an "I'll Be Seeing You" sash. Glassware and honorary degrees glitter in their display cases.

The final room begins with a large oil painting of mother Liberace, with candelabras on either side. In the center of the room, a rhinestone-covered grand piano twinkles as it turns. As Liberace's renditions of "Theme from *Chariots of Fire*" and "Send In the Clowns" waft in from above, you can see many of his gaudy furs and stage outfits; everything from his first gold lamé jacket to his red, white, and blue hot pants outfit. The World's Largest Rhinestone is given its own display case.

On the way to the gift store, you pass his replica office, and then walk into his replica bedroom suite, with two tastefully furry single beds separated by a bottle of champagne on ice. The gift shop features porcelain Libbos for $150. "I'll Be Seeing You" chocolates featuring the entertainer's likeness can be purchased for anyone who still wants to say, "I ate Liberace."

Lawrence Welk Resort Village is a mobile home retirement community in Escondido, CA. The symbol of the village is a quarter note, with the number 18 on its flag, symbolizing Welk's two passions, music and golf. The sidewalk is studded with bronze musical notes and miniature musical instruments. Outside are a large bronze quarter note fountain, and a life-sized statue of the maestro himself, baton in mid-twirl. And at the resplendent center of things is the Lawrence Welk Museum.

Inside the museum, along with photos and old posters, are two items of spectacular note. One is the world's largest champagne glass, bubbling water, lit from inside, and raised on a velvet pedestal. It was given to him in honor of his twenty-fifth TV anniversary.

Next to it is a real roadside treat. A life-sized Lawrence Welk band-stand has been constructed, complete with the famous "LW" music stands. The band is on break, perhaps to the village's par-3 course, but their instruments are ready for their return. Patiently waiting for them to get back is a life-sized cardboard color cutout of Mr. Wunnerful, baton at the ready. Studio lights illuminate the stage, and every three minutes an applause sign flashes. A vintage color TV camera is trained on Welk, and a studio monitor allows you the choice of viewing his image either "live" or on the TV, where you're used to seeing him. The museum invites visitors to "Be on TV with Lawrence Welk," and allows you to stand next to LW while a friend snaps precious souvenir photos off the monitor.

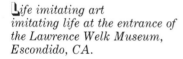
Life imitating art imitating life at the entrance of the Lawrence Welk Museum, Escondido, CA.

Anita Bryant Theater

—Eureka Springs, AR

The twin meccas of Eureka Springs, AR, and Branson, MO, are famous for their nightly hoedowns and jamborees, featuring their own unique, if anonymous, brand of hillbilly music. But Eureka Springs is also home to a star. It is the new home of **Anita Bryant Theater.**

For now, Anita Bryant Theater is the reconverted banquet room of a USA Inns Motel. Low ceilings and cafeteria-style chairs add to the intimacy of the place. Lest you wonder what a famous entertainer and Miss America runner-up is doing here, Ms. Bryant answers these very questions during her one-woman performance.

The first half of her show is a musical autobiography, in which she talks, jokes, and sings about her life from birth to breakdown and back. She sings her jingles, "Come to the Florida Sunshine Tree" and all five seconds of "Things go better with Coca-Cola, things go better with Coke." She sings "San Francisco" and "Somewhere over the Rainbow" to exorcise her gay tormentors, and "Men" to get over her painful divorce. In between, Bryant tries hard to sell the assembled a special Anita Bryant life story photo book. Holding up a copy, she explains many, many of the individual photos.

The second half of the show—a killer—is devoted to patriotic and spiritual numbers. The fifty-something Bryant opens by walking up center aisle in a majorette's outfit, twirling a baton. She marches around the small stage, and then stops at attention and sings two verses of the "National Anthem." The audience stands. The second verse is about conquering other people if we know we're right. This was offered as proof that our forefathers knew the price of freedom.

With a Vietnam flight jacket wrapped around her blue evening gown, Anita closes the show with the "Battle Hymn of the Republic."

Anita was born a baby full of black poison, but her family stuck her head in a bucket of cold water, fed her whiskey and black coffee, and she lived. She knew God had put her on earth for a reason, and first sang publicly in a church when she was two. She recreates the event by singing "Jesus loves me, this I know . . ." in a little-girl-of-two voice, until the last note, which she holds deep and womanly and triumphant.

Later she dons a flight jacket given to her by a Private Bryant when she was touring Vietnam with Bob Hope. Private Bryant was killed there, with Anita's letters on his person. Wearing that jacket tightly around her blue evening gown, she ends with "Battle Hymn of the Republic." A large American flag waves behind her. Smoke pots quickly fill the room and help close the show.

Afterward, she sits in the lobby with Charlie, her second husband and manager, autographing things, chatting, and selling her records and books. Charlie talks of plans for a new, stand-alone Anita Bryant Theater and Museum, featuring videotaped messages from Bob Hope and Billy Graham. God has put her in Eureka Springs for a reason. But, as Bryant said several times during the show, and again afterward to well-wishers, she never expected that her life would turn out this way.

Our Television Favorites

The worst part of spending a vacation in a car is the extreme lack of television. Being on the road can get mighty lonely with only your family and the radio to keep you company. Fortunately, there are attractions based on our TV favorites that ease the hours until nightfall, when the ice bucket is full and the motel TV, floating near the ceiling, locked above you on a metal arm, is going.

According to several polls, the most recognizable face in America still belongs to Fred Flintstone. This type of popularity was bound to be exploited, so it is no surprise that not one, but two **Flintstone Bedrock City** attractions exist, one in Custer, SD, and one near the Grand Canyon in Vail, AZ.

South Dakota's Bedrock City was the first, the brainchild of several local concrete makers. Up went Fred's house, then Barney's, then Mr. Slate's. At one end of Main Street is Mt. Rockmore, a mini Mt. Rushmore, with Fred, Barney, and Dino included as the famous heads. Ride in a Flintmobile and have a Brontoburger. At the Black Hills location, live Freds and Barneys walk around and shake hands. At Arizona's less-opulent version, their molded figures speak, and Dino barks.

*F*red and Barney wave from Main Street, Bedrock City, Custer, SD.

*T*he Beverly Hillbillies Car, complete with Granny's rocker, is on display at **The Ralph Foster Museum,** School of the Ozarks, Point Lookout, MO.

The attractions will postmark mail with cartoon Flintstone heads and "Bedrock City," so save months of unpleasant letters to mail during your visit. How can someone get mad at a person who quits a job from Flintstoneland?

It is a disappointment visiting **The Ponderosa Ranch,** in Incline Village, NV (right where the "Bonanza" map used to burst into flame every week). One is happy to see that a television show has legs enough to keep an attraction going this long. But Ponderosa is too sterile and sedate. This is a farm machinery display, a sparse "Kiddieland," a petting zoo, and a Hoss Burger stand (probably only *named* after him). There are no uncontrollable savages running rampant, no mean bad guys to hate. The featured souvenir is a tin cup.

And when Michael "Little Joe" Landon died in 1991, The Ponderosa Ranch had a series of memorial services at The Church of The Ponderosa to which they charged admission. PU. Better to visit the **Dan Blocker Memorial Head** in his hometown of O'Donnell, TX. Hoss is on a granite stand in the town square.

Now that sit-coms are being recognized as an American art form like jazz and no-money-down real estate, you can find places to pay homage if you look hard enough. **Lucille Ball's Hometown** is Jamestown, NY. She's enshrined in the local Hall of Fame, located in the Lucille Ball Little Theater. Her childhood home is at 59 Lucy Lane, and a Lucy display beckons from the Victorian Fenton Historical Center. LucyFest happens every Memorial Day weekend. A dedicated museum is planned.

Donna Reed's Hometown is Denison, IA. It is also home to the Donna Reed Center for the Performing Arts. Her childhood home is located off Donna Reed Drive, and the Donna Reed display at the Victorian W. A. McHenry House features her *From Here to Eternity* Oscar. The Donna Reed Festival happens every July. A dedicated museum is planned.

Al "Grampa Munster" Lewis has his own Italian restaurant, **Grampa's Bella Gente,** in New York City's Greenwich Village. He hangs there— when he's not working.

Finally, at the border of "Ohio's Colonial City," Mount Vernon, is a sign still reading **"Hometown of Paul Lynde,"** the late actor who was "Bewitched's" Uncle Arthur, and the best center square there ever was.

$teve Canyon Statue, *Idaho Springs, CO. In 1947, Squirrel Gulch, CO, was renamed Steve Canyon, after the Sunday comics' charmed aviator, as a tribute to the servicemen and -women of WW II. In 1949, residents commissioned this forty-foot statue, which still graces the landscape. Its plaque reads, in part, "The United States Treasury salutes Steve Canyon and through him, all American cartoon characters who serve the Nation."*

Hometown Heroes

The Superman statue stands in downtown Metropolis, while a lady hogs the phone booth. A speeding bullet has put a hole in his chest.

Two midwestern towns have tried to fight civic anonymity by claiming to be the homes of mythical superheroes. Metropolis, IL, is **The Hometown of Superman,** while Riverside, IA, maintains that they will be the **Future Birthplace of Captain James T. Kirk.**

Metropolis was first to act. In the early 1970s, faced with a decline in local industry, the town cautiously began its first associations with the Man of Steel. Fanned by early success and irresponsible prodding by the media, the town was quickly deluded into starting a huge "Amazing World of Superman" theme park, to be complete with a 200-foot statue of the man of steel, legs open for cars to drive through. When the novelty wore off and the media quit reporting, visitors stopped dropping by, and Amazing World was scrapped halfway done. Metropolis still blames the gas crisis of 1973–1974.

Today's statue is only ten feet tall, though a fifteen-foot-tall one should be up by press time. It rests on Superman Square, an island in the middle of the main drag. Still, the biggest statue in town is of Big John, a Clark Kent-ish bag boy in front of a local supermarket.

Superman is seen flying on "Welcome To" signs, and above Metropolis Drugs. The chamber of commerce office has his phone booth, where you can pick up the receiver and talk to Supe. Other Superman memorabilia are displayed inside, including photos of the unfortunate goings on back when. The chamber gives away packets of multicolored Kryptonite, akin to handing out bullets in Dealey Plaza, to children.

When we asked if Superman's real hometown wasn't Smallville, a nice chamber of commerce lady said, "Nobody's ever questioned that." She seemed nervous, as if the town had realized it years ago, in the hungover aftermath of civic folly, and was keeping quiet about the whole thing.

Ten years after Metropolis got going, a Riverside, IA, town council member read that "Star Trek's" Captain Kirk is to be "a man born in a small town in Iowa," and persuaded the council to beat other crossroads towns in Iowa to the punch. Riverside is still building toward a final insane blow-off, as national recognition and media enthusiasm for its project grow.

A twenty-foot long Starship *Enterprise* replica sits in the town park, and at the city limits reads a sign "Riverside: Where the Trek Begins." Local businesses include Flower Trek and Future Designs by Carol, but the Bar Trek saloon sold out and is no longer here. A white ex-barber shop on the main street serves as Kirk HQ, and a shapeless concrete blob behind it marks the spot upon which Kirk will be whelped.

Townsfolk want to put up a bronze bust of their hometown hero, but Paramount Pictures, not run by small-town Iowans, wants $40,000 to license the image. The annual Riverfest was changed to Trek Fest, and they now get ten to fifteen thousand pale technonerds and their technodollars materializing each year. They come dressed in Starfleet uniform, as Vulcans, and as Captain Kirk himself, to pay homage.

Whereas Metropolis must answer the hard questions about its claim to fame, Riverside still has two hundred plus years to get its act together. We feel that Riverside must try to breed Kirk, using the husbandry skills learned in its agricultural past. Invite Nobel Laureates, Olympic Hopefuls, Gulf War Heroes, and Men of State to visit and impregnate the local cheerleaders. Other attributes must be ingrained: duty to ship, leadership, sex drive. Practice on grain silos and at little league games. And whatever you do, make sure visiting technonerds don't roll in your hay and infect the gene pool.

Captain Kirk's ancestor, Bob Wieland, watches the skies above Riverside, IA, for possible Klingon sneak attack.

One of the Seven Wonders of The New Roadside America

TWITTY CITY

—HENDERSONVILLE, TN

Conway Twitty has recorded more number-one songs than anyone else in history. Frank, Elvis, and the Beatles are all somewhere forever further down the list. This alone is enough to mix up the way you always thought things were. Now, try to imagine how your world view will change after visiting a tourist attraction not only dedicated to *the* superstar of music, but actually built with his home, and the homes of his mother and children, as living parts of the experience. This is **Twitty City,** the wonder built by Conway Twitty about Conway Twitty.

Twitty City comprises two souvenir shops, a snack bar and a stage, and a multimedia auditorium/museum called the Conway Showcase. But it is the promise of viewing the homes of Conway and his family that is the main tourist draw. There is the faint but ever-present hope that your tour group might meet Conway as he gets his morning paper or mows his lawn.

The tour begins in the Showcase, a labyrinth of thickly carpeted, heavily air-conditioned rooms. You're seated in a small theater and shown a multiscreen slide extravaganza about Conway's philosophy of life, love, and music. It's here that you're told the Russian language version of Conway's hit "Hello Darlin' " was the first earth music ever broadcast from outer space.

Introducing the next phase of your journey is a four-foot-tall fiberglass model of Twitty Bird. Twitty Bird, in case you haven't already guessed, is a close copy of Warner Brothers' hateable Tweetie Bird, outfitted with a cowboy hat, boots, and a guitar. Twitty Bird's annoying visage is everywhere at Twitty City, but only in the Showcase does it speak—punctuating everything with psycho monster movie giggles.

In between laughs, Twitty Bird introduces life-sized photographs of Conway's band members as if they were alive. They respond with musical solos from speakers concealed behind their poster-board

instruments. Twitty then directs your attention to eight-foot scale models of Conway's two tour busses, Twitty I and II.

Next stop is the Wall of Gold room, with a 1956 T-Bird (get it?) as its centerpiece. Along the wall behind it are mounted dozens of gold records commemorating Conway's many hits. The tour group hears clips of these songs as a disco ball spins and projectors flash scenes of Conway in concert. Finally, "It's Only Make Believe" plays, and the doors to the outside world open, signaling the conclusion of the Showcase tour.

But the best is still to come. Tour groups emerge into Conway's actual front yard, shielded from nonpaying passersby by a high brick wall. Conway's classic music is still audible—this time from speakers hidden in the trees.

Above the Showcase exit is a window to Conway's conference room. When Conway is there, you are told, he sometimes looks out and waves a cheery "Hello Darlin' " to visitors. Along the Showcase wall is a giant Twitty Bird, masoned out of multicolored brick. Nearby, a large "CT" is embedded in the sidewalk. "This is Conway's favorite spot for signing autographs when he's around," the group is told.

Next stop is Observation Point. From this strategically located spot, visitors can view the houses of Conway's four children. There

Visitors stand in Conway Twitty's front yard. He might choose this moment to stick his head out a window or take out the trash. You just never know.

they are. Right over *there!* Maybe his kids are just inches of brick away from being seen! After much clicking of camera shutters, the tour finally heads to, as the brochure describes it, "home sweet home for Conway . . . a charming Colonial house in a unique location—the center of Twitty City." And you're going in!

The group is allowed inside only briefly, for a quick peek at Conway's dining room and breakfast nook. Then they are escorted back outside where they can look at Conway's home over a metal fence. Conway wanted to open his entire twenty-four-room, seven-bath home to his fans, but was afraid some of them might not be able to climb the stairs. "He didn't want to leave anyone unsatisfied," the tour guide explains. The group is shown the driveway where his car might be parked, if it were around.

You have to wonder, just how close does anyone really come to rubbing elbows with Mr. T? Twitty City has thought of a way to combat this element of disappointment. As the tour group breaks up and heads for the parking lot, the guide calls after them, "If it hasn't already occurred to you, you can now brag to your friends that you were on the front yard of a big star's home."

Lest We Forget

Emilio Carranza—Aviator Emilio Carranza was known as the "Lindbergh of Mexico." Attempting to become the first to fly nonstop from New York City to Mexico City, he only got to New Jersey, where he crashed. They say he died with a flashlight in his hand, still looking for a place to land. The cairn on the isolated crash spot is complete with a bas-relief eagle heading straight down. Planted around it are scrawny cacti, no bigger than broken beer bottles, stunted by cold New Jersey winters. But every July, a group from the U.N.'s Mexican Consulate still drives down to Tabernacle, NJ, and has a little ceremony.

Frank Kindell—Frank Kindell, another doomed aviator, was known as "The Flying Paperboy of the Guadalupes." When Kindell and his plane crashed into a mountainside while making deliveries in 1964, saddened newspaper subscribers erected a big propeller affixed to a granite obelisk, marking the lonely spot in New Mexico's Guadalupe Mountains where Kindell "flew across the great divide into eternity."

Hi Jolly—When the U.S. Army was over in the Middle East gathering camels for possible use in the American deserts back in the nineteenth century, Hi Jolly was picked up to train them. He was called Hi Jolly because his real name could not be pronounced by the soldiers. The camel experiment was not successful, but such was the fondness and appreciation for HJ that when he died, a multicolored stone monument, topped by a camel, was erected to him in Quartzsite, AZ. Modern Quartzsite adds its own tribute, being home of The Hi Ali Motel and Hi Jolly's Liquor Box.

A Little Bit Country, A Little Bit Rock and Roll

The road is kind to country music fans, far less so to rockers. For whatever reason—rock's reputation as drug-crazed defiler of the status quo or country stars' longer career span—it is easy to find a well-kept country tribute, and painfully hard to find rockin' reminders.

One need only look at the Halls of Fame for each. **The Country Music Hall of Fame** in Nashville, TN, is beautiful. Clean, well laid out, and with enough sparkly costumes and Elvis Cadillacs to make it well worthwhile. The **Rock and Roll Hall of Fame,** scheduled since the mid-'80s for Cleveland, hasn't even broken ground yet. We are assured that it should be open by sometime in 1994, you know, if they can get it together.

When it comes to museums, country wins hands down. Nashville is littered with them, honoring Barbara Mandrell, Hank Williams, Jr. and Sr., even Boxcar Willie. **Meridian, MS,** honors "The Singing Brakeman," Jimmie Rogers, and **Turkey, TX,** will always be the home of Bob Wills and the **Bob Wills Monument.**

About the best rock offers is the **Motown Museum,** in Detroit. But aside from the Michael Jackson room, with a flower power costume he wore as a youngster on Ed Sullivan, a glove, and a hat, the museum is mostly dull photos.

What about rocker birthplaces? Going to Hibbing, MN? Great if you want to see **The Greyhound Bus Origin Center,** or the **World's Largest Open Pit Iron Ore Mine.** But on the bus ride to the open pit mine, look quick as it passes **Bob Dylan's Boyhood Home** or you'll miss it.

If you were a rocker fortunate enough to die prematurely, fate is a little kinder. Lubbock, TX, **Buddy Holly's Hometown,** has erected a bronze statue of Buddy playing his guitar. It is the centerpiece of a Walk of Fame honoring other local musicians, like Waylon Jennings and Mac Davis. Holly is buried in The Lubbock Cemetery. His grave is planted with guitar picks left by fans. At the **Surf Ballroom,** in Clear Lake, IA, a monument marks the spot where Holly, Ritchie Valens, and The Big Bopper played their final gig.

The Museum of The Gulf Coast in Port Arthur, TX, contains, for our money, the best rock tribute. Port Arthur was the **Birthplace of Janis Joplin,** and this museum shows off some of Joplin's childhood religious artwork. Displayed are her "Christmas Lawn Ornament Jesus and Mary," "Paint by Numbers Garden of Gethsemane," and a crucifixion scene she did when she was thirteen. ("Notice she left off the crown of thorns," says the librarian.) Other paintings and photos are around, as is a stage

The Woodstock Monument, Bethel, NY. *The plaque commemorating all the performers has been repeatedly recemented because some visitors aren't content to take home mere vibes.*

outfit, her Bible, and her slide rule. A bronze multibust on a marble pillar shows the many moods of Janis Joplin.

But even being part of heaven's helluva band doesn't guarantee you a decent tribute. The **Jimi Hendrix Viewpoint** is a rock with a star-shaped bronze plaque overlooking the African Savanna exhibit at his hometown's Woodland Park Zoo. The plaque reads like a P.C. Civics text: we "gain a new perspective on the African animal world, and pause to remember the perspective that Jimi Hendrix gave to the musical world." The rock was supposed to be heated, so people could sit on it during Seattle's rainy weather ("The Jimi Hendrix Hot Rock." Get it, man?), but that never happened. Around the rock, purplish bushes symbolize Purple Haze, a brand of LSD popular with Hendrix before he died of a drug overdose.

Whereas visitors to country superstar **Loretta Lynn's Ranch,** Hurricane Mills, TN, are invited for hayrides and miniature golf, and Conway lets tourists wander through the first floor of his house at **Twitty City,** don't try something like that at **Berry Park,** in Wentzville, MO. Though the marker in front reads "Welcome. Established by Chuck Berry and his family, For The People," this grassy retreat with picnic tables, band-

The welcoming gates of Loretta Lynn's Ranch, Hurricane Mills, TN, and the ominous tombstone greeting at (Chuck) Berry Park, Wentzville, MO. Mean Berry went to prison for transporting a female minor across state lines for immoral purposes. Nice Lynn was a female minor when she had her first child, but that was okay, because she was married. Interestingly, both have last names that can also be first names.

stand, and a pond is on the far side of a chain-link fence. Away from the road at the back of the park is Chuck's own house! And if you stop in the parking lot and try to get out for a quick picnic at one of the tables For The People, mean scary dogs and even ex-jailbird Chuck himself could well advise you to stay in your car, turn around, and get the hell out!

None of country's overall hospitality excuses **Dollywood,** Dolly Parton's cutely named ripoffarama in Pigeon Forge, TN. It costs a family of four $62 plus tax just to get in, and once in there's nothing to do, except watch them blow glass, and buy food and souvenirs. A free **Dolly Parton Statue** is up nearby in Sevierville, in front of her hometown's courthouse. Go there instead. Her breasts should be rubbed for luck.

Elvis

Elvis Presley is the number-one tourist celebrity in the country. And while there's not enough good stuff to do a whole book about him, we'd be derelict in our duties if we omitted the best of El Elvis.

First stop, **The Elvis Presley Museum** in Kissimmee, FL. Elvis's "personal friend" Jimmy Velvet rotates exhibits here with his Nashville museum, and one can see Elvis's reading glasses prescription, the instruments used by the obstetrician who delivered him, and a pair of his karate pants. Elvis loved karate, and, as a sign tells you, "He achieved 9th degree black belt, making him the highest ranked entertainer." Everything is labeled for sale.

Don and Kim Epperly have built a miniature **Elvis City** (including Graceland with guitar-shaped pool, his Tupelo birthplace, and a performance hall) in their Roanoke, VA, front yard. A new building a year goes up, and visitors are welcome from 10 A.M. to 10:30 P.M.

The **Elvis Museum** in Pigeon Forge, TN, has a display of Elvis beauty aids: his razor, hair dryer, Brut, and nasal spray applicator. You want more? How about two sets of Elvis X rays? Buy copies of Elvis's shopping list in the gift store.

Next on the itinerary is **Elvis's Birthplace** in Tupelo, MS! It is a small railroad-style home, and you can see it in its entirety by simply looking through the screen door. An Elvis memorial meditation chapel is adjacent—a popular place for Elvis fans to wed. The Elvis-theme McDonald's in town is popular for the receptions.

Memphis is the site of the ultimate tribute to Elvis, his beloved home, **Graceland.** It is located on Elvis Presley Boulevard, and Elvis tribute gift stores, museums, and restaurants line the street across from the mansion.

Join with a half million other annual visitors, and see the dining room and the gold-leaf piano. Visit the TV room in the basement, nerve center of Elvis's entertainment system. The King often watched its three TVs at once, and was within arm's length of the wet bar. Don't miss the Jungle Room, designed by Elvis himself. Lamp shades look like leopard skins, sofas like zebras. The ceiling is covered in green shag carpet. A world-weary Elvis recorded his last two albums here.

See the shooting room. This is where Elvis took target practice! Shell casings are still on display. In the trophy room pay special attention to the fantastic Aztec Sunburst outfit, his wedding tux and Priscilla's wedding dress, and the TV given him by RCA for selling 50 million records. Outside, the walk from the pool leads to the Meditation Garden, where Elvis is buried along with his mother, father, and grandmother. Here

An Elvis suit displayed at Graceland. Elvis is one of the few entertainers in the world who can be recognized even if his likeness has no head.

guests grow unusually quiet, unless you get in their way when they try to take a picture.

The museums and gift complexes directly across from Graceland are now all controlled by official interests and they have put the squeeze on unlicensed and undignified souvenirs. The unofficial gift stores "Of Elvis Presley Blvd." are separated by a tall wooden fence from the official Presliana, but play their music louder.

These shops have the decanters and busts, and tell-alls by many once- and twice-removed relatives. Graceland stores eschew all that, selling classy merchandise like "Elvis Razor Relief Cologne," and "Moments by Priscilla Presley" perfume.

★ Motorcade of the Damned

Buford *Walking Tall* Pusser's Death Car
Carbo's Police Museum, Pigeon Forge, TN
1974 Corvette

Hank Williams, Sr.'s Death Car
Hank Williams, Jr. Museum,
Nashville, TN
1952 Pink Cadillac

Exotic World

—Helendale, CA

Halfway between the glitter of Los Angeles and the glitter of Las Vegas, in the remote desert town of Helendale, exotic dancers have pitched their mansion. It takes some doing to find this ranch-style retreat, but the unmistakable wrought-iron **Exotic World** sign haloing their dirt driveway lets you know when you have arrived. This museum to all that was good about Burlesque is also headquarters of the Exotic Dancers League of America, and is run by the former "Marilyn Monroe of Burlesque," Dixie Evans.

Dixie greets visitors and personally leads the tour, which is by appointment. It begins in the main house, whose comfortable suburban living/dining room has been converted into a memorial to the all-time greats of stripping. Soft drink bottles are on the breakfast counter and the TV is on, like in your neighbor's home. Except where your neighbor would have Audubon prints, Dixie has packed dozens of 8×10s of beautiful nearly naked women with big breasts and long legs.

Old strippers often visit from parts unknown, and share the couch and conversation with you. Dixie is effervescent and entertains a mile a minute. "The girls love coming by. They enjoy knowing that someone cares about preserving their work."

The tour features a tribute to league founder and Exotic World's first hostess, "The Bazoom Girl," Jennie Lee. Jennie died in 1989 of breast cancer, but her ashes and a large portrait remain above the fireplace mantel. Jennie's *Juggs* magazine work is on the walls, between the likes of Tempest Storm and Chesty "Double Agent 73" Morgan.

Hirohito's Limousine
Imperial Palace Auto Collection,
Las Vegas, NV
1935 Packard

Jayne Mansfield's Death Car
Tragedy in U.S. History Museum,
St. Augustine, FL
Buick Electra 225

Friendly greeters Sadie Burnett, Dixie Evans, Trina Lynn (left to right), and Dusty Sage (kneeling) pose underneath the famous Exotic World entrance gate.

Bonnie and Clyde's Authentic Death Car
Whiskey Pete's Casino, (near) Jean, NV
1934 Ford V-8

Tammy Faye Bakker's Cadillac
Cars of Yesteryear, Freeport, OH

Next the tour proceeds outside toward a newly constructed wing. As you walk past the Exotic World Rolls-Royce, little dogs scamper around your feet and bark. Greek-like plaster goddesses, fountains, pools, and horses are in view as you walk around. "I'm trying to make it look like a fairyland," says Dixie.

The new wing consists of three rooms, all of them full of stripper 8×10s. The first room contains Jayne Mansfield's couch and bookcases of stripper autobiographies. In this room, Dixie recreates part of her act. As the Marilyn Monroe of Burlesque, she had an act that paralleled events in MM's life. "After she and Joe DiMaggio split, my routine went like this . . ." Evans vamps into a breathless impression, ending with "Am I worried about our breakup? No, because I've still got his . . ." She pulls out two imaginary baseballs, kissing each before throwing them toward you. If you ever wondered what Monroe would look like today, Exotic World is the place to find out.

In the next room, Dixie tells stories of some of the strippers on the walls. "Industrialists will write in asking about a certain stripper they saw as a young man. Many ask about Siska and her macaws. Siska's birds would fly onstage and take off a piece of her clothing, fly offstage, drop it, and come back. Right when they got down to her G-string, she'd start dancing too fast for the birds to catch up to her, and one macaw would turn to the audience and yell 'Hellllpppp. Helllllppppp me.' "

The last room has a small gift boutique, where one can buy Exotic World T-shirts and Exotic Dancers League of America lapel pins. "The Burlesque era was a renaissance era for the United States," says Dixie. For emphasis, she holds up a thick doctoral thesis on the subject, written recently by a female graduate student in Alaska, copies of which are on sale in the store. Some 8×10s are also for sale, "but I don't emphasize it, because I don't want people to get the wrong idea. We're not here to sell girlie pictures. We're here to preserve memories."

Hitler's Staff Car
The Thing?, Cochise, AZ
1935 Rolls-Royce

John Q. Drunk's Death Car
Highway Patrol Safety Education Museum,
Jefferson City, MO
1987 Ford Escort

Graves

Famous faith-healer evangelist **A. A. Allen** was a staple of Mexican radio. In 1958, he founded the town of Miracle Valley, AZ, near Bisbee. In the midst of his great popularity, he announced that he could raise the dead, in accordance with scripture, having done so to two children. Followers shipped their dead to Miracle Valley for the cure until authorities clamped down. Allen died in 1970, but for many months, his taped broadcasts saying "I am not dead" caused people to think he himself had risen. Today, Miracle Valley's population has fallen way off, after wars with another religious group left several dead. But if you drive through the decaying Miracle Valley Bible College to the nearly empty cemetery in the back, at the apex of the dirt drive is Allen's small crypt, emblazoned "God's Man of Faith and Power." His body remains above ground, in case.

James Dean is laid to rest in Fairmount, IN, and weeping fans still make vigils to his grave and memorial at Park Cemetery. Unlike many towns that seem to have forgotten that their soil is the eternal vessel for an exploitable personality, Fairmount has historical exhibits, galleries, look-alike contests, and fun runs honoring JD. For those wishing a more remote, quieter place to contemplate fickle fate, we recommend Dean's actual death site in Cholame, CA. A rich Japanese admirer has built a mysterious shiny tribute with an infinity symbol on it where the car crash occurred.

Sex novelist **D. H. Lawrence,** noted for *Women in Love* and other late-night cable fare, was cremated after he passed on. Instead of being scattered to the four winds, he had himself mixed with the plaster of the D. H. Lawrence Ranch in Questa, NM. This is probably the only chance you'll get to walk around inside a noted author.

Tom Mix's Death Car
(and the suitcase that killed him)
Tom Mix Museum, Dewey, OK
1944 Cord

JFK's Death Car
Henry Ford Museum, Dearborn, MI
1961 Lincoln Limousine

Uncle Sam's grave, and mourner, Oakwood Cemetery, Troy, NY.

Mother Goose is buried in The Old Granary Burying Ground in Boston, MA. Her grave is the most popular in the place, far outshining those of Samuel Adams, John Hancock, and Paul Revere.

Sitting Bull was originally interred in a military cemetery in North Dakota. South Dakota wanted his old bones, and asked North Dakota for them. North Dakota said to forget it. So one night, South Dakota snuck across the border, and, under the cover of darkness, dug him up

Billy Carter's "Redneck Power" Super Service Station Tow Truck Smoky Mountain Car Museum, Pigeon Forge, TN

Ray Tse, Jr.'s Full-sized Mercedes Benz Gravestone Linden, NJ Granite 240D and hauled him off. Before North Dakota knew what was going on, South Dakota had him safely buried in their town of Mobridge. A big stone bust was placed over Sitting Bull to keep North Dakota from stealing him back.

Colorado saw what happened to Sitting Bull, and made sure no such shenanigans befell their fallen fella, **Buffalo Bill Cody.** When he died there in 1917, Wyoming and Nebraska immediately put in dibs for him. Colorado said no way, and buried him way up on top of Lookout Mountain in Golden. Then they covered the grave in concrete, reinforced with steel bars, just to make sure.

Uncle Sam is laid to rest in Troy, NY, and frankly, we are surprised that a photo of his grave has not appeared in some commie workers' paper, accompanied by a poorly structured joke. But it hasn't. Perhaps it has something to do with the vigilance of the Uncle Sam Council of Boy Scouts that maintains the site, and makes sure that the flag is raised every day above him.

*alk of Relative Fame: The further you get from Hollywood, the less famous you have to be to get your name in the sidewalk. Out at the state fairgrounds in Indianapolis is the **Indiana Walk of Legends.** Among the hands in cement here are those of Orville Redenbacher and former Secretary of Agriculture Earl Butz. America thanks you, Indiana.*

Science

Part of the fun!
American Museum of Atomic Energy, *Oak Ridge, TN.*

*S*cience appeals to both young and old. The young want to see what breakthroughs will give them limitless energy and wardrobes. The old want to know if they're going to miss anything. "Mission to Mars? Forget it, Gramps! We spent all your tax money on bilingual signs!" Scientists are pretty smug about their achievements, their little tinkerings with nature and reality. You can see it in the new breed of science museums that parcel out knowledge like they were spoon-feeding amoebae. Turn a crank and find out how hard it is to pump blood through a clogged artery. Put your face on this magnet. Ha! It's an optical illusion. That's not how gravity works at all. Are you some kind of idiot?

Yeah, those scientists think they know it all. Even when they accidentally unleash a plague or melt the glue that holds together the universe, they can say, "Hey—it was just a theory." The best science on display shows off their sociopathic bounty—stuff from the future or space, toxic nightmares and atomic gadgets, with little or no math involved.

Doctors are even worse than scientists. They're *sure* they know it all. While scientists delve into abstractions before they accidentally kill people, doctors go right for the jugular. We're busy saving lives, dammit. Don't interrupt us. Make an appointment.

Medical institutions and private physicians have quietly hoarded startling collections of surgical scraps and medical oddities—*for further study by those with proper medical credentials*. A few collections are open to strong-stomached civilians. The rest of you can go crank an artery.

Space Junk

Nineties teenagers must be terribly confused by America's space program. NASA left a bunch of early '70s junk on the moon, and the guys that walked there are now grandparents. Scientists astonish us with an orbiting, out-of-focus telescope; the military develops experimental city-killers, or maybe just expensive wrenches—they aren't saying. Space is a vacuum that just plain sucks.

Or does it? Perhaps a perusal of our space legacy—on display to the public—can ignite our candles of stellar enthusiasm.

Moon rocks—what mysterious force is exuded by these lunar barnacles? Several hundred pounds were carted back to earth. Scientists soon established that the rocks weren't coated with a freaky alien fungus that would kill all life. So scores were sent to museums and positioned in sparkling, sealed chambers—as if they were the rarest of jewels. In a sense they are; they cost taxpayers millions in extra thrust-design requirements and fuel. Many museums display "replica" moon rocks, and visitors are still awed!

At the **International Space Hall of Fame,** Alamogordo, NM, visitors can see moon rocks, then take a simulated stroll on Mars and prowl around the highly optimistic Space Station 2001. The **Michigan Space Center,** Jackson, MI, features a moon rock "that you can touch"! They also display an unused moon rover and the Apollo 9 capsule.

Capsules—now we're talking primo space junk! Heroes floated through outer space in these tiny cans for days on end, eating paste out of a tube and pissing into a bag.

*Your family here! Another capsule, at **Meteor Crater,** Leeup, AZ.*

The coolest capsule? Try the command module from the ill-fated Apollo 13 mission, exhibited at the **Museum of History and Science,** Louisville, KY. At the overrated **Kennedy Space Center,** FL, check out the armrest from the Aquarius, sole surviving artifact from the lunar lander that kept the Apollo 13 astronauts from dying a horrible death in the vast loneliness of space. The first unmanned Mercury capsule and the Gemini 9 capsule are among the discards here. Their moon rock is enshrined in a clear Plexiglas pyramid.

The prize exhibit at the **Kansas Cosmosphere and Space Center,** Hutchison, KS, is the spacesuit of Svetlana Savitskaya, the first woman to walk in space. It's the only Soviet spacesuit the USSR ever allowed to be displayed in the West, probably because it was at the "Cosmosphere."

The **U.S. Air Force Museum** in Dayton, OH, shows off a "Zero-G Razor" and a space can opener in its "Space Gallery." A display on consumer bounty resulting from space R&D includes Velcro, Tang, freeze-dried ice cream, Dustbusters, and premoistened towelettes. Without the space program, research for this book might have been impossible . . .

The **Astronaut Hall of Fame,** Titusville, FL, has a peculiar assortment of original Mercury 7 bric-a-brac. See the toothbrush Alan Shepard used on Apollo 14, one of Gus Grissom's spaceflight souvenir dimes, and the flag that draped his coffin. The **USGA Golf Museum,** in Far Hills, NJ, possesses one of our greatest lunar treasures—the six-iron used by Alan Shepard to drive a golf ball on the moon in 1971.

The **Neil Armstrong Air and Space Museum,** in Wapokoneta, OH, proudly displays the droppings of man's first moonwalker. See Neil's survival machete, perfect for the jungles of the moon, and a moon rock presented by Tricia Nixon Cox in 1972.

Teen visitors at the **Museum of Science and Industry,** *Chicago, IL, see ancient space attire and quaint lunar excursion vehicles from the 1960s.*

Moon trees flourish in several states, with little or no mutating impact on the surrounding flora. These trees miraculously sprouted from terrestrial seeds that traveled to the moon and back with Apollo astronauts. A moon tree in Atchison, KS's **International Forest of Friendship** co-exists peacefully with a nearby Amelia Earhart statue. In **Lansing, MI,** an Apollo 14 sycamore seed planted by a governor in 1976 continues to bear no ill will toward the human race.

At the **Virgil I. Grissom State Memorial,** Mitchell, IN, "Star Voyager Gus" is honored with a display of his spacesuit and a Norman Rockwell painting. Mercury 4 was the flight on which he allegedly panicked and accidentally sank the capsule. The painting shows him getting ready for the Apollo flight in which he was killed. America's hapless astronaut was in the ground four years before this unremarkable building, far away from everything in a state park, was dedicated. A very lonely tribute to a hard-luck explorer.

Lots of foreigners videotape the **Astronaut Memorial** at the Kennedy Space Center. It honors the famous and the obscure dead of our bygone aerospace era, with lots of room to add on more names. This black monolith thing was designed to rotate away from the sun, so it's impossible to get a good photo of it. American tourists seem much more interested in the turtles and alligators that swim at the base of the memorial than in the memorial itself.

Welcome to the Hall of Micro-Processors . . .

With computers becoming obsolete, underpowered scrapheaps every five minutes, it was only a matter of hours before someone recognized their retooling potential as valuable museum relics.

The **Computer Museum,** Boston, MA, leaves no doubt that "thinking machines" are worthy historical topics. Three floors of slick "interactivity" tell us that the past is catching up much too quickly. Piles of clunky useless equipment, some only a few years old, have been donated by corporations all too happy to get it off the books.

Exhibits include hypnotic 3-D "PHS Colorgrams" using "stealth negative technique"; the computer offices from the 1964 New York World's Fair; the Hollerith Tabulator (used to compute the 1890 census); and famous computers like the NEAC-2203, Illiac IV, Univac I, and the 1940s

SCIENCE

Tech-heads laugh at this hysterical inside joke at Boston's Computer Museum.

MIT Whirlwind. Watch the work of Aaron, the '70s computer-art machine, as it creates the kind of nervous line drawings that used to keep people in mental hospitals. A soothing computer voice in the elevator tells visitors, "Come . . . stroll inside the walk-through computer," which features the world's largest trackball and electrical outlet. Visuals assault you throughout the galleries, from old industrial films about robots to clips from "Star Trek." Most visitors plunk down at one of the assorted terminals to experience ancient interfaces or solve engaging computer puzzles.

The gift shop is ready for a future when computers will have the last laugh. They sell old circuit boards as artsy wall hangings, coffee table computer repair manuals, keypad earrings and brooches, floppy disk beer coasters, and fading color slides of old circuit schematics, all for ridiculously inflated prices.

At the **National Video Game and Coin Op Museum** in St. Louis, you can relive your first moments of face-to-face combat with a computer, playing Pong or Space Invaders. They're here, along with Donkey Kong and the complete Pac-Man family. The first thing one notices is the familiar trilling sounds of spaceships and blinking cartoon characters, from games like Q-Bert, Gauntlet, and Karate Champ. Signs give brief histories of each machine.

Industry pioneers are ready for play, like Dragonslayer (the first laser disk game), although they break down as much as when they were first released. Certain machines evoke emotional explosions from visitors, who run toward them like loved ones they were sure were long dead.

The museum, which opened in 1990, nearly succeeds in presenting an interesting historical collection rather than an arcade bypassed by the technological interstate. The crucial catch that may doom this place is that you pay two admissions—the entry fee, and the cost of tokens to play the games.

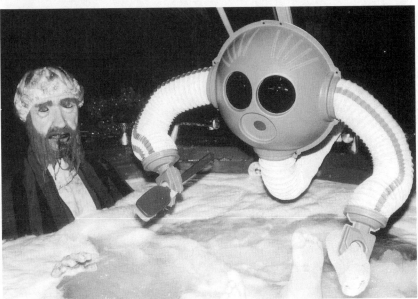

Look forward to a future living in the puffy foam homes of **Xanadu**
*(Wisconsin Dells, WI and Kissimmee, FL). In Lake Delton, WI, the helpful
servants of* **Tommy Bartlett's Robot World** *will scrub you from head to toe.
The Xanadus are rapidly falling apart, while Bartlett's cheap-looking robots
continue to twitch and tell jokes from their dated dioramas.*

THE ATOMIC TOUR

Don't get scared about your country's nuclear heritage—go out and learn about it. Then get scared. Nukes don't get much good press these days, but that doesn't stop government and industry from paying tribute to the fissionable little buggers whenever they can. Everyone, clip on your Radiation Exposure Badges, and move forward in a single file . . .

DAY 1: Start your atomic tour in Washington, DC, where important pronuclear legislation is signed regularly. Your first target is the **Smithsonian Institution's Museum of American History,** where you can size up the replica Fat Man and Little Boy bombs. Not quite the same as seeing the real thing . . .

Streak down to tiny **Mars Bluff, SC,** the spot where an air force B-47 accidentally dropped the real thing on Walter Gregg's farm in 1958. The high explosives' trigger detonated, leveling a farmhouse and leaving a 35-foot-deep crater. This nonnuclear dimple is now a swampy pond.

Take Route 125, the Road of Doom, from Millet, SC, to the notorious **Savannah River Nuclear Defense Site** in Jackson. You'll need to get a pass, and have to promise to stay in your car on this risky twenty-mile stretch. Chronic seepage problems are still reported; watch for radioactive turtles.

DAY 2: A fusioning ball explodes on the eastern horizon, sunrise, as you arrive in **Oak Ridge, TN**—"Home of the Atomic Bomb." This

Manhattan Project boomtown still churns out fissionable uranium for peaceful purposes. The original graphite reactor is open to the public, in the 10X building. The **Museum of Science and Energy** is disappointing for gung-ho atom fans; it's loaded with interactive energy displays instead of "You Be the Bombardier" simulations. See the short film on testing nuclear waste containers, as railroad cars and trucks smash into walls and each other at speeds of sixty to eighty miles per hour! Blam!

Next stop—a town whose postcards once proclaimed it "Atomic City." Since 1951, the **Paducah, KY,** weapons works has buried locally some seven million pounds of plutonium. It's enough plutonium to kill everyone in Paducah 330 trillion times, but who's counting?

DAY 3: Start your day at the squash courts of the **University of Chicago,** Chicago, IL. The monument says: "On December 2, 1942, Man Achieved Here The First Self-Sustaining Chain Reaction And Thereby Initiated The Controlled Release Of Nuclear Energy."

Drive, drive, drive, until you reach "Freedom Park," in Junction City, KS. This is where you can gawk up close at the **Atomic Cannon,** a huge piece of artillery built in the mid-'50s to hurl nuclear shells far enough that they wouldn't kill the people who fired them. There's another on display at **Fort Sill, OK.** Can you see both in one day? If your car was atomic powered you could!

DAY 4: At the **Strategic Aerospace Museum** in Bellevue, NE, reach out and touch the largest bombers ever built—ten different models! Seven different types of deadly missiles are in the outdoor garden. Pick up a replica red phone and overhear an end-of-the-world scramble. Watch a slide show reenactment of "Red Alert," and *see* the button glow. No milquetoast energy exhibits here! Pure nuclear firepower!

Drive quickly past the **Rocky Flats Weapons Plant,** Golden, CO, site of numerous calamitous "incidents." This place keeps catching on fire, and only a scant fifteen miles from downtown Denver! Have a quickie snack in **Grand Junction, CO,** a town built out of uranium scraps. Hundreds of houses were mistakenly built on or out of uranium mill tailings, which emit low-level radiation.

Check your exposure badge and move on, to Montana!

DAY 5: Pause for a breather at the **Merry Widow Radon Health Mine** in Basin, MT. The "healthful radon" industry arose after WW II, in abandoned uranium mines that give off this concentrated

TITAN MISSILE MUSEUM—GREEN VALLEY, AZ

When the Green Valley ICBM launch site was decommissioned by the military, townspeople turned it into a museum. Featured attraction: a tour deep into a missile silo housing a 103-foot-tall Titan.

Retirees staff the **Titan Missile Museum.** These forgotten guardians of Cold War sensibility lead the one-hour guided tours and man the cash registers. After a briefing room video explains the missile's history and "Peace Through Power," you select a hard hat and follow the guide outside to the entrance of the rocket's den.

The massive sliding door that once protected the missile that once protected us has been permanently sealed halfway open, and a two-foot hole has been cut in the reentry vehicle nose cone. "So Russian satellites can tell it's deactivated," says the guide.

It's time to go 100 feet down into the silo, as if your group is a missile crew coming in for its twenty-four-hour shift. The whole silo is on springs. Walls are not connected to floors. "Designed to withstand anything but a direct nuclear hit," says the smiling guide.

In the war room, an old punched-tape reader is ready to feed secret target directions into the guidance system. The scariest part is not the missile itself, but the antiquated equipment that national security once rested upon. Could this low-budget computer hardware really deliver a payload 6,500 miles away?

With a retiree's special combination of thoroughness and forgetfulness, we learn about the very typical boring day of a missile crew. Visitors look at each other. Everyone knows what everyone is waiting for: "Hurry up and shoot it!"

An audiocassette of the order to detonate from the movie *War-Games* is played, and the nightmare countdown begins. First to the safe where launch keys and codes are kept. Two different keys are inserted into two different parts of the computer. The guide turns the keys—and there's no turning back. Different sets of lights blink on, then alarms, bells, and quiet. "That's it."

Your group is led down the cableway for an underground view of the missile. Then, without even checking to see if the blast doors are hot, you are booted back to the surface and into the gift store.

On the way back north toward the rest of the country, you breathe a sigh of relief that we have maintained Peace Through Power, and then you notice that all the highway signs along I-19 are *metric only!* Whaaa . . . ? Hey, who won that Cold War anyway?

decay product of the ore. Many people swear of miraculous cures by this radioactive nemesis of superstitious realtors. Old people sit and chat or play cards while soaking up the beneficial radon aura.

Uncontaminated dust billows from the Idaho roadbed as you screech into the only town actually named **Atomic City.** The gas station is also the post office, general store, and motel. In nearby Arco, ID, take a self-guided tour of **Experimental Breeder Reactor #1,** and see "the hot cell," protected from you by thirty-four layers of oil-separated glass!

Now drop that third stage and rocket into the wasteland . . .

DAY 6: You're lost in the dead zones, purified patches of the DOE's Nevada Test Site Range at **"Jackass Flats."** The government has exploded over 700 bombs. They really let this place have it!

Roll down your windows again, and hurtle on to spend the rest of your day at the **Titan Missile Museum** in Green Valley, AZ. High-heeled shoes cannot be worn in the missile silo!

DAY 7: The tour concludes where the fireworks started, New Mexico. In Artesia you can visit the **ABO Elementary School,** built underground, just in case! The **Scientific Museum** in Los Alamos has its own replica Fat Man and Little Boy bombs, as does the **National Atomic Museum** on Kirtland Air Force Base in Albuquerque. Another slippery blockbuster, this time an H-bomb, dropped in 1957 five miles from Albuquerque's main streets. The Mark 17 bomb was 625 times more powerful than Hiroshima's noisemaker, but only the detonation explosive went off. Today, the crater is a small sand pit surrounded by desert sagebrush.

Our last stop is the **Trinity Site,** Alamogordo, NM. The first atomic bomb was detonated here at the first ever Ground Zero, marked by a stone cairn. The site is only open to the public once a year, on the first Saturday of October. You can turn in your exposure badges now. You should be fine.

They don't make 'em like this anymore! The replica Fat Man at the National Atomic Museum, Albuquerque, NM.

Marvelous Medical Museums

The **Mutter Museum** at the Philadelphia College of Physicians promises—and delivers—an afternoon of esoteric and incredible sights. The sophisticated, high-ceilinged gallery that houses this collection of medical monstrosities helps us rationalize our interest in it. Designed for perusal by present and future members of a dignified overpaid profession, the museum is two floors of dark-wood-trimmed display cases and a library-like stateliness. Shouts of "Will ya look at this *PICKLED FREAK?*" are entirely inappropriate.

The museum collection of pathological specimens is largely ignored by the general public. But where else can you see a plaster cast of Siamese twins Chang and Eng—*and* their actual attached livers? The Chevalier Jackson Collection of objects swallowed and surgically removed—you don't say! Brains of murderers and epileptics—I guess we could take a peek . . .

Gallery of human skulls at Philadelphia's Mutter Museum.

"Aieeee! It's starting to rain!!!" the Soap Lady at the Mutter Museum appears to be saying.

In deep glass cases around the walls are latex versions of eye diseases, a cavalcade of skulls, fetuses, and the skeletons of a giant and a midget. Two celebrity body parts are must-sees: the Secret Tumor of Grover Cleveland, and the Piece of Thorax of John Wilkes Booth. Grover's growth floats in a small jar, surreptitiously removed from his jaw while he was in office so as to avoid a financial panic.

One highlight is a giant colon that looks like a sand worm from *Dune*—arranged with one end rearing up from the tastefully underlit display. Doctors sent the owner of this whopper home with the diagnosis of a simple enlargement of the colon. His digestive distension now helps to educate new generations of doctors not to make the same hasty error.

Oddest is the body of the Soap Woman, who died of yellow fever in 1792 and was buried in soil with certain chemical properties . . . that turned her into soap! An accompanying display shows an X-ray cross-section and tells her story. A Soap Man, buried alongside the Soap Woman in the same cemetery, is hidden somewhere at the Smithsonian.

The smell of ancient insanity still hangs in the corridors of the **Glore Psychiatric Museum,** in St. Joseph, MO. It takes up one of the wards of St. Joseph State Hospital, a fortress-like mental health complex, now, thanks to modern medication, nearly empty of patients. The museum was started in 1967 by George Glore, a lifetime employee of the Missouri mental health system.

Dioramas span the history of treatment for mental illness: witch burnings and devil stompings; the Bath of Surprise, a gallows-like platform that dumped a patient into icy water; and a working model of O'Halloran's Swing, in which strapped-in patients spun at up to 100 RPMs.

Many devices are shown in use on an assortment of female glamour mannequins donated by department stores. Three are chained to the wall of the Bedlam Asylum scene. "Bedlam used to charge admission—people would visit as recreation," Glore says, shaking his head, as he leads recreating visitors through his museum.

The mid-twentieth-century exhibits include items used during the early days of Glore's own career: hydrotherapy and the wet sheet pack (patients rolled in wet sheets), lobotomy instruments, Fulton, MO's hospital cage, electroconvulsive treatments, and a fever-cabinet used for heating syphilis victims.

On one wall are displayed the 1,446 items swallowed by a patient and removed from her intestines and stomach. She died during surgery from the bleeding caused by 453 nails, forty-two screws, and assorted safety pins, spoons, and salt and pepper shaker tops. Displayed in a large crate are 100,000 cigarette packs collected by a patient under the delusion that the cigarette companies would redeem them for a new wheelchair for his ward.

The museum has no budget; it has gotten this far mainly on Glore's

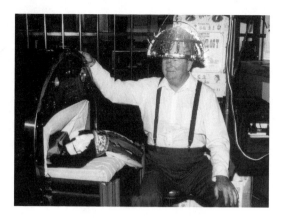

Bob McCoy with the MacGregor Rejuvenator. It was invented by a Seattle man in the 1930s to reverse the aging process. The patient was bombarded with radio waves, infrared and ultraviolet rays, and magnetic fields until he or she became a kid, or until his or her money ran out.

ingenuity. Glore always has a new diorama under development; he hopes to build a giant gerbil-like wheel that early patients used. Medicated ex-patients drop by and are glad to see that straitjackets are now museum pieces.

The **Museum of Questionable Medical Devices** is prominently situated in a mall in Minneapolis, MN. You will recognize Bob McCoy's establishment by the large phrenological reading devices out front. When we visited, Bob was demonstrating quackery to a group of children by linking them to an electrical "healing" device. "Now all of you hold hands and I'll just turn this knob . . ." RZZZZ! Mr. Anti-Wizard smiled as kids first grimaced, then yelled at the weakling who broke the chain.

Some of the other displayed treasures include a Prostate Warmer that plugs into a light socket and stimulates the "abdominal brain"; a Nemec-tron Machine that uses different-sized metal rings to "normalize" breasts; and a glowing Ultraviolet Comb (with penile and anal attachments).

The **National Museum of Health and Medicine,** Bethesda, MD—for some crazy reason—is trying to change its image and emphasize its so-cially conscious AIDS and mental health displays. Plow through this glitzy facade and get to the back, where the interesting stuff is. Like the wax head of a nineteenth-century alcoholic sailor with a horribly deformed nose. " 'Rhynophyma,' colloquially known as 'brandy nose,' " reads the sign. Really disgusting.

Also on display is a gangrenous human foot, the mummified head of a Kentucky girl preserved with alum (1858), microscope slides of Ulysses S. Grant's tumor, a mummified Siamese twin baby, a hat struck by light-ning, shorts found in a shark's stomach, and another big colon—this one from a soldier who had diarrhea for four months. Don't miss the leg bone of Major General Daniel E. Sickles and the twelve-pound cannonball that shattered it at Gettysburg. "For many years he visited the museum on the anniversary of its amputation."

The only decent new thing here is an interactive computer terminal that lets you play Lincoln's deathbed doctor. "Congratulations! You've scored an 84 out of a possible 100. The nation applauds your effort as a doctor and as a responsible member of society. Unfortunately, the president is dead."

Transparent Women

We've run into a number of transparent women: TAM, the Transparent Anatomized Mannequin at the **Museum of Science and Industry,** Chicago, IL; Varta, at the **Kansas Learning Center for Health,** Halstead, KS; Juno, at the **Cleveland Health Education Museum,** Cleveland, OH; and the perky transparent twins at the **Ft. Crawford Medical Museum,** Prairie du Chien, WI.

The twins are a well-preserved anatomical light show from an era of health education traveling displays. Organs glow, arteries pulse, and nerves shimmer in cool blue. They rotate to display their transparent backsides. The twin on the right does all the talking—probably because her sister has no face. "My eggs, when fertilized by sperm from my husband, will turn into a child . . ." Mysterious pelvic organs blink on. Two higher bulbs brighten. "My breasts provide milk for the newborn . . ." So this is why Superman could never enjoy a peep show.

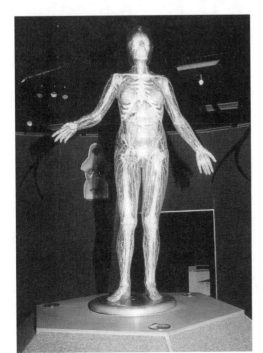

Juno, *the Talking Transparent Woman, at the Cleveland Health Education Museum.*

THE BODY ECLECTIC

Trephined Skull, **International. Museum of Surgical Sciences**, Chicago, IL: 2,000-year-old Peruvian skull with a hole drilled in it. The patient lived on for many years; skull chips were used as currency. Also see Napoleon's death mask, the Hall of Immortals, and kidney stones arranged like a rock collection.

Hair, **Hair Museum**, Independence, MO:Seventy-five framed human hair objects, a weird nineteenth-century art form exhibited at cosmetology school. Includes hair wreaths, hair jewelry, hair bookmarks, and a convict's hair diary. After you tour, get a discount haircut by fully licensed students.

George Washington's Dentures, **New York Academy of Medicine**, New York, NY. Made of real teeth, including one of his own.

Jawbone, **DeSoto Caverns**, Childersburg, AL: From a 2,000-year-oldWoodland Indian, who "scientists believe was over seven feet tall."

Half-inch man and woman cross-sections, **Museum of Science & Industry**, Chicago, IL: On a stairwell landing. Both bodies were sliced deli-style in the 1940's — the man horizontally (ear to ear) and the woman vertically (profile head to toe). About sixteen slices are on display in lit glass panels, which can be observed from either side. You can no longer flip through them like a book.

Chest of Sylvester mummy, **Ye Olde Curiosity Shoppe**, Seattle, WA: Handsome Sylvester puffs it up for mummy-mate Sylvia.

Twin livers of Chang and Eng, **Mutter Museum**, Philadelphia, PA: They're buried in North Carolina, but their liver is in Philly, in a pan under a life-sized plaster cast of the famous Siamese Twins.

Right arm, Body Parts Museum, **University of Pittsburgh Medical School**, Pittsburgh, PA: Big collection for student and professional perusal. Wear a stethoscope.

Section of James Garfield's vertebral column with bullet path, **National Museum of Health and Medicine**, Bethesda, MD.

Mystery pelvis, **The Thing?**, Benson, AZ.

Fingers in a jar, **Wood County Museum**, Bowling Green, OH: Used as evidence in a murder trial.

Petrified Finger, **Creation Evidences Museum**, Glen Rose, TX: Disproving evolution once again!

Lucky Finger, **Capital Punishment Museum**, Trenton NJ: Bitten off by a convict and worn as a necklace. Pickled in a jar by curator Joe Baranyi and on display with other prisoner contraband.

Dillinger's penis, **Smithsonian Institute**, Washington, DC: Just a rumor, but we know they're holding the Soap Man and 15,000 Indian skeletons somewhere . . .

Mummified Princess Foot, **Zorayda Castle**, St. Augustine, FL: Found in a cat hair rug by an ignorant fisherman.

Club Foot George's Foot, **Virginia City Museum**, MT: Mummified foot of a frontier town character lynched by the overzealous "Vigilante" group of the 1860's.

Composing "That New Look" From Body Parts On Public Display

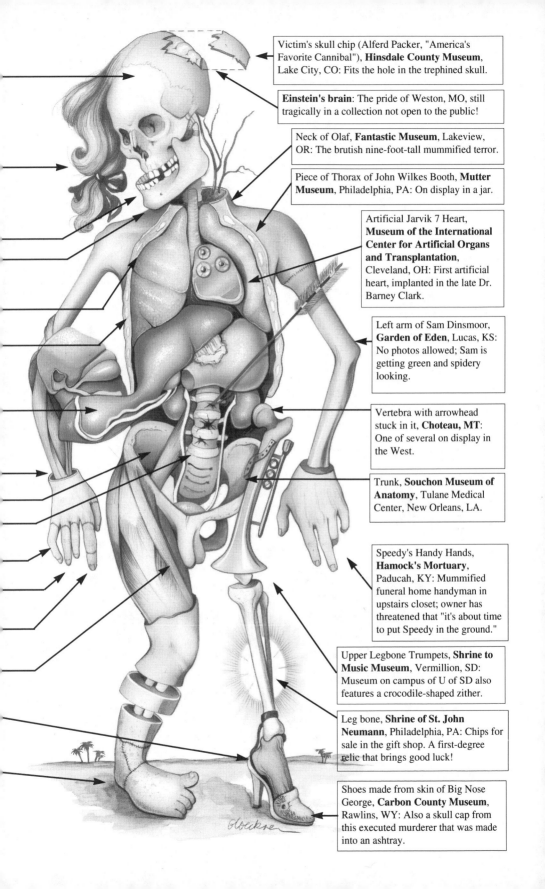

Victim's skull chip (Alferd Packer, "America's Favorite Cannibal"), **Hinsdale County Museum**, Lake City, CO: Fits the hole in the trephined skull.

Einstein's brain: The pride of Weston, MO, still tragically in a collection not open to the public!

Neck of Olaf, **Fantastic Museum**, Lakeview, OR: The brutish nine-foot-tall mummified terror.

Piece of Thorax of John Wilkes Booth, **Mutter Museum**, Philadelphia, PA: On display in a jar.

Artificial Jarvik 7 Heart, **Museum of the International Center for Artificial Organs and Transplantation**, Cleveland, OH: First artificial heart, implanted in the late Dr. Barney Clark.

Left arm of Sam Dinsmoor, **Garden of Eden**, Lucas, KS: No photos allowed; Sam is getting green and spidery looking.

Vertebra with arrowhead stuck in it, **Choteau, MT**: One of several on display in the West.

Trunk, **Souchon Museum of Anatomy**, Tulane Medical Center, New Orleans, LA.

Speedy's Handy Hands, **Hamock's Mortuary**, Paducah, KY: Mummified funeral home handyman in upstairs closet; owner has threatened that "it's about time to put Speedy in the ground."

Upper Legbone Trumpets, **Shrine to Music Museum**, Vermillion, SD: Museum on campus of U of SD also features a crocodile-shaped zither.

Leg bone, **Shrine of St. John Neumann**, Philadelphia, PA: Chips for sale in the gift shop. A first-degree relic that brings good luck!

Shoes made from skin of Big Nose George, **Carbon County Museum**, Rawlins, WY: Also a skull cap from this executed murderer that was made into an ashtray.

A life-sized (eight-feet-eleven) bronze statue of Robert Wadlow, "The World's Tallest Man Who Ever Lived," is located in his hometown of Alton, IL. Alton claims to have buried him in their **Upper Alton Cemetery** in a twelve-foot-long reinforced concrete sarcophagus. California's Loma Linda University maintains that it has his skeleton hanging in the **Shyrock Museum of Embryology.** Whom to believe? The nice trusting people of Alton, who invite all to visit? Or Loma Linda, who last shocked the world when they transplanted a baboon heart into newborn Baby Fae, and who keep the door to their museum locked?

Animal Freaks: Finding living freak animals is not easy, but one scholarly institute seems to specialize in their study. **Prairie Dog Town,** Oakley, KS, has both a living five-legged cow and six-legged steer, along with other animal anomalies. Inside the gift shop, a stuffed two-headed calf stares from the wall. PDT administrators bristle at the suggestion that they are crossbreeding mutants to produce even more spectacular monsters.

Aliens, Monsters, and Bugaboos

The world of the unexplained gets creepier every day. While smug skeptics bewail the lack of scientific evidence to support "Forteana" (named after the legendary researcher of mysteries, Charles Fort), we are under siege by the supernatural. Bug-eyed mothmen chase your car, friends spontaneously combust, and saucers leave burn holes on your front lawn. Ack!

Unexplained phenomena threaten roadside safety. Skyfalls—literal downpours of fish, rocks, and frogs—affect visibility and make asphalt slippery. Gravity hills, like the one behind the state capitol in **Salt Lake City, UT,** strain parking brakes and cause cars to roll uphill. Spooklights—glowing plasma balls—challenge night vision by bobbing for annoying and fleeting instants on back roads and above railroad beds. The **Tri-State Spooklight,** in Quapaw, OK, is a notorious chimera on State Line Road. The **Blue Ghost Lights** of Silver Cliff, CO, dart among gravestones along Highway 96 regularly. The **Brown Mountain Lights,** Brown Mountain, NC, are noted on a National Forest Service sign, visible on clear nights as ascending globules.

Monsters stalk the landscape. Big Foot still rules in the Pacific Northwest, and his stomping grounds near **Willow Creek, CA,** are marked with a statue. The Lizard Man still mucks around **Scape Ore Swamp,** near Bishopville, SC. A **Sea Serpent** statue in Crosby, MN, seems to be the only public acknowledgment of the multitude of water-borne midwestern monsters. The horned, sharp-taloned **Hodag** controls the Wisconsin town of Rhinelander, while the **Piasa Bird** continues to buzz the citizens of Alton, IL.

The **Bell Witch,** of Adams, TN, was America's nuttiest poltergeist. She drove the Bell family nuts, flew freely around the state wreaking havoc, and invited her drunken poltergeist friends over to abuse the mortals. Andrew Jackson even met her. She's still seen in a cave on the property, "they say." **Resurrection Mary,** the notorious Chicago phantom hitchhiker, thumbs on South Archer Avenue every so often. The enticing blonde in the white gown gets picked up mostly by lonely guys; when we pass her cemetery, she disappears!

A Fortean vacationer shouldn't focus solely on erratic events; it's wise to temper these superstitions with crackpot science and outlandish theories. The **Unarius Academy of Science,** in El Cajon, CA, features displays that teach followers of UFO-contactee Ruth Norman about their Space Brothers in the Intergalactic Confederation. The **Nikola Tesla**

Museum, Colorado Springs, CO, is trying to rediscover the "secrets" Tesla unearthed during his 1899 series of electrical experiments. This storefront is filled with plasma jars, a Tesla coil, and a photo of Tesla surrounded by a halo of sparks, "showing the Inventor in the Effulgent Glory of the Myriad Tongues of Electric Flame after he has saturated himself with electricity."

Chesterfield, IN, has a Museum of Spiritualist History at its **Spiritualist Camp,** but to bolster your theories on the unseen forces, visit Cassadaga, FL, the **Town of Spiritualists.** Five separate spiritualist groups battle for tourist attention: the Psychic Therapy Center group, the Spiritualist Camp group, the Universal Center group, the Hotel group, and the Grocery Store group. You can sense the animosity in vandalized signs and negative auras. If you want some magnetic healing, spirit guide drawings, or "Out-of-Body Traveling Tips," this is the place for you, but be wary. Third-eyed residents watch outsiders from screened front porches, silently plucking information from your head about competing spiritualist groups.

For a palpable fragment of Forteana, check out the **Lightning Portrait of Henry Wells,** in Carollton, AL. Former slave Wells was accused of burning the County Courthouse in 1876. He was arrested two years later, and placed in the garret of the new courthouse. A local mob gathered outside to lynch him. As Wells peered out the garret window, a bolt of lightning struck nearby and permanently etched his terrified expression on the windowpane. Wells died less than two months later "of wounds received while attempting to escape." The lightning photo is visible from the outside. Science tries to explain it, but we know better!

*This space roadster can park anywhere it pleases in **Mars, PA.***

Mythical Animals

 Genetic Engineering, or Inter-Species Love Children?

The jackalope, with its jackrabbit body, antelope speed, and deer antlers, is a reproductive mystery. Jackalope territory ranges as far south as Arizona and Texas, north to the Canadian border, and west to Idaho. Its birthplace is in **Douglas, WY,** marked by an eight-foot-tall painted fiberglass statue that has to be repaired every two years. A jackalope to ride can be found at **Wall Drug,** Wall, SD. An even stranger hybrid, the fur-bearing trout, can be found in the streams of northern plains states. We can only speculate about other elusive animals, still to be captured on postcards. Was there never so strong a love between raccoon and moose, coyote and vulture, or skunk and sidewinder?

The Merman at the Arkansas Alligator Farm in Hot Springs.

 Mermen, Alligator Men, and FeeJee Mermaids

The **Peale Museum,** Baltimore, MD, is hosting the "FeeJee Mermaid," half-man, half-fish, on sabbatical from Harvard's Peabody Museum. P. T. Barnum bought the FeeJee from Japanese sailors in 1822. Since then, others have come forward. The largest of these creatures, "Merman," has been an ennobled fixture of the **Arkansas Alligator Farm,** Hot Springs, AR, for over ninety years. Ripley's is reportedly attempting to buy up all of the world's Mermen. If you don't wait too long, other Mermen can be seen at the **Bird Cage Theatre,** Tombstone, AZ, the **Milwaukee Public Museum,** WI, the **Delaware State Museum** in Wilmington, and the **New York State Museum** in Albany.

Jake, the Alligator Man, hangs out at **Marsh's Free Museum,** Long Beach, WA. **Ye Olde Curiosity Shoppe,** in Seattle, WA, boasts the nation's only Mer-family: a Merman, Merwoman, and Merbaby.

Mermen and Alligator Men often find themselves torn from their freak shows and thrust into a cold, uncaring society. The Merman Support Group is sensitive to the hardships that these special creatures must undergo to cope in a changing world. They meet twice a century to share experiences and network.

Mystery Spots

Unexplained phenomena are best conveyed by an old codger, wise to government cover-ups and the shifty vagaries of science. Listening to the ravings of the **Mystery Spot** expert at Santa Cruz, CA, is half the fun. Many Mystery Spots fail miserably, employing fourteen-year-olds to convince skeptical summer visitors. "Scientists think it's caused by the 'igmmeous' rock in the hill, I think . . ." offered one bored, gum-clicking expert. Other spot-wranglers sheepishly point out the optical illusions, moving through a set of wall-walking and seat-balancing tricks.

The **Mystery Spot,** St. Ignace, MI, was discovered in 1953 and boasts that "Even a blind person could be affected." The **Wonder Spot** at Wisconsin Dells, WI, predates St. Ignace by five years, but proximity to such a bloated tourist mecca makes its claims suspect. Other spots include the **House of Mystery,** Hungry Horse, MT, **Mystery Hill,** Blowing Rock, NC, **Wonder World,** San Marcos, TX, and the **Cosmos Mystery Area,** Rapid City, SD.

America's premier mystery spot is the **Oregon Vortex,** Gold Hill, OR, 165 feet in diameter—perhaps the most mysterious spot on earth! The folks who maintain the vortex are careful to call it just that—"the vortex"—and not "the mystery spot," which they consider insulting. It's their claim that the only other real magnetic anomaly is at Santa Cruz, CA, and it isn't half as powerful as the Oregon Vortex. The other 300 mystery spots and "gravity hills" scattered throughout the United States are, according to Vortexophiles, pure hokum.

At the Oregon Vortex, you'll find the original House of Mystery, a slanted shack familiar to all mystery-spot devotees. Shacks are always present at mystery spots, having "slid down the hill" to their present position. Within these shacks, all the forces of nature "go haywire." Of course, the folks at the Oregon Vortex insist that their shack really *did* slide down the hill. After subjecting many spots to rigorous, very scientific tests, our Mystery Spot Test Kit™ indicates that the Oregon Vortex is the most disturbed.

What causes the mysterious goings-on? Nobody knows. One theory is that a great beam of "high velocity soft electrons" exits the earth through the vortex. Another claims that a giant underground manufactured device produces the weird effects. One man who apparently knew the secret of the Oregon Vortex—John Lister—lived at and studied its effects for more than forty years. He even corresponded with Einstein on the subject. What he uncovered no one will ever know, for he burned all his notes before his death.

"The world isn't yet ready for what goes on here," he warned.

Gabriel's Footprints and Glen Rose Man Prints

If you want more evidence of conspiracy by the superrich, here it is. Angels rarely land on earth, and when they do, it is even more rare for them to leave footprints. But that is exactly what Gabriel did when he visited **New Harmony, IN,** way back when. Much of the former Lutheran colony has been restored, but one home, in the backyard of which lie the controversial footprints, has been left in tatters. It's not open to the public, and a high fence keeps out prying eyes. Who'd think twice, if a religious superhero hadn't pulled a Grauman's Chinese in its backyard? The old postcards are missing from the town's artsy-craftsy notions shoppes, and only the older townspeople know anything about it.

Are rich people hogging the footprints for themselves? Are special secret powers transferred to those who stand in them?

More puzzling evidence sits right under the turned-up nose of Science in Glen Rose, TX. Near Dinosaur State Park, Giant Man tracks are on display at the **Creation Evidences Museum.** Fifty-seven humanoid footprints are in the same strata as the thunderlizards, conclusively disproving evolution.

The museum is building a forty-six-ton "hyperbaric biosphere." According to the director, they "are simulating the pre-Flood atmosphere which led to the dinosaurs. If this experiment is successful, it will upend the theory of Evolution." They predict that the pressure and heat will turn sphere lizards into dinosaurs, and lobsters and flying squirrels into . . . who knows what?

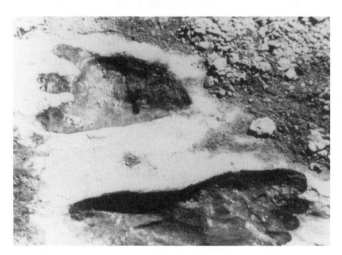

Man and dinosaur walk together at the Creation Evidences Museum, Glen Rose, TX.

The Thing?

—Cochise, AZ

"Mystery of the Desert." "Ghost of the Past." "Large selection of collectable liquor miniatures." These are only some of the many billboard advertising slogans used to draw the unwary to **The Thing?**. America's most purposefully mysterious attraction resides just off I-10, near the town of Cochise, AZ.

From outside, The Thing? looks like any other interstate gas station, aside from "The Thing?" written on the roof to attract curious air travelers. Behind the gas pumps is a gift shop that mysteriously offers nothing pertaining to The Thing?: no postcards, no logo T-shirts, no cedar burl dare speak its name.

What is The Thing? To find out, pay seventy-five cents and head through a door at the back of the gift shop. No photos—the better to preserve The Thing?'s strange mystique. What the gold footprints painted on the floor lead you to first, however, is less than startling: a small courtyard housing three prefab corrugated steel sheds. These sheds ring a collection of mobile homes for either The Thing?'s vestal virgins or its gift shop owners.

The first shed is filled with several old cars, wagons, and tractors. "1932 Buick," reads one sign. "This antique car was really THE THING."

"1937 Rolls-Royce," reads another. "This antique car was believed to have been used by Adolf Hitler . . . THE THING is, we can't prove it." The final exhibit is a metal cage filled with life-sized wood carvings of people being tortured. These carvings are the work of one Ralph Gallagher. Ralph signs his name, "Ralph Gallagher, artist," just so you know. "This display is worth many thousands of dollars," a sign reminds you. Root and driftwood simulacra painted to resemble animals hang all about the ceiling.

The second shed also has these wooden objects along its ceiling, as well as two rows of glass exhibit cases. A 1654 Matchlock rifle is in one. "It is beyond price. Take a good look," the sign explains. Also on display is a tarantula diorama, "Mandarin Stool—1467," and two water-damaged prints labeled simply "French 1800."

Now it's on to number three. The big moment. And there it is, real as life, right as you walk through the doorway. "THE THING—What is it?" reads a sign over its concrete container. Hmmmmm. Uh-huh. Then a quick denouement. Next to The Thing sits the top half of a clothing-store mannequin enclosed in a glass box. "This statue, showing a man being tortured, was located in Italy." Then a pioneer bedroom, more "folk art sculpture," and reentry into the gift store.

Several questions come to mind. How many thousands of people have visited The Thing? At seventy-five cents a tour, the proprietors must be making their profit on volume, and Rolls-Royces don't come cheap. Why are they located out in the middle of nowhere? Why? WHY?

Should The Thing? forever remain "The Mystery of the Desert"?

Over There Over Here

The mysterious **Pyramid House**,
guarded by its sentinels in Wadsworth, IL.

*T*here's not a single good reason to ever leave the continental United States. Not one. Anything you'd ever want to see or experience lies somewhere within a few hours' drive of a good old American interstate.

You probably think we're crazy, right? Myopic isolationists, flag-waving jingoheads, ignorant of the rapture of world travel. Well, Mr. World Traveler, just what do you get for the misery and expense of your globe-girdling adventures?

A lot of trouble, that's what. Dangerous, unsafe jets carry you to fetid, foreign lands, where alien people don't speak English and would rather kill you than give the proper directions to your decaying hotel. Want to be kidnapped by terrorists? Tortured by secret police? Sold into slavery? Then travel to foreign countries. They'll fix you up good, with their execrable food and poison water. Earthquakes strike, diseases and plagues spread unchecked, people pee in the street, and governments topple every five minutes—leaving the typical American running from angry mobs toward the nearest airport, to ride another unsafe jet that contains terrorists or bombs or God knows what.

Is it any wonder that Americans are turning away from the grisly horrors of world tourism and looking inward, to the varied treasures of their own continent?

America, the Great Melting Pot, also displays the finest parts of its great melting populace. Little lumps of unmelted ethnicity still stick to the sides of the pan—Bavarian Villages, Chinatowns, Dutch Wonderlands. Of course they're not distributed in a very orderly fashion, and with four Statues of David, a dozen Little Norways, and a hundred Holy Land replicas, nobody's promoting originality. But at least they're safe, and easy to visit.

If you want to see the world, don't bother to get a passport. It's all right here.

Holland, MI's
*Klompen Dancers
celebrate the annual
Tulip Time Festival
held in mid-May.*

America Unhenged

The most frequently replicated old-world site in the United States isn't the Tower of Pisa or the Parthenon. It's Stonehenge. Psychologists and historians advance all sorts of fancypants theories as to why this is so, but never see the obvious: It's easy to build.

The prettiest Stonehenge stands on a lonely bluff overlooking the Columbia River in Maryhill, WA. **Sam Hill's Stonehenge** was planned by Hill, a legendary road-builder, as a memorial to the WW I dead of Klickitat County. It originally stood at the center of Maryhill, but Hill forgot to put in a water system and everything except Stonehenge burned down. The monument was dedicated in 1918 but it wasn't completed until twelve years later. Sam Hill was by then in a "manic state" and short on cash. He died in 1931, living just long enough to see his Stonehenge finished. He is buried at the base of the Stonehenge hill, but there is no easy path to his grave because he wanted to be left alone.

The Georgia Guidestones in Nuberg, GA, stand on a windswept hilltop overlooking GA 77—six granite slabs, nineteen feet tall, a kind of mini-Stonehenge. They were erected in 1980 by a mysterious man named R. C. Christian and "a small group of Americans who seek the Age of Reason." On the upright slabs, carved in twelve different languages (including Swahili, Hindi, and Sanskrit), are ten "laws" encouraging readers to "unite humanity," "guide reproduction wisely," and "avoid useless officials." The Guidestones warn, "Be not a cancer on the Earth!" Does that refer to us, or to bad Stonehenge replicas?

The **stubby Stonehenge** on the University of Missouri's Rolla campus was built to showcase the stone carving capabilities of its High Pressure Water Jet Lab. According to its designer, this Stonehenge is "accurate to within fifteen seconds" when used as a clock.

America's Stonehenge in North Salem, NH, doesn't look a bit like its namesake, but it is the only Stonehenge site in America that claims to have spooky powers, astronomically configured rocks, and rumors of human sacrifice. Was it built by the "ancients" in 2000 B.C.? Or maybe renegade Irish monks in 1000 A.D.? Or crazed eighteenth-century farmers with nothing better to do? This jumble of rocks originally promoted itself as "Mystery Hill" but too many tourists showed up wanting to see their cars defy gravity.

It's hard to imagine, but there was a time when the residents of Alliance, NE, wanted to tear down **Carhenge** and the Nebraska Department of Highways wanted to label it a "junkyard" and build a big fence around it. Not any more! Now signs on the outskirts of town proudly identify Alliance as the "Home of Carhenge" as does the sign in front of the local Best Western. A gift shop down the road proclaims, "We sell Carhenge souvenirs."

If you haven't already guessed, Carhenge is a Stonehenge replica built out of junked cars. It was erected in the middle of a dusty field by six local families during a reunion in 1987. The junked cars, ranging in size from a '58 Cadillac to a '79 Honda, have since been painted a uniform gray to make the monument even more beautiful.

According to Carhenge's self-appointed caretaker, only about 40 percent of the people who visit know about Stonehenge. "We get a lot of remarks like, 'What the hell is this?' in our comments box," he sighs. "But the people come from all over just the same."

Sam Hill's Stonehenge in Maryhill, WA. Complete, the way the Druids would have wanted it.

Oyotunji African Village

—Sheldon, SC

Adelana and Adegbolu pose next to the giant head of Olokun at Oyotunji African Village. Though its mailing address is Sheldon, SC, it is not part of the United States.

This wayward scrap of Africana was born in 1970, when its twenty-seven marshy acres officially seceded from the U.S. Its ruler, His Royal Highness Oba Ofuntola Oseijeman Adelabu Adefunmi I, is a former used-car dealer who saw the tax benefits of starting not only his own religion but his own country.

A painted plywood sign beckons visitors to drive down a potholed dirt road to visit the village "as seen on TV." Actually, the only part of **Oyotunji** that's ever been on TV is the king—on Oprah and Phil defending his right to practice polygamy.

Oyotunji juts up between tall cedar trees, a bug-infested conglomeration of clapboard shacks, infrequently painted concrete gods, and a "royal Osha-giyan Palace" that looks like a bargain basement V.F.W. hall. Oyotunji literature pictures its happy residents strutting about in colorful, flowing robes, dancing and playing percussive instruments. In fact, if you ignore their ritual scars, Oyotunji's inhabitants look and dress like anyone else in South Carolina who lives in a town with dirt streets.

The colony used to contain over 200 Olorishans; only thirty-seven remain. Even more alarming, the king's wife count has dropped from seven Yoruban queens to four.

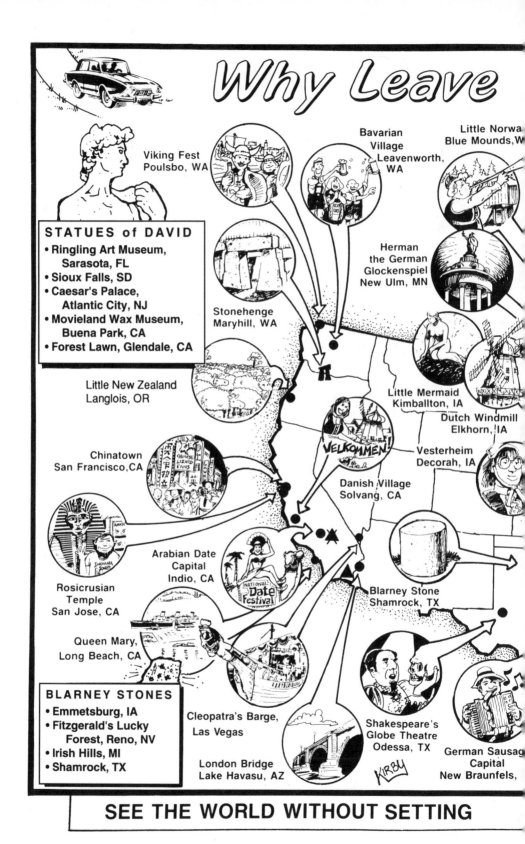

Why Leave

Viking Fest
Poulsbo, WA

Bavarian
Village
Leavenworth,
WA

Little Norwa
Blue Mounds,W

STATUES of DAVID
- **Ringling Art Museum,**
  Sarasota, FL
- **Sioux Falls, SD**
- **Caesar's Palace,**
  Atlantic City, NJ
- **Movieland Wax Museum,**
  Buena Park, CA
- **Forest Lawn, Glendale, CA**

Herman
the German
Glockenspiel
New Ulm, MN

Stonehenge
Maryhill, WA

Little New Zealand
Langlois, OR

Little Mermaid
Kimballton, IA

Dutch Windmill
Elkhorn, IA

Chinatown
San Francisco, CA

VELKOMMEN!

Vesterheim
Decorah, IA

Danish Village
Solvang, CA

Arabian Date
Capital
Indio, CA

Rosicrusian
Temple
San Jose, CA

NATIONAL
Date
Festival

Blarney Stone
Shamrock, TX

Queen Mary,
Long Beach, CA

BLARNEY STONES
- **Emmetsburg, IA**
- **Fitzgerald's Lucky**
  Forest, Reno, NV
- **Irish Hills, MI**
- **Shamrock, TX**

Cleopatra's Barge,
Las Vegas

Shakespeare's
Globe Theatre
Odessa, TX

KIRBY

German Sausag
Capital
New Braunfels,

London Bridge
Lake Havasu, AZ

SEE THE WORLD WITHOUT SETTING

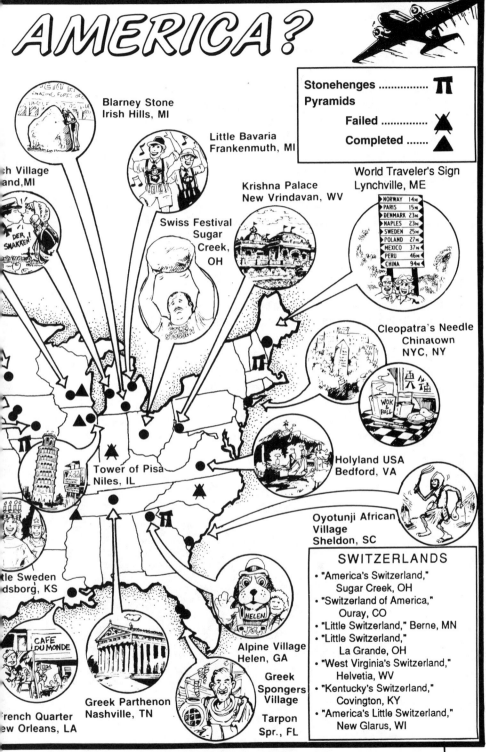

AMERICA?

Stonehenges .... π
Pyramids
      Failed .... ✕
      Completed .... ▲

Blarney Stone
Irish Hills, MI

Little Bavaria
Frankenmuth, MI

:h Village
and, MI

Krishna Palace
New Vrindavan, WV

World Traveler's Sign
Lynchville, ME

NORWAY	14mi
PARIS	15mi
DENMARK	23mi
NAPLES	23mi
SWEDEN	25mi
POLAND	27mi
MEXICO	37mi
PERU	46mi
CHINA	94mi

Swiss Festival
Sugar
Creek,
OH

Cleopatra's Needle
Chinatown
NYC, NY

WOK
&
ROLL

Tower of Pisa
Niles, IL

Holyland USA
Bedford, VA

Oyotunji African
Village
Sheldon, SC

tle Sweden
dsborg, KS

SWITZERLANDS

- "America's Switzerland,"
  Sugar Creek, OH
- "Switzerland of America,"
  Ouray, CO
- "Little Switzerland," Berne, MN
- "Little Switzerland,"
  La Grande, OH
- "West Virginia's Switzerland,"
  Helvetia, WV
- "Kentucky's Switzerland,"
  Covington, KY
- "America's Little Switzerland,"
  New Glarus, WI

CAFE
DU MONDE

HELEN!

Alpine Village
Helen, GA

Greek
Spongers
Village

Tarpon
Spr., FL

rench Quarter
ew Orleans, LA

Greek Parthenon
Nashville, TN

FOOT OFF THE CONTINENTAL U.S.

THAT LOONY CUCKOO BATTLE

In the mid-1980s, the owners of the Bavarian Clock Haus in **Frankenmuth, MI** ("Michigan's Little Bavaria"), converted the front of their building into a giant cuckoo clock, complete with a big bird that emerged and wagged its tongue and tail on the hour. Surely, they thought, this was the largest cuckoo clock in the world, and they promoted it as such.

Then a letter arrived from a lawyer representing a Mrs. Grossniklaus, owner of the Alpine Alpa Cheese Haus in **Wilmot, OH.** *Her* establishment, the lawyer claimed, had the world's largest cuckoo clock, and she had Guinness to back up her claim. Frankenmuth decided to do a little checking.

Mrs. Grossniklaus, it was true, had her clock featured on the cover of the *Guinness Book of World Records*. But there was no cuckoo clock category within, and this was no oversight. Guinness had determined before the book was published that there was no way to compare such different cuckoo clocks and they weren't about to start. Despite what Mrs. Grossniklaus's lawyer claimed, Guinness wanted nothing to do with her battle.

We aren't so timid. While it's true that the Frankenmuth cuckoo clock isn't a separate timepiece like the one in Wilmot, it certainly is one in spirit. Mrs. Grossniklaus's clock may delight purists, but if you're a fan of pure size, Frankenmuth blows doors.

Wilmot, OH's giant cuckoo clock.

*Bug-laden Menagha, MN, offers us **St. Urho,** who chased the grasshoppers out of Finland. His roadside statue defiantly impales a giant grasshopper on a pitchfork.*

Desert of Maine Snow Globe

A few foreign attractions promise more than they can possibly deliver. The **Desert of Maine,** in Freeport, ME, is a large patch of land where bad farming practices eroded the topsoil and left a bunch of sand dunes. Technically a desert, but no more amazing than your local dirt-bikers' sand pit. The concrete camels look especially sad during torrential downpours. "Every weekend's been beautiful up until today!" insisted the gift shop lady, but the London Fog outlet store down the road hints at a different story. There was a mix-up at the snow globe factory, and the whole Desert of Maine order ended up with ocean liners instead of camels. Not exactly the "ships of the desert" they had in mind.

Spongeorama

—Tarpon Springs, FL

"The sea and men . . . men who search the sea for treasure. But the treasure they seek is not gold or jewels . . . it is a gift from the sea taken for granted by most. Since the beginning of recorded history, man has sought and prized the natural sponge . . ."

So begins the horribly deteriorated '50s vintage film, now video-projected in the Cinematic Theatre of **Spongeorama.** Onscreen, craggy toothless men scan the horizon for favorite sponging spots. This grainy, jumbled documentary convincingly conveys the murky terror of deep-sea sponge diving. So does the fishy-smelling Sponge Diving Museum next door, with its crude dioramas of blood-splattered mannequins dying from the bends. Exhibits such as "Popular Greek Foods" and "How Spongers Are Paid" beckon from behind grimy glass, while peppy balalaika music plays everywhere.

Tarpon Springs is a predominantly Greek community, drawn to the Florida gulf to harvest "rich sponge beds." Artificial sponges have absorbed most of the market, and the gulf beds are all but exhausted, yet you'd never know it from the restaurants selling souvlakis and sour cheese pies, and the souvenir stands hawking classical statuary, sponge plant-holders, and rubber sharks and divers.

A diver's helmet photo opportunity is one of the many surreal touches offered at Florida's Spongeorama.

Prabhupada's Palace of Gold

—New Vrindaban, WV

The Hare Krishnas are conspicuously absent from today's airport begging zones, displaced by panhandling LaRouche cold fusion fanatics and other fringe politicos. Where did those glassy-eyed, shaved-head zombies go with our spare change? The answer is surprising.

West Virginia.

The winding mountain road is longer than we remembered. On nearby hills, arrays of Christian crosses seemingly ward off bad karma from our destination—**Prabhupada's Palace of Gold.** This is the place the Krishnas have chosen to erect a glittering glimpse of the old India of the Bhagavad-Gita. The Palace was originally designed to be a home for His Divine Grace A. C. Bhaktivedanta Swami Prabhupada. Favor-currying curry favorers finished the "Taj Mahal of the West" in his memory in 1980.

Today, the palace plays a dual role: It's a destination for spiritual pilgrimage (the only official Hindu holy place outside of India) and a tourist attraction. Krishna chant tapes play on a droning loop over the palace grounds. Tourists remove their sneakers or sandals to tour the beautiful interior.

We pass a forty-foot-tall concrete couple, frozen in acolyte aerobics over the time-share cottages. The Deity Swan Boat is moored inside a shuttered gazebo. At the Temple of Understanding doors, a few Krishnas sit, sore of foot and dog-tired after three days of "festival." They pleasantly answer questions about their latest projects: a new teen center, and progress on the City of God, about two miles up the road.

The Temple of Understanding holds the answers to our other questions. Musical instruments are piled near a jumble of chairs. A wax Prabhupada sits serenely enthroned, Jesus by his side. Stranger gods sit in alcoves, including three brightly colored cartoon creatures with giant eyes like divine Scrubbin' Bubbles. A "What Are Deities?" display brings more anxiety than enlightenment.

The final chamber is the City of God map room, which contains a scale model, blueprints, and computer renderings of a planned 100-acre Transcendental Theme Park. The new Temple of Understanding will be 216 feet tall and will last a thousand years. Trams, a Swan Skyride, and live elephants will transport faithful throngs from the Land of Krishna Hotel to the Plaza of Light and the Trinavarta Victory Tower. New computer designs make the T. of U. look more like a crystal starship, poised for launch.

The Krishnas are on the golden path, despite some unpleasantness a few years back with the authorities over some bodies illegally buried on the property. Live elephants are already giving rides, and a nearby hill bears the stigmata of heavy construction.

If you don't mind feeling like you're trapped on the cover of *Sgt. Pepper*, come chant at the Palace of Gold.

Shoes are a no-no in Prabhupada's golden prayer pad.

The Curse of the Pyramids

Pyramids are cursed! Who dares taunt the yelping dog demons of Anubis? Time and time again puny Man ignores Unknowable Force, as ego trips his rightful fear of gods.

The pyramid at the center of the world, Felicity, CA.

Nowhere is this malevolent power more evident than in **Bedford, IN,** "The Limestone Capital of the World." The town received over $700,000 in government grants to build an eight-story replica of the Great Pyramid out of native limestone. Work began, with restaurants and heliport proceeding smoothly. However, as the pyramid's base was being laid, funds ran out and new monies could not be raised. The project has been long abandoned. Weeds grow up through the foundation as the earth reclaims the land.

The Ames Pyramid in Laramie, WY, is sixty feet tall, monolithic in the middle of windswept, barren pastureland, and only accessible by a two-mile dirt "road." It was built in 1882 to honor the financiers of the Union Pacific, and to give rail passengers something to look at in Wyoming. While it still stands, the railroads inexplicably declined, and the tracks that used to run alongside were removed. Now all that remains is the stark and scary pyramid, perhaps a warning to others.

The Pyramid, a supper club shaped like one in Beaver Dam, WI, seemed to have appeased mighty Isis. Some credited its Yummy Mummys, a specialty after-dinner refresher. But! The owner of this popular eatery suffered a stroke in 1986, immediately after excitedly viewing an ill-publicized travel book in which his pyramid was mentioned.

Who dares now mock the gods? Tiny Felicity, CA, tempts all fate with its twenty-one-foot-high **Center of the World Pyramid.** Inside, mirrored walls focus attention on a circular plaque in the middle of the floor, marking the exact center of the world. While this helps Felicity in its ecocentric Ptolemic polemic with rival world center **Hartwell, GA,** the mayor closes Felicity during the summer and flees to Europe. The pyramid is always visible, but why do you run, mayor?

Official green highway signs lead the way to the five-story **Pyramid House** in Wadsworth, IL. A wall topped by Egyptian heads and a desert-like no-man's-land separate casual onlookers from the house. While official tours are booked six months in advance, the brave may park and look through the gate. This is a private estate that includes a moat, a long line of mini-Sphinxes, and a three-pyramid garage, built by a mysterious foreign-looking man (his license plates read "RAMSES II"). 'Bagos full of strangers give him no peace.

While the pox goes on all around it, Memphis, TN, has completed **The Great American Pyramid.** Standing 321 feet tall, this is the largest pyramid ever built in the Americas (not even the Aztecs could match it), complete with a stainless-steel exterior and an outdoor inclinator ride to its glass-enclosed apex. But it is already $200 million over budget. A sister pyramid on Festival Island has been scrapped. Some locals call the developers "New Age Priests." Spray-painted near an adjacent statue of Ramses is "Millions for this while Memphis rots." Is anyone surprised?

The Pyramid supper club, Beaver Dam, WI.

The Great American Pyramid, Memphis, TN.

Romantic Rome? Hah! It's romantic Niles, IL, where America's very own Tower of Pisa teeters impressively.

One of the Seven Wonders of The New Roadside America

SOUTH OF THE BORDER

—DILLON, SC

The automobile trip from the bleak cities of the Northeast to the sunny shores of Florida via I-95 takes two good days of driving. Halfway there, as you speed between the pine stands, visible heat coming up off the road, a huge alien sombrero, nearly 200 feet high, suddenly appears in the distance.

You grin, speed up, and turn off at the next exit, as if compelled by some otherwordly force. The sombrero is Sombrero Tower, landmark of the **South Of The Border** tourist complex. There can be no doubt. After enduring an accelerating onslaught of 120 billboards for the past 200 miles, this is what you've waited to see.

South Of The Border (SOB to insiders) is a unique amalgam of Dixie and Old Mexico. Odd at first, but in a remarkably short time you'll come to accept SOB as a neon yellow and pink Tijuana, with the added benefit that its inhabitants speak English and understand proper concern for hygiene.

The lovable mascot of the place is pedro, a grinning mustachioed caricature who wears an outsized sombrero. It is pedro who speaks from the billboards. It is pedro who straddles the SOB entrance as a ninety-seven-foot-tall statue/sign. You can drive through his legs.

Once parked, a visitor can venture into fourteen different gift stores, and browse through figuratively millions of souvenirs. Quantity rules, with, for example, eight types of backscratchers and twenty-two types of coffee mugs. Bins are packed to o'er brimming with each gewgaw and doodad. Big ticket "classy" items, like $2,000 crystal Eiffel Towers, are for sale in pedro's exquisite Rodeo Drive Shop.

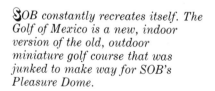

SOB constantly recreates itself. The Golf of Mexico is a new, indoor version of the old, outdoor miniature golf course that was junked to make way for SOB's Pleasure Dome.

Take a ride up the glass elevator to the top of Sombrero Tower, the same monolith that caught your eye in the first place. As you walk around in the brim of this huge hat, look out at the surrounding fields. Nothing. A desolate terrain cut in two by the highway. SOB is a real oasis.

Relief from the heat and the loudspeakered pop music is afforded by a restaurant stop. The Sombrero Room serves the best Mexican food in northern South Carolina. Pedro's Casateria offers food in short order, and Las Maracas puts to rest the myth that one simply cannot get a good steak in a building shaped like a Mexican hat.

If you find yourself spending more time here than originally scheduled, and it starts getting dark, don't worry. SOB has both RV campgrounds and 300 motel rooms spread over its 135 acres. And staying here allows access to pedro's Pleasure Dome, with its indoor pool, steam room, Jacuzzi, bar, and wedding chapel.

A dozen weddings are performed here every summer weekend. Ninety-nine dollars gets you married, a night in an "heir-conditioned" honeymoon suite (complete with champagne and waterbed), and a free breakfast the next morning!

South Of The Border continues to evolve, amazing return visitors. Giant Vegas-like electric signs now announce special deals. Mini Mex Golf has been replaced by The Golf of Mexico, an air-conditioned, indoor putt-putt extravaganza. The Top Hat is a swank new private bistro, located above the Rodeo Drive Shop.

SOB's man of vision is Alan Schafer, who began his rise to roadside immortality in 1950 with a simple beer stand. When supplies started being delivered to "Schafer Project: South Of The [North Carolina] Border," a neon light went on in his head. He started importing Mexican souvenirs, and on one such trip arranged for two boys to come work for him. As Schafer says, "Since it fit into the theme, we began calling them both 'Pedro.'" Today, all SOB workers, regardless of race, creed, or color, are called pedro.

At age seventy-eight, Schafer is still the guiding genius. All the major projects at SOB are conceived by him. All the billboard slogans are his creation. Inside his office, a half dozen desks are scattered about, each covered with charts and drawings—ideas in formation. A battery of computers and telephones sits in the outer office, ready to close a deal for plastic backscratchers in Taiwan or check the sale of camouflage condoms in SOB's Dirty Old Man shop.

SOB's proximity to military bases means its Dirty Old Man shop is a Times Square–style outlet, stocking videos and various latex helpers. Of course, that's like the "real" Tijuana, but where will that sort of logic end? With a donkey show out behind SOB's post office? No thank you, sir. South Of The Border has the best of both worlds right now!

Founder Alan Schafer still runs things at South Of The Border. He continues to write all the billboards. Our favorite: "Keep yelling, kids! They'll stop!"

History

*A typical American family ponders the memorial to the Truman family at **Truman Corners Shopping Center,** Grandview, MO.*

istory is only interesting to uninteresting historians," someone probably once wrote or thought, and on the whole we'd have to agree. Most of us shy away from historical sites for the same reason we avoid dietetic candy and public television. If it doesn't sing, wiggle, or explode, why bother?

We don't have a lot of history in America, and that's good. In Europe, on the other hand, there's so much history that you can't move without tripping over some dusty relic or grave. Europe has no room for a Children's Crusade Goofy Golf or a Diet of Worms Water Slide, and even if it did, it probably wouldn't want them.

In the U.S.A., however, we've got the space and the time to make history that will at least look good on a postcard. Want to blast bas relief cartoon characters into that rock commemorating a gruesome Indian massacre? Go right ahead! Want to immortalize your great-granduncle, the Chinese Noodle King, by building a giant replica of his first pot? Feel free! Why don't you build a Goofy Golf or a Water Slide while you're at it?

Tourist attractions have done their best to pep up what little history we do have, and their efforts are usually commendable. Wax dummies drip blood and give us insight into the lost art of torture. Bombs and rocketry bring back memories of wars fought in colorful, faraway lands. Wild West tourist towns regularly succumb to exciting, mysterious fires—just as the real places once did.

History is what we decide it should be, and it should be as loud, fast, and wiggly as possible.

*Yankees beware! Chattanooga, TN, is the home of **Confederama,** which recreates "the battle that sealed the fate of the Confederacy" on a giant electromechanical map.*

War and Peace

The Revolutionary War took place almost exclusively in the Northeast, which does not bode well for its commercial exploitation. After spending an afternoon at stultifying **Plimouth Plantation** in Plymouth, MA, or **Colonial Williamsburg** in Williamsburg, VA, you'll swear all our fore-fathers did all day was dip candles, play the fife and drums, and sit in the stocks and pillory.

WW II was more exciting, but it wasn't fought anywhere near American soil—or so one-worlder history profs would have you believe. However, near the town of Brookings, OR, stands **Mt. Emily,** which is one of several targets along the Oregon coast bombed by the Japanese in 1942. You can hike a half-mile trail to the marked site. Why the Japanese would want to bomb Mt. Emily, or **Mt. Avery** in nearby Sixes, remains a mystery, but they did. The close proximity of **Bomber Gas** in Milwaukie, OR, and the **Flight 97 Restaurant** in McMinnville, OR, both made out of old B-29s, shows that the citizens of Oregon won't be caught with their pants down again.

If you want to take a gander at some slam-bang modern military hard-ware, stop at the **USAF Armament Museum** in Valparaiso, FL, and

The Mickey Mouse gas mask was supposed to appeal to kids. It didn't. "Not even the Smithsonian has one of these," chuckled the curator at the **U.S. Army Chemical Corps Museum** *in Fort McClellan, AL.*

This XB-70 Valkyrie, "the world's most exotic airplane," is the only one of its kind that didn't crash. See it at the U.S. Air Force Museum in Dayton, OH.

view their collection of smart bombs, AMRAAM missiles, and an SR-71 Blackbird. The **U.S. Air Force Museum** in Dayton, OH, is even better, with its F-117A Stealth video show (accompanied by groovy fusion jazz), and Thunderbird Leader, the chatterbox host of the Air Power Gallery. His goony face is projected onto a dummy clad in a bright red jumpsuit as he directs visitors to nearby water fountains and rest rooms.

You can walk around old battleships in Wilmington, NC, Fall River, MA, La Porte, TX, and Mobile, AL, but you'd be better off visiting the **Concrete Outline of the U.S.S. *South Dakota*** in Sioux Falls's Sherman Park. When the government mothballed the *South Dakota* in 1962, land-locked Sioux Falls stripped all the parts they could carry, poured a foot-high concrete outline onto the grounds of a city park, and combined the pieces into a weird, minimalist pseudo replica. Now a museum occupies the spot where the bridge once stood, and for two dollars you can be commissioned an admiral in the South Dakota navy.

On the distaff side, the **Women's Army Corps Museum** in Fort McClellan, AL, places most of its emphasis on uniform development. You'll learn everything you ever wanted to know about the café brown accessories introduced in '51, the silver taupe summer outfit of '54, and the 1952 elegant Evening Dress Uniform with its blue tiara. All are modeled on glamour mannequins. Ask the director to show you the storage room, packed solid with everything this large museum doesn't have room to display, including WAC garter belts and tiger skin hatboxes.

In the interests of balanced journalism, we attempted to visit the **Peace Museum** in Chicago. It is closed.

Blacks and Confederates: Parallel Lives

Montgomery, AL, bills itself as "birthplace of the Civil War and the Civil Rights Movement." As home to both the **First White House of The Confederacy** and the **National Civil Rights Memorial,** who can blame them? The injustices foisted upon Confederate President Jefferson Davis

*Jefferson Davis and Robert E. Lee don't look very happy at the **Hall of Presidents Wax Museum** in Colorado Springs, CO. You can't please everybody.*

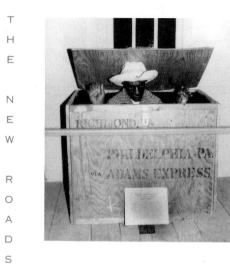

*Henry "Box" Brown mailed himself to Philadelphia and freedom. One of the many inspirational displays at the **Great Blacks In Wax Museum** in Baltimore, MD.*

after the noble war are revealed at the stately White House. The injustices foisted upon thirty people killed in the twentieth-century struggle for civil rights are revealed at the stately memorial. The best souvenir photo in town? Try the corner of Rosa Parks Avenue and West Jeff Davis.

Take your choice of the Robert E. Lee Bridge or the Martin Luther King Bridge into downtown Richmond, VA. On Clay Street is the **Museum of The Confederacy,** located next to the (second) **White House of The Confederacy.** Here we learn of the heroic "Victory in Defeat: Jefferson Davis and the Lost Cause." Also on Clay Street is the **Black History Museum,** where we learn of blacks' heroic victories and defeats against guess who.

Atlanta, GA, is the site of the **Martin Luther King Historic District,** featuring the nonviolent leader's birthplace and grave, and the church where he preached. At #1 Martin Luther King, Jr. Drive, hop aboard The New Georgia Railroad for a trip to **Stone Mountain,** featuring the world's largest bas relief sculpture—honoring Confederate leaders Robert E. Lee, Stonewall Jackson, and Jefferson Davis.

The Wild West

Wild West towns still exist in the wild West, but it's hard to tell which are worthwhile. **Central City,** CO, bills itself as "the richest square mile on earth," and when you see what they charge for parking in this congested nightmare of a town, you'll understand why. **Boot Hill** in Dodge City, KS, has to stage its gunfights with noisy downtown traffic as a backdrop. **Deadwood,** SD, is being rebuilt from the ground up in order to accommodate legalized casino gambling and now the good stuff is being pushed out. The **Chinese Opium Tunnel Museum** has already been re-named the "Chinatown Tour," and more limp-wristed yuppification is expected. Can Wild Bill Hickok's poker hand of death, still defiantly displayed in the **#10 Saloon,** survive?

At **Tombstone,** AZ, arguably the most famous wild West town of all, death and mayhem are forced to share space with the corner FINA station and trailer park. However, one attraction that should not be missed at Tombstone is the **Historama,** narrated by Vincent Price. Through the miracle of "missile-age electronics," tiny moving figures teeter across a five-sided revolving turntable. "See . . . licking flames engulf the town!" "Hear . . . the dread Apache war cry pierce the air!"

We heartily recommend **Old Tucson,** AZ, and **Buckskin Joe's** in Canon City, CO. Old Tucson is a nearly full sized replica wild West town, built by Columbia Pictures in 1939 as a set for the film *Arizona*. The well-choreographed multiple-shootout mayhem here is satisfying, and the post-cards are excellent.

Buckskin Joe's is a relative newcomer, with the usual complement of creaking buildings and historical exhibits, but it also features hourly gunfights and superrealistic HANGINGS. "Hell, I ain't gonna wait for no jury!" declares the sheriff as he drags a struggling bad guy up onto the scaffold and kicks the trapdoor out from under him. As the bad guy's neck breaks and he dangles in the breeze, a voice over a loudspeaker proclaims, "In the old West, justice was swift!" The sheriff thoughtfully leaves the bad guy hanging for several minutes ("Take yer pictures before he turns blue!") while moms, dads, and kids pose in front of the dangling dead man. *That's* history!

The citizens who are not dead in Tombstone, AZ, are proud of their heritage.

Indians!!!

When the White Man arrived in the New World 500 years ago, there was a lot of room for everybody. Soon, more White Men arrived, and then their wives and their bratty kids. And soon after that, there wasn't so much room anymore. This foreseeable set of circumstances led to friction between Those Who Were Here First and Those Who Could Care Less and left us, their descendants, with (1) guilty consciences, and (2) lots of good massacre sites to visit.

"Just a little off the top, chief." Bloody wax fun at the **Lone Star Hall of Texas History** in San Antonio.

The **Alabama Historama** in Mobile devotes itself to recreating the Massacre at Fort Mims. "You can relive the action: smoke, fire, dying settlers, and Creek victory cries, the largest Indian Massacre in the history of the entire North American Continent!" If you've only got time for one massacre it might as well be the largest, and 537 men, women, and children were put to the Creek hatchet here in August, 1813.

The **Tippecanoe Battlefield Monument** in Battle Ground, IN, salutes the military genius of future President William Henry Harrison. In all fairness, it should salute the bonehead generalship of Tecumseh's idiot brother, The Prophet, who convinced his followers that the White Man's musket balls would pass right through them. This led to ill-advised bravado, a lot of dead Indians, and the election of WHH as president number nine. Harrison died after only a month in office, perhaps from a lingering Cherokee curse.

The Red Man also got the worse of it in Penacook, NH, where the **Hannah Dustin Monument** honors a woman who scalped her ten Indian captors, and in Mankato, MN, site of the **Largest Legal Execution in U.S.** A granite marker on the corner of Front and Main Streets shows you the spot where thirty-eight Sioux were simultaneously hanged after murdering unarmed citizens in some long-forgotten uprising.

Colorado had plenty of Indian massacres and thus now has plenty of Indian ruins. This was good news for history-hungry tourists, but bad news for tourist-hungry Manitou Springs, which didn't have any. So Manitou Springs decided to build the **Manitou Cliff Dwellings Museum,** an ingenious cliff dwellings replica that looks just like the real thing, but isn't. It has forty rooms and is tucked into a convenient sandstone overhang right next to the fast-food outlets and chain motels of Colorado Springs. We have to admit, it's much better here than off in some godforsaken desert.

Government has once again poked its nose into Indian affairs with disastrous results. We initially cheered Public Law Number 101601, which forced the **Smithsonian** to give up the thousands of dead Indians

*This **Indian Burial Ground** was once next to the St. Augustine, FL, Fountain of Youth—which didn't speak very well of the Fountain of Youth. The Indians were removed.*

they'd been hoarding for years. We hoped that this dusty old museum would turn their Indian bones over to tourist attractions, where they could be displayed with proper horror-movie lighting and sound effects. Instead the Smithsonian gave them back to the Indians! Now the Indians, smelling easy prey, have mounted a savage attack against *all* dead Indian attractions. The Indian Burial Pits in New Cambria, KS, were the first to go, then the burial mounds in Wickcliff, KY, and Moundsville, AL. The **Dickson Mounds** in Lewistown, IL, may soon follow suit, as they fend off a siege by Indians, the police, the press, and local politicians. Circle the wagons, Dickson!

If you can't see dozens of dead, anonymous Indians, perhaps you'd like to visit the grave of a dead, famous Indian. **Geronimo's Grave** is at Fort Sill, OK, where this legendary Apache died in 1909. He was on his way home from selling souvenirs to tourists when he fell off his horse and rolled into a ditch (he'd apparently had too much to drink). Geronimo lay there all night. In the morning he was found and put to bed, but the ditch in which he lay had been filled with water, and Geronimo contracted pneumonia and died. What happened to his body? The spokesperson at Fort Sill "didn't know anything" about reports we'd heard that Geronimo's skull was stolen by George Bush's dad and given to the supersecret **Skull and Bones Club** at Yale University. We dug up Zachary Taylor on less evidence, why not Geronimo? Or will we have to send our own children to cootie-puss Yale before we know the truth?

The ancient ruins of **Casa Grande** in Coolidge, AZ. No one knows why it was built, but the WPA erected a giant steel umbrella over it anyway.

Presidential Paternalia

Monuments to our presidents vary widely in their impact. Some are inspired, some are stupid, and those that display inspired stupidity are the tributes we like best.

The **George Washington Memorial Stump** stands (sort of) in St. Mary's, GA. For many years, when the stump used to be a giant oak tree, this was St. Mary's top tourist draw. It had been planted the same year that George Washington died, but in 1986, unfortunately, the tree also died. Now all the town has left to promote is the stump, which it does.

Rubbing the nose of any Lincoln statue is supposed to bring good fortune. This legend started because Abe's children used to pull on his nose for luck. Most of them died young, and Lincoln was assassinated. Oops.

Truman Corners Shopping Center in Grandview, MO, occupies the land once farmed by the Truman family, with signage that looks like it hasn't been changed since give-'em-hell Harry was in office. A bas-relief plaque, standing on a pedestal near Osco Drug, honors Harry and his clan—but more so their land, which, we are told, contributed "to the great American dream of opportunity and progress by becoming the site of one of America's finest shopping centers."

In Plattsburg, MO, you'll find the **President Atchison Monument**, a statue honoring Plattsburg's favorite son, David Rice Atchison. As a result of an inauguration snafu, Atchison was President of the United States for one day, in 1849, in between James K. Polk and Zachary Taylor. Atchison's influence on the Republic is debatable, since he spent the entire day sleeping off a drunk.

The **Gerald Ford Museum** in Grand Rapids, MI, is a place befitting America's only unelected president, chock full of such dreary displays as Ford's baby booties and a pompous time line chronicling the *Mayaguez* incident as if it was Seven Days in October. The museum has the gun with which Lynette "Squeaky" Fromme tried to kill Ford, but it's not on display. The counter help—who have an instinctive distrust of people under forty not wearing golf shirts—curl their lips when you ask why not. If it's important enough to keep, why isn't it important enough to display? Perhaps the best thing about this place are the original Ford White House matchbooks that you can buy in the gift shop for $1 apiece.

Our favorite presidential tribute would have to be the **urinal used by JFK,** in the men's room at Reilly Stadium in Salem, OH. The urinal is marked by a small plaque, and when the stadium's rest rooms were renovated in the late '80s, it was reverently left untouched.

The **Ronald Reagan Memorial Tree** stands in Arcata, CA. Enjoy it while you can; it will one day become the Ronald Reagan Memorial Stump.

JFK travels back in time to assassinate Lincoln. A bold hypothesis brought to life at **Wax World** *in Wisconsin Dells, WI.*

Richard Nixon Library and Birthplace

—Yorba Linda, CA

The new **Richard Nixon Library and Birthplace** is like the new Nixon. The facts are all there. We just see them differently today.

Inside, The Road to the Presidency takes you past a replica hollowed-out Alger Hiss pumpkin, the Nixons' Campaign Woody, and the sheet music for 1960's "Nixon Victory Song." On to the triumphs of 1968 and beyond. Then one of the museum's centerpieces, a room of former world leaders, cast in bronze, engaged in happy dialogue. It's a popular spot to pose with the deposed.

Next into a pagoda of peace—purposely unfinished because President Nixon's work for peace was also unfinished. Then into the mock living room of a suburban tract home, the outside wall of which has white siding and a garden hose attached. At the touch of a button, a '60s-style TV broadcasts the famous "Silent Majority" speech, explaining Nixon's support for the Vietnam War.

In the Gifts of the People room, displayed, among the knitted eagles from regular people is one of Sammy Davis, Jr's "Love and Peace" medallions, and a handgun presented to Nixon by Elvis Presley. "The President Meets the King" photos are on sale in the gift store (as are replica Nixon Birthplace bird houses for $45).

Next into the dark hall: Watergate: The Final Campaign. Visitors can listen to the "Smoking Gun" Watergate Tape through headphones. But pay attention to the narrator. "It was Nixon critics who call this 'the smoking gun.' But it is not what it once appeared to be . . . This conversation resulted in no obstruction of justice, and no cover-up resulted from the conversation." Unfortunately, the president had to resign to heal the nation.

After seeing the resignation speech on video, you move to a small theater where you can ask President Nixon, via interactive videotape, a number of questions about his administration. "If it were 1972 all over again, what would you have done differently about Watergate?" "I would have paid more attention."

Crime ...

Most of our glorified crime occurred in the nineteenth century. Possibly this is because the lawbreakers who lived in that era were more colorful and exciting. More likely it's because all the people who could possibly sue are now dead.

*Al Capone's favorite chair is a prize exhibit at the **House of Cash** in Hendersonville, TN.*

The **Dalton Museum** stands in Coffeyville, KS, where two Dalton brothers (and two gangster buddies) were shot dead. A wall-sized photo of their corpses lets you know that. After marveling at the plaster replica of the world's largest hailstone (which fell in Coffeyville), visitors can walk across the actual threshold and through the vault doorway of the two banks the Dalton Gang robbed just before the irate citizenry blew their brains out.

In St. Joseph, MO, visitors can tour the **Jesse James Home** and "see the bullet hole" that was made after the bullet took a shortcut through Jesse's head. Generations of souvenir hunters have picked away at the hole until it is now an unrecognizable, fist-sized blob in the plaster wall. Current management has sealed the hole under a sheet of Plexiglas, thus preserving an important relic.

Lizzie Borden was New England's contribution to the bloody 1800s, and her accomplishments have been enshrined in the **Fall River Historical Society Museum** in Fall River, MA. Lizzie was charged with the 1892 murders of her well-to-do mom and stepdad, and among the displays here are Lizzie's whackin' hatchet and gruesome crime scene photos of Mr. and Mrs. Borden's pulpy heads. You have to suffer through a narcotizing, hour-long tour of local Fall River junk to see the Lizzie Borden display, unless you tell them you're travel writers and in a hurry.

If John Dillinger wasn't dead, he'd enjoy the **John Dillinger Historical Wax Museum,** which occupies two floors of a stately old house in downtown Nashville. This place is everything a museum dedicated to a ruthless outlaw should be: quirky, bloody, and altogether satisfying.

The primary focus of the Dillinger Museum, "offered without social or moral comment," is the gory death of John Dillinger. Instead of skirting the issue and offering some namby-pamby display or plaque, this place rips the lid off the subject and fills two whole rooms with Dillinger death exhibits. One even has a red light that flashes as you enter, warning those with faint hearts to stay out!

JD's original tombstone is prominently displayed, as is a replica of the electric chair he never lived to die in. A battery of 8 × 10 glossies lines one wall, showing Dillinger awash in a pool of blood outside the Biograph Theater; another selection shows his bullet-ridden corpse in the morgue. Many angles are offered for your viewing pleasure. Off to one side stands a transparent skull with a Lucite bullet piercing it at the trajectory of the original death slug. Next to this are Dillinger's trousers of death, with their pocket contents displayed alongside, and his baseball shoes. The focal point of the museum is an exact, life-sized wax recreation of Dillinger on the slab, blood and all.

Educational? You bet!

. . . and Punishment

As is only just, the places where you can see punishment far outnumber those where you can see crime.

One of the best is **The Old Jail** in St. Augustine, FL, where crumbling mortar adds nicely to the ominous atmosphere. Dozens of broken-down dummies in prisoner stripes fill the exercise yard; most have had at least one limb torn off or a face whittled away. The Old Jail's real-life residents probably didn't fare any better.

The **House of Frankenstein Wax Museum** in Lake George, NY, features more torture tableaus than you can shake a stick studded with impaled heads at. Prerecorded screams fill your ears as dummies are flayed alive, garroted, and boiled in oil. A skull sticks out of a pile of sand; "Ant Torture—a thousand deaths before the end," reads the sign. A woman screams as an axe cleaves into her face. "The Hatchet Man— another innocent victim is murdered," reads this one. We won't even

These dummies are happy they're not being ripped apart by tourists at The Old Jail in St. Augustine, FL.

New Mexico's first electric chair, tastefully displayed at the Santa Fe Trail Museum in Springer, NM.

begin to describe what's happening to the poor devils in "The Amazing Room of Rats."

Capital punishment is the ultimate punishment, and also the ultimate thrill. The **Old Wyoming Prison Museum** in Rawlins features a real gas chamber. The **Santa Fe Trail Museum** in Springer, NM, displays New Mexico's only electric chair, while "Old Sparky" stops 'em dead at the **Texas Prison Museum** in Huntsville. **The Museum of Capital Punishment** in Trenton, NJ, has the chair used on Bruno Hauptmann. "Lethal injection is no deterrent to a junkie," laments curator Joe Baranyi. "It's just a longer trip. Cook 'em."

Several places allow you to don the hood and participate. At the **1869 Territorial Prison and Wax Museum** in Virginia City, NV, dropping a dime into a slot can bring an animated execution to life, complete with buzzers, flashing lights, and a quivering victim. At **Wall Drug** in Wall, SD, the premise is the same but the punishment is different; for a dime you can hang an animated cowboy. Watch that neck s-t-r-e-t-c-h comically! It's loads of laughs.

The Witch Dungeon —Salem, MA

The Witch Dungeon is a most entertaining presentation of justice. It's located right where it all happened back in 1692 and features a live witch trial, something you can normally only see in our nation's Capitol.

The show begins with several minutes of preparatory narration, piped into a "courtroom" filled with tourists. Stage curtains slowly pull back to reveal a shadowy court bench and jury box, containing roughly a dozen trial participants. The proceedings get underway quickly, but it soon becomes apparent to the more attentive audience members that only two of the performers are actually alive. The rest are thinly disguised dummies that fail to move an inch or utter a syllable during the entire show. However, the prosecutor and the accused, Sarah Goode, are animated—animated enough to make up for a whole dungeon of dummies.

Every summer a new duo of aspiring actresses work their thespian magic here. The witch gets to be spooky by cackling and prancing about in a moldy, hooded cape, but it's the prosecutor who has the lion's share

The People's Court—seventeenth-century style. A burning desire for justice is evident at the Witch Dungeon.

of great moments. Our favorite is her twitching struggle with some invisible demon as she shrieks, "She has the devil's mark! She's biting me!!!" The audience accepts all this in dead earnest, even at the climax when the witch, ranting incoherently, plunges into the crowd, whacks the pressure bar on the nearest exit door, and disappears!

Audience members, still awestruck, are then led on a tour of the dark, lower dungeons, where the dummies that are too deteriorated to stay upstairs in the courtroom are flogged and tortured. It is here that the economy of the Witch Dungeon becomes apparent, as it is the prosecutor who leads the tour while the witch pops out of murky cubbyholes screaming at the top of her lungs.

Police Museums

Standing somewhere between Crime and Punishment, straddling—as one brochure proclaimed—"the thin blue line between criminals and those who break the laws," are the police. **The American Police Hall of Fame and Museum,** Miami, FL, bills itself as "a crime-prevention multiplex"

The American Police Center and Museum in Chicago shows that the law can be just as terrifying as the lawbreaker.

and proclaims, simply, "This country is at war." In order that you might better understand this, the museum displays a blood-splattered guillotine, a "hands on" electric chair (good for gag photos), human skulls with entry wounds, and bricks from the St. Valentine's Day Massacre garage. An entire wall is filled with grisly crime and accident scene photos, with shots of birth defects tosssed in for good measure. It's as if the police wanted to say, "Look, the real world is gross and disgusting. Aren't you glad you have us to keep it away from you?"

The **American Police Center and Museum** in Chicago keeps its employees behind bulletproof glass, which adds to its atmosphere. Among its displays are John Dillinger's Biograph Theater seat, a gun used by Bonnie Parker, and the terrific Horror of Drug Addiction exhibit. Here, an open coffin is upholstered with drugs of all descriptions, while a recorded drumbeat plays. Next to the coffin stands a disgusting, life-sized photo of a sixteen-year-old female "drug user," oozing from head to toe with hypo abscesses. "NOT VERY PRETTY, IS IT?" asks a voice from the tape.

At the **Buford Pusser Home and Museum** in Adamsville, TN, you can visit the basement where Buford spent most of his off-the-job time. "There were so many attempts on his life," visitors are told, "it was the only place he felt safe." The displays here used to be out in the open, which meant tourists could actually touch such exhibits as the *Walking Tall* sheriff's shoes of death. Then someone stole Buford's wallet of death and now all the display cases are locked.

NO MORE HUMILIATIONS! ARISE, MY ZOMBIE BROTHERS! EEYAAGH!

What ho! It's the stolen head of Geronimo, winging its way back to Ft. Sill, OK!

The Tragedy in U.S. History Museum

—St. Augustine, FL

Just inside the majestic gates leading to St. Augustine's snooty Fountain of Youth sits a tiny house covered with large, yellow signs. "Old Spanish jail—See human skeleton!" one announces. "See Jayne Mansfield's death car—learn the truth!" proclaims another. This is **The Tragedy in U.S. History Museum,** the creation of L. H. "Buddy" Hough and a perpetual bone in the throat of the St. Augustine Chamber of Commerce. "That place is closed," the chamber snaps if you ask about it. Happily, it is not.

The first thing you'll encounter inside is the gift shop, selling snapshots of Bonnie and Clyde's graves. On top of the souvenir counter sits a book listing every American who died in Vietnam, and behind it is a display of Lee Harvey Oswald's bedroom furniture.

"See each shot as they hit President Kennedy in the Dallas parade!" declares another sign. This exhibit is nothing more than several old *Life* magazines laid end-to-end in a display case, their pages opened to blow-up frames from the Zapruder film. Buddy didn't even rip them out.

In the back room of the house stands a mummy in a coffin. "Lonesome?" beckons the sign beneath it. "Take me home with you. $4,500." Across the room are the Last Will and Testament of Elvis Presley (poorly photocopied) and a leather jacket once worn by James Dean. This is displayed with the box in which it was shipped to the museum, which adds to its authenticity.

Out in the backyard, your eyes are immediately drawn to the glass garage housing "famous movie star" Jayne Mansfield's death car, and astute observers will quickly learn the "truth" alluded to in the sign out front—Jayne's death car was a Cadillac, while the car on display is a Buick Electra 225. The human skeleton (in a box, under a sheet of plate glass) lies next to this, and next to it is what purports to be the Bonnie and Clyde getaway car "as depicted in the famous movie." "Crime does not pay! 137 bullet holes!" declares the sign.

For those wishing to enjoy these exhibits more fully, a picnic area has been thoughtfully provided, offering a fine view of the Bonnie and Clyde car and the human skeleton.

Museum of Museums

Between Tucson and Phoenix, a curious collection of bombed-out buildings appears along northbound I-10. A truck perched atop a sign shows that these ruins had once been a tourist attraction. Upon inquiry at the gift store across the highway, we learned that it was once a museum belonging to a Mr. Furrer. "But it wasn't too popular," the salesperson told us. "All he had in it was old stuff."

Many collections suffer from this "old stuff" affliction. Sometimes little distinguishes the local Pioneer Museum from the local Goodwill store. And you don't have time to sort through all the dull droppings to get to the truly neato stuff. But we did.

Here then, in no particular order, is *The New Roadside America*'s new "Museum of Museums." Like good curators, we have rotated some exhibits since the last time you visited.

- J. Edgar Hoover's bronzed baby shoes **(House of the Temple,** Washington, DC)

- Herbie, the Love Bug **(Elvis Presley Museum,** Kissimmee, FL)

- Isabel (TV's "Weezie Jefferson") Sanford's bra **(Frederick's Bra Museum,** Hollywood, CA)

- Wax display: Superman using X-ray vision to look at Lois Lane's panties **(World of Illusions,** Gatlinburg, TN)

- Rock touched by Helen Keller **(Walk of Fame,** Rollins College, Winter Park, FL)

- Full-scale replica of world's first Piggly-Wiggly **(Pink Palace Museum,** Memphis, TN)

- Jake LaMotta's leopard skin robe **(National Italian-American Sports Hall of Fame,** Arlington Heights, IL)

Jim Watson, assistant curator of the UDT-SEAL Museum, proudly displays Manuel "Pineapple Face" Noriega's chair.

- Bugle from Custer's last stand (**Wyoming Pioneer Memorial Museum,** Douglas, WY)

- The key to Hitler's Berchstegaden bomb shelter (**Baldpate Inn,** Estes Park, CO)

- Some of Gandhi's ashes (**Self-Realization Fellowship's Lake Shrine,** Pacific Palisades, CA)

- Life-sized replica Liberty Bell made out of wheat (**Mennonite Heritage Center,** Goessel, KS)

- Whiskey bottle smashed by Carrie Nation (**Museum of Whiskey History,** Bardstown, KY)

- Manuel Noriega's chair (**UDT-SEAL Museum,** Fort Pierce, FL)

- Sand from President Eisenhower's putting green (**Sand Museum,** Desert of Maine, Freeport, ME)

- Sioux headdress worn by Hubert Humphrey (**Nobles County Museum,** Worthington, MN)

- "The beam on which Bill Young was hung by a mob, after his acquittal on mass murder charges" (**Clark County Historical Museum,** Kahoka, MO)

- Gold nugget shaped like Jimmy Durante's face (**Northwest Bank Museum,** Helena, MT)

- Plaque memorializing Nikolai Ivanovich Kibalchich, builder of the bomb that killed Czar Alexander II. "While waiting to be executed, he invented the rocket engine." (**International Space Hall of Fame,** Alamogordo, NM)

- Floor safe kicked in anger by Jack Daniel, which infected his toe and killed him (**Jack Daniel's Distillery,** Lynchburg, TN)

- The world's first traffic light (**Ashville Heritage Museum,** Ashville, OH)

- Altimeter from the *Hindenburg* (**The Fantastic Museum,** Redmond, OR)

- Top fuel slingshot dragster that exploded and blew off Big Daddy Don Garlits's right foot. With shrapnel display (**Don Garlits Museum of Drag Racing,** Ocala, FL)

- Barbara Mandrell's wedding nightie (**Barbara Mandrell Country,** Nashville, TN)

- A piece of Grover Cleveland's 1886 wedding cake (**Grover Cleveland Birthplace,** Caldwell, NJ)

- Lee Harvey Oswald's can opener (**Gafford Family Museum,** Crowell, TX)

Civic Pride

The fifty-five-foot-tall Jolly Green Giant casts his leafy shadow over **Blue Earth, MN.**

$\mathcal{M}$adness grips many towns. It is not spawned from fluoridation or industrial spillage or the Playboy Channel. The madness is civic pride.

Civic pride usually spreads unchecked through tiny burgs with inadequate video outlets and underused chambers of commerce. One day, an order comes down from on high: Make our town exciting! Then the lunacy strikes. "Let's build a giant skunk!" cries one chamber member. "No, no, let's claim we have the world's oldest toothbrush!" It spreads from City Hall to the Elks Lodge to the Beauty Boutique until soon the entire town is smitten; Friendlyville has become Zardoz.

Nutty, however, is not nearly enough. A good civic boast must be exciting; something to brag about in front of people who might otherwise not recognize the importance of your hometown. "You live in Paris? Hah! That is merely the capital of France. I live in the Pipe Cleaner Capital of the World!"

Civic chauvinism based on mortal things (such as trees or animals) is time bomb waiting to pop off. Wise civic leaders recognize that their claims to fame must always be made out of something permanent—such as concrete or fiberglass—to capture the public's imagination. Home of the largest cantaloupe ever grown? Where is it now? Why didn't you preserve it in a big jar? Let's go over to the next county and look at their giant, fake cantaloupe instead!

Towns are waiting, eager to infect you with their delirium. And every single good one sells postcards.

*A sign of pride: **Cadiz, OH.***

Treasures, Boasts, and Swell-Headed Hokum

In 1986, the Lions Club of **McRae, GA,** got patriotic. Since it was the centennial year for the Statue of Liberty, they decided to build a scale replica "as a reminder to citizens what America really means." Liberty's head was a gum stump dredged out of a local swamp, sculpted with a chainsaw. Her upraised arm was made of marine Styrofoam, and the hand that held her torch was actually an oversized electrician lineman's glove. "We never knew it would be so pretty," said one Lion, admiring his handiwork.

McRae, GA, built their Statue of Liberty out of local junk.

Things were not looking good financially for the town of **Pineville, KY.** Then the Pineville Kiwanians came up with an idea; they attached a giant chain (3,000 pounds, 101 feet long) to an equally giant rock that appeared ready to roll down a mountainside onto the town. In fact, the rock wasn't about to roll anywhere, but that wasn't the point. The Kiwanis club got great press as "the town was saved" and the only thing that rolled into Pineville was tourist money.

Kokomo, IN, is not the only town to base its civic pride on a tree stump—which is odd enough—but theirs is the biggest. Fifty-seven feet in circumference and twelve feet high, Kokomo's stump stands next to the stuffed carcass of Big Ben, the world's largest steer—yet another claim to fame. Perhaps buoyed by its premier stump and steer status, Kokomo proclaimed itself America's "City of Firsts." This promptly got them into a brawl with **New Bern, NC,** which claimed the same thing. For the record, Kokomo boasts that it is the birthplace of the *first* push-button car radio, the *first* Dirilyte golden-hued tableware, and the *first* aerial bomb with fins. New Bern counters by claiming it was the *first* town to celebrate George Washington's birthday, the site of the *first* federal hanging in America, and the *first* town in North Carolina to decorate its streets with varicolored electric lights at Christmas.

Liberal, KS, is a town that really wants you to visit. Their drive for civic individuality began in the '30s, when Liberal built their new library in the shape of an open book. But Liberal was ambitious; they wanted more. So the town proclaimed themselves "Gateway to the Land of Oz," built a replica of Dorothy's house and the yellow brick road, imported a pair of supposedly genuine ruby slippers, and opened an Oz minimuseum. Still, Liberal wasn't satisfied. Then they hit upon a title that would propel them out of orbit entirely: "Pancake Hub of the Universe." In order to nail down this claim, Liberal competes in a flapjack-flipping race with Olney, England, every Shrove Tuesday. "It has been suggested that the Pancake Race has established a grass-roots international understanding that might never have been possible at even top-level diplomatic sessions."

Many world capitals dot the U.S. map. Though they may be transient acne to ivory tower cartographers, there's no denying that **Dalton, GA,** is the Carpet Capital of the World; **Martinsville, VA,** is the Sweat Shirt Capital of the World; and **Central City, NE,** is the Pump Irrigation Capital of the World. Chester Greenwood invented the earmuff in 1873, thus making his hometown of **Farmington, ME,** Earmuff Capital of the World by proxy. **Cedar Springs, MI,** the Red Flannel Capital of the World, backs up their claim with flannel factory tours and a museum, and anyone caught not wearing red flannel on Red Flannel Day (the first Saturday in October) is arrested.

In some instances, separate towns can share the spotlight by boasting about nearly the same thing. For example, the **Amana Colonies, IA,** are

the "Bratwurst Capital of the World" while **Sheboygan, WI,** is the "Wurst Capital of the World." **Worthington, MN,** and **Cuero, TX,** each claim to be the Turkey Capital of the World. Rather than fight, the two towns stage a race—the Great Gobbler Gallop—every October, in which one turkey from each town competes. The first across the finish line wins for its town the Turkey Capital crown for the following year.

This live-and-let-live attitude, however, does not apply to **Claxton, GA,** and **Corsicana, TX,** which both claim to be Fruitcake Capital of the World (Claxton fruitcake, locals point out, was the only fruitcake exhibited at the 1964 New York World's Fair). There's also no love lost between **Punxsutawney, PA,** and **Sun Prairie, WI,** which both claim to have America's only official weather-forecasting groundhog (this battle has already reached the floor of Congress). The battle for the title "First Town Named for George Washington" is especially murky. **Washington, NC,** claims George actually visited in 1791. **Washington, GA,** says that doesn't matter, and besides, they were the first city in Georgia to hang a woman. **Washington, KY,** seems to be backing out of the fray; they merged into neighboring Maysville in 1990, and now prefer to be called Old Washington. Meanwhile, the civic leaders of **George, WA,** maintain a wooden-jawed silence.

Bigger Is Always Better

When civic pride is at stake, it's best to stake it on something big. It doesn't matter if a town's claim to fame is dumb or ugly, so long as it casts an impressive shadow across the face of gawking tourists. Bigness is what brings the 'Bagos to a burg.

The statue of Vulcan in **Birmingham, AL,** is a fifty-six-foot monstrosity, the world's largest cast-metal statue and the largest statue ever made in the U.S. The local JayCees gave Vulcan a neon torch in 1946, making him the "World's Largest Safety Reminder." The torch changes color if there's been a traffic fatality in metro Birmingham; green means everybody is okay, red means somebody kissed asphalt. A plaque at Vulcan's base reads, "Thousands must work to keep it green. One careless chance could turn it red!" This threat of postmortem public humiliation probably does more for traffic safety in Birmingham than any mandatory seat belt law.

The statue of Vulcan in Birmingham, AL. Cast in 1904, it once held a giant Coke bottle.

The small Set

The World's Smallest Public Library is in **Coalfield, TN.** It's only five by six feet and has propelled librarian Dot Byrd onto the late-night talk show circuit. **Arthur, NE,** recognizing that their World's Smallest Courthouse was a potential yawner, built it next to their other claim to fame—the only church in America made out of straw.

Salvo, NC, concedes that their claim of having the World's Smallest Post Office is spurious when compared to **Ochopee, FL'**s letterbox, which currently holds the record at a microscopic seven by eight feet. Or is the smallest P.O. in the remote hill town of **Silver Lake, WV?** Our scientific test (mailing each a four-by-eight-foot sheet of plywood) has yielded inconclusive results.

In happier days, the Big Stack belched lead and arsenic over Anaconda, MT.

The World's Largest Man-Made Illuminated Star stands eighty-eight and a half feet tall on a mountain overlooking **Roanoke, VA.** It's neon, so it emits a pleasant little hum. It's best appreciated at night, but before midnight, please, because that's when Roanoke goes to bed and turns the star off. It glows an eerie blue most of the time, but turns red, white, and blue on the Fourth of July or—shades of Birmingham—whenever a traffic fatality occurs in Roanoke Valley.

The biggest claim to fame belongs to **Anaconda, MT,** home of the aptly named Big Stack. Anaconda didn't have a lot going for it, and when the Washoe Smelter Complex shut down in the early '80s it had even less. But Anaconda did have the smelter's smokestack—at 585-plus feet, "the largest free-standing brick structure on earth." The Federal DEP came in with bulldozers to knock it down, but local citizens formed the Anacondans to Save the Stack Committee, and "sold" its individual bricks to raise money for its preservation. It has since been designated an official Montana state park. A big fence currently keeps people away, but Anacondans hope that when "environmental stabilization" of the plant site is complete (the DEP claims it leaks arsenic), they will actually be able to walk up and embrace their beloved civic symbol.

Mondo Smiley

Everything's all smiles in Makanda, IL.

We don't remember when we first noticed it. Maybe it was **Calumet City, IL.** Maybe further south in **Makanda, IL.** But by the time we reached **Adair, IA,** we knew something was going on. Each of these midwestern towns has painted its water tower to resemble a huge, bulbous, yellow Smiley Face, the "Have a nice day" symbol that spread through '70s hippies like a case of the crabs. Adair has made "Smiley, The Friendly Greeter on I-80," its civic symbol, and local merchants have him printed on their business cards, and display "Evening In Adair, Made With The Extract Of Ol' Smiley" shampoo in their windows.

Didn't Smiley's grin go out with bell bottoms and peace with honor? Why would a faggy flower child symbol catch on in the robust small-town heart of the heart of the country? Passing the visage again at the Oklahoma/Kansas state line on U.S. 69, we wondered: What strange powers do these Smiley Faces possess?

When we happened upon another one looming above **Oconto Falls, WI,** it hit us. It's depressing living here! Farm auctions, yard sales, flea markets, and "hand-crafted" extra income items for sale on front lawns spell economic "sluggishness." Secondhand stores like Stuff 'n' Things outnumber firsthand stores downtown, selling all the things left in the bedrooms of a generation that got the hell out. John Mellencamp's a dick, but he's right. With the exception of Fort Wal-Mart guarding the interstate gates to town, nothing new gets built. One needs to see a reassuring countenance in these dark days. Someone there, seeming to say, "It's all right. I'm here above you, watching over you, protecting you. Smile."

But it's more than "Don't Worry, Be Happy." And future anthropologists will certainly put two and two together. It's a Central Time Zone Cargo Cult that's built the big Smiley Faces—totems to appease the Gods. After all, it was the smiling yellow Gods who were responsible for the plant closings and the layoffs in the first place. But find favor with them, and they'll drop their factories from the air into our fallow enterprise zones and industrial parks. The prosperity will return and all will be well. And until it does, Ol' Smiley serves as a beacon, grinning over our cruising youth with their declining SAT scores and rusting Rivieras.

Meet the Town Pet

Some towns are daring. They stake their civic pride on something that not only is alive, like a tree or a shrub, but is ambulatory, like a bird or a burro. Towns such as these can complicate your travel itinerary; you have to get to them before their animal flies out a window or gets hit by a truck.

Griggsville, IL, has titled itself the Purple Martin Capital of the World. Behind the program is J. L. Wade, president of the Trio Manufacturing Company, the town's only industry. Purple martin bird houses are installed all over town, on every street. Anchored within the median strip

*Griggsville, IL,
the Purple Martin
Capital of the World.*

*The skull of
Geronimo, which may
have been stolen by
George Bush's father,
visits the statue of
Andre the Seal, who
may have been run
over by George Bush's
speedboat.*

of Griggsville's main thoroughfare is a seventy-foot purple martin tower supporting 562 purple martin apartments. The result: Griggsville has very few mosquitoes or other flying pests. Guess what Trio manufactures?

Wild burros infest **Oatman, AZ,** which at one time was a gold-mining boomtown. Unfortunately, the boom went bust and Oatman wisely fell back on their only remaining natural resource, the burros abandoned by Oatman's miners. Now the burros are protected by the National Wild Horse Act and freely roam the streets, trying to get you to stop your car and give them handouts. Residents who run the gift shop and gas station don't mind a bit.

Fairplay, CO, had two very special town pets. Prunes and Shorty were Fairplay's beloved burros, studies in contrast in life as they now are in death. Fairplay's memorial to Prunes is a self-supporting stucco wall, into which is cemented a brass plaque recounting Prunes's sixty years of service to the miners in the area. Also embedded in the wall is his collar, which is protected under glass. Shorty's memorial is less os-tentatious, a tiny pink marble tombstone on the courthouse lawn. Shorty was the town mooch (the exact opposite of industrious Prunes) but he was beloved all the same. Interred along with him is Bum, his dog pal, who was so grief-stricken upon Shorty's demise that he lay down on Shorty's grave and refused to move or eat until he died as well.

Let the story of **Rockport, ME,** serve as a sober warning to all animal-dependent towns. For twenty-five years, Rockport basked in the publicity lavished on Andre the Seal—actually a sea lion—who would surface in the town's tiny harbor every spring and hang around for the next several months, entertaining the locals and attracting the tourists. That ended in 1986, when Andre died. In desperation, Rockport erected a statue of Andre—hoping, perhaps, that their many Canadian visitors wouldn't notice the difference—but it didn't work. When we revisited Rockport to check out their much-ballyhooed hundredth anniversary celebration, we were the only ones there.

Eat We Must

When you live in the world's breadbox, agricultural prowess becomes a popular civic claim to fame. Farm colleges teach our tillers of the soil that it's best to stick to what they know, and what they know, we eat.

The battle for the World's Largest Egg is up for grabs. **Mentone, IN,** erected an eleven-foot-high, 3,000-pound cement blob in 1946, painted "Eggbasket of the Mid-West" across it, and proclaimed that it was the world's largest egg. Two thousand miles west, **Winlock, WA,** erected an egg that was also eleven feet tall and claimed that it was the world's largest, though they concede that Mentone's is the world's heaviest.

Nobody likes vegetables unless they're giant and inedible. California claims the World's Largest Artichoke in **Castroville** and the World's Largest Olive in **Lindsay.** The battle for the World's Largest Ear of Corn used to be exclusively a Minnesota affair; **Olivia, MN,** went to the trouble of building an ear twelve feet tall; **Rochester, MN,** took the easy way out and simply painted one on a husk-shaped forty-foot water tower. Both must soon step aside for **Coon Rapids, IA,** which is planning an ear fifty feet tall. "Whatever ear of corn is biggest now, ours will be bigger," they promise.

A chicken large enough to lay the Mentone Egg would consume enough corn each day to fill the Liberty Bell.

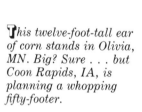

This twelve-foot-tall ear of corn stands in Olivia, MN. Big? Sure . . . but Coon Rapids, IA, is planning a whopping fifty-footer.

Cheese exists somewhere off to the far side of the dairy products spectrum; it's smelly, rubbery *stuff* and no one can really tell you how it's made without sounding disgusting. That hasn't stopped Heine's Place, a dairy products outlet located north of **Berlin, OH,** from boasting that it has the World's Largest Wheel of Cheese. It's a ten-ton monster, enshrined in a refrigerated glass kiosk. Stranger still is the World's Largest Replica Cheese, housed in a glass-sided tractor trailer (next to Chatty Belle, the world largest talking cow) in **Neillsville, WI.** The real cheese weighed 35,000 pounds and was eaten at the 1965 annual meeting of the Wisconsin Dairymen and Cheesemakers Association.

Cornelia, GA, bills themselves as the "Apple Capital of the South," and wanted a giant apple to reflect their civic pride. In 1925, for reasons no one can remember, Cornelia asked rival apple town **Winchester, VA,** to build them a giant apple. Winchester built Cornelia's apple, all right—

The world's second largest—but most photogenic—apple, in Cornelia, GA.

The behemoth of berrydom towers over Strawberry Point, IA.

STRAWBERRY POINT

a seven-foot-tall, 5,200-pound behemoth—and then promptly built themselves a bigger one.

The civic leaders of **Strawberry Point, IA,** felt proud of their town's name, and built a strawberry fifteen feet tall and twelve feet wide in its honor. That's probably news to **Poteet, TX,** which has three giant strawberries. The World's Tallest is a 130-foot water tower crudely painted to resemble the red fruit, but painted water towers don't count. Poteet, perhaps sensing that chicanery might not net them the title, built another giant strawberry ("the world's largest," they claim) in front of the fire department. Yet this one isn't even as big as the misshapen concrete berry that sits next to the Poteet Food Mart! Strawberry Point's is bigger than both.

Yakima, WA, simply calls itself "Fruitbowl of the Nation" and stays out of trouble.

THAT KOOKY LOON BATTLE

When **Mercer, WI,** set out to nail down the title of World's Largest Loon, they did it right. They knew that **Virginia, MN,** had a fourteen-foot loon, and paid a company that specializes in giant animals $10,000 to build a bigger one. The result was impressive: a sixteen-foot photogenic loon that weighed 2,000 pounds. Mercer gave it a name, Claire de Loon, titled it the "world's largest," and built a tape loop into its belly so that it would "talk" to visitors. Mercer thought they had it made.

They hadn't reckoned on Minnesota tenacity. Virginia promptly rebuilt their loon so that it was twenty feet long and ten feet high. It is, once again, the world's largest. It's also the world's largest floating animal, spending the summers bobbing on the end of a tether in Silver Lake. Mercer should either fess up and admit they've only got the world's largest *talking* loon, or build a bigger one.

The world's largest floating loon, Virginia, MN.

The Corn Palace

—Mitchell, SD

Mitchell, SD, is corn crazy. It calls itself the Corn Capital of the World. Its high school teams are the Kernels. Its radio station call letters are KORN.

Mitchell's greatest tribute to its favorite seed is what it calls the "agricultural showplace of the world"—**The Mitchell Corn Palace.** It's a mad combination of minarets, turrets, and kiosks that's been standing in downtown Mitchell since 1892. If the Soviet Union could grow enough to feed itself, this is what the Kremlin would look like.

The Corn Palace was originally built to compete with a rival "grain palace" in neighboring Plankinton, twenty-two miles to the west. Plankinton lost the battle and its palace was torn down, but the Corn Palace remains. It stands five stories high, covers a square block, and is built out of reinforced concrete, not corn. Its exterior, however, is completely covered with native South Dakota corn, grain, and grass murals. Ears of corn are sawed lengthwise and then nailed flat to outside panels that are changed yearly. Typical recent themes have been South Dakota Birds and A Salute to Agriculture.

*T*hree thousand bushels of corn adorn The Mitchell Corn Palace, America's agricultural showplace.

WORLD'S LARGEST CHAIR BATTLE

The Duncan Phyfe in Thomasville, NC.

Civic nuttiness reaches full flower in the giant chair battle. Not two, but fully five towns are currently involved, and at least four others have spent some time in the ring before getting knocked out.

It started quietly enough, when the town of **Gardner, MA,** erected a twelve-foot Mission chair in 1905. Word got around and soon a rebel yell came from the reconstructed South; in 1922 **Thomasville, NC,** decided to construct a chair thirteen feet, six inches tall.

Up went eyebrows in Gardner; pride was hurt. With typical Yankee determination, they countered with a fifteen-foot Mission in 1928. Then, to add insult to injury, Gardner replaced it with a sixteen-foot Colonial Hitchcock chair in the depression year of 1935.

Thomasville fought back, in 1948, by building an eighteen-foot steel and concrete Duncan Phyfe on a twelve-foot pedestal. They even convinced LBJ, over Lady Bird's protests, to take time out from politics and sit in their big chair.

Next, **Bennington, VT,** decided to enter the fray and put up a wooden Ladderback nineteen feet, one inch tall. However, this was not to be Bennington's fight either, as Gardner, outraged, built a brown Heywood-Wakefield, twenty feet, seven inches tall. It was ten feet wide, nine feet deep, and for a year, the world's largest.

Then private enterprise stepped in, escalating the fight and putting it on new terms. Pa's Woodshed in **Binghamton, NY,** erected a twenty-four-foot-nine-inch-tall Ladderback, with a twelve-foot-square seat. Visible from both I-81 and I-88, it shocked the world.

But even as Pa was glorified in the 1979 *Guinness Book*, his crown was being stolen. In 1978, the Hunt Country Furniture Company of **Wingdale, NY,** used more than a ton and a half of wood to build a huge Fireside Chair, twenty-five feet tall and fourteen feet wide, which was soon recognized as World's Largest. Was. The owners were finally forced to remove the chair because "young people were climbing up and doing unsafe things on it."

The South watched and waited. In the early '80s, Millers Office Supply of **Anniston, AL,** built a thirty-three-foot-tall office chair in front of its building. It was made of ten tons of steel, causing would-be vandals to throw up their crowbars in despair. It could withstand 85 MPH winds, and a special staircase led to the seat. Here was a chair for the ages. It quickly became the town landmark; the chamber of commerce flew visiting businessmen over it.

Underhanded rivals could not attack the chair, so they attacked the company. Miller's has moved crosstown and the lot is up for sale. The chair is in need of a paint job. And amid all this, we hear rumors of a Swiss chair larger than them all. The Swiss, bloodless superbankers harboring the accounts of dictators and strongmen, are easily capable of bringing economic hard times to one neighborhood in Anniston. Neutral, our ass. The big chair battle is now beyond civic pride. National pride is at stake.

The Office Contemporary in Anniston, AL.

One Town and Its Relic

Everybody remembers the *Maine*, but who remembers its bathtub?

When the *U.S.S. Maine* was raised from Havana harbor in 1911, every Congressman wanted a piece. Frank B. Willis of Ohio snagged a prize— Captain Sigsbie's enameled-steel bathtub—and planned to give it to Urbana. Urbana clubwomen said they'd use the bathtub as a horse trough before they'd put it on display, and told Willis to get their town a respectable ten-inch shell instead.

Neighboring **Findlay** saw their opportunity. They asked Urbana for the tub and got it, fending off competitors and guffaws. Boston demanded the bathtub because they were Captain Sigsbie's hometown. The *Cincinnati Enquirer* suggested that Findlay sink the bathtub in the Ohio River. Findlay hung on. Meanwhile, the bathtub was sitting in the chicken house of Urbana's mayor. He wasn't giving it to anyone until he got his ten-inch shell. In desperation, Findlay appealed to Congressman Willis, who pulled strings at the Navy Department. The shell arrived by the end of the week and Urbana shipped the bathtub to Findlay.

On March 3, 1913, the bathtub arrived. Findlay's heart sank faster than the *Maine*; its prize bathtub was rusty and pitted, having been underwater for fourteen years. No one could figure out how to display such a cruddy relic, so the town stored it in its municipal building.

Less than a year later, the bathtub had become the Findlay city hall coal bin. Lima, a covetous rival town, found out and raised hell, demanding the tub. Sleepy Findlay stirred to action. Local Spanish War veterans promised to bronze the bathtub and display it in Riverside Park. Lima backed off. So did the Spanish War veterans. Instead of bronzing the bathtub they stuck it into a display case, which was then shoved into a little-used hallway of the Findlay courthouse. It sat there for fifteen years. The courthouse janitor eventually taped a *"U.S.S. Maine* Bathtub" sign to the case because he got tired of explaining it to visitors.

In 1929 the bathtub was placed along the wall of the courthouse rotunda, where it sat for another thirty years. When the courthouse was renovated in 1960 the bathtub was removed and shipped to the Findlay College Museum. They cannibalized its case for another display and stored the bathtub in an old cigar factory. In 1974 it was turned over to the Hancock Historical Museum, which dumped it into their basement.

This story might have had an unhappy ending. However, the bathtub was recently retrieved from the basement and can now, once again, be seen by visitors. Most of its enamel is gone, but that doesn't detract from the fact that it is the bathtub from the *U.S.S. Maine*, the only one you're ever going to see, and you should.

Earth

*Journey to the center of the earth in luxurious comfort at **Fantastic Caverns**, Springfield, MO.*

ome of our most precious roadside wonders revolve around human history, ethnic origin, even individual characters or clever animals. But these are short, fleeting station breaks on the big geologic projection TV called Earth. Over the long haul, it's the natural wonders that last. Nature's indigenous tourist attractions—rocks, caves, big trees, bodies of water—will be here for thousands or millions of years, even if we are not. While some are shaped by the forces of erosion or growth, others are shaped by the hand of Man, coaxing Ma Nature's juices into magnificent fountains, tunneling into her for beautiful gems, or carving the living guts out of her trees so his cars can drive through.

National parks were created specifically to worship natural wonders and protect them from those shape-crazy hands of Man. If you want to see this untouched wilderness—on a two-lane road jammed with thousands of obnoxious nature seekers—go ahead. You'd do better subscribing to *National Geographic* or buying an Ansel Adams print.

We like the places where attraction owners and their wonders have struck a pact—a pact to entertain you, the attentive visitor. With a touch of neon here, a hint of loudspeaker there, attraction owners nurture nature and guarantee an indelible memory. What's a spring without a bunch of mermaids in it? What's a forest without a one-log house and a statue of Paul Bunyan, the great tree-biter?

The Roadside Rock Garden

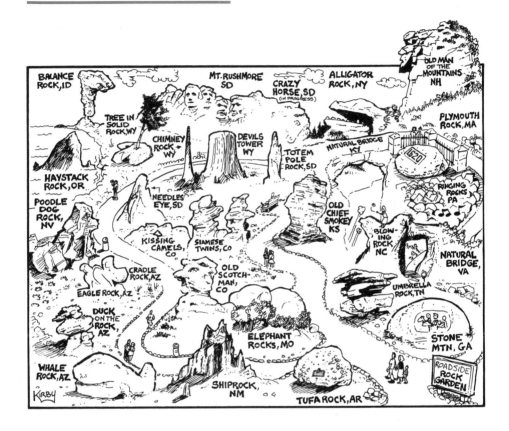

They are the rocks! Geologic appendages ignored for eons by the continent's transient tenants are thrust into the scenic limelight by a familiar shape and evocative name. Witness the imposing **Whale Rock** of Texas Canyon, AZ, or the whimsical **Mexican Hat Rock,** Mexican Hat, UT. Weather-carved faces leer at us from mountainsides, like the **Old Man of the Mountain,** in Franconia Notch, NH, or the **Great Stone Face,** Deseret, UT, which resembles Mormon prophet Joseph Smith. Our favorite monolith monicker? "Seal Making Love to a Nun" Rock, at the **Garden of the Gods,** Colorado Springs, CO. The visionary publicist who named it was quickly fired, and it was retitled "Seal and Bear."

*S*unset at **Toilet Rock,** *City of Rocks, NM.*

*T*he incessant hammering *of semiprecious gem-happy geotourists reverberates across the* **Ruggle Mine,** *Grafton, NH. Rabid rockhounds rent flashlights, helmets, goggles, and picks to chip away at everything— including the main support pillars—in search of giant beryls and smoky quartz. It's refreshing, in an age of "Take only photos, leave only footprints," to find a place that says, "Go ahead! Destroy our attraction!"*

Big Brutus vs. Big Muskie

A mighty machine once ran around the clock, clawing out house-sized chunks of ground in search of coal. **Big Brutus,** sixteen stories and 11 million pounds of earth-moving muscle, mined the flat, southeastern corner of Kansas. Some said he worked too hard, used too much electricity. In 1974, teary-eyed, the owner finally pulled Big B's plug in West Mineral, KS; the great shovel sagged to stillness. But locals rallied to have him declared a state landmark and turned into a museum. Postcards of Big B were mailed far and wide. The big-hearted earth-mover would not be forgotten.

Meanwhile, in Cumberland, OH, another great machine toiled—**Big Muskie.** This 27-million-pound leviathan could scoop 325 tons per bite as he moved backwards, powered by the largest extension cord ever made. The Ohio Power Company boasted of Big Muskie's digging prowess. He must be the largest "Walking Dragline Machine" in the world!

Then, times changed. Electricity got expensive. Other energy alternatives wooed the power company. Big Muskie was given an office "upstairs." The company offered tours by advance arrangement, and sold postcards that were mailed far and wide.

With so many postcards flying around, who can say when Big Brutus and Big Muskie will find out about each other? Two sleeping giants, awakened by the idea of a blood rival, closing a gap of some 700 miles of unmined landscape. Traveling at top speeds—Muskie creaking west at $\frac{1}{10}$ MPH, and Brutus trundling east at $\frac{1}{5}$ MPH—they could lock shovels in fourteen weeks, south of Bloomfield, IN.

Big Earth Mover Statistics

Big Brutus		Big Muskie
1963	Dedicated	1969
5,500 tons	Total Weight	13,500 tons
160 feet	Total Height	160 feet
150 feet	Boom Length	310 feet
135 tons/90 cubic yards	Scoop Capacity per Bite	325 tons/220 cubic yards
660 feet	Overall Length	151 feet
Three	Minimum Crew	Seven
$\frac{1}{5}$ MPH	Top Speed	$\frac{1}{10}$ MPH
15,000 homes	Uses as Much Power as	27,500 homes

The Wonderful World of Caves

The claustrophobic novelty of a cave tour keeps over 150 commercial caves around the U.S. in operation, from national park giants like **Mammoth Cave,** KY (over 250 miles in passages), to small, family-owned holes that spackle the map. Caves have bricked walkways, artificial lighting, "expert" guides, and are usually adjacent to (if not covered by) a gift shop.

The natural tendency of travelers to head for the "biggest" or the "longest" is pointless when it comes to caves—most tours are limited to an hour and cover only a small portion of the passageways. The best caves are lit like a '70s Italian horror movie, and the "subterranean experience" is enhanced using completely fabricated natural wonders, like waterfalls. Bold manipulation indicates a cave owner who has a finger on the throbbing neck vein of the vacationing corpus.

The cave entrance at **Meramec Caverns,** Stanton, MO, contains a neon sign that proudly proclaims "Jesse James Hideout," not far from Loot Rock, where replicas of Jesse and Co. divide the booty. Nearby is a moonshiner's cavern, transplanted from the Ozark hills above. The high-

*The Lake of the Moon room, **Inner Space Caverns**, Georgetown, TX, features one of several Sound 'n' Light shows. Hear the "Flowing Stone of Time" read from the Book of Genesis as your tour guide skillfully manipulates spotlight dimmer switches. "And God said . . . let there be light," proclaims the rock. You don't have to be religious to guess what happens next.*

light of any trip to Meramec is the Stage Curtain and Flag show, known as "the greatest show under the earth." Visitors seated in the Theater Room face a massive limestone drapery formation (the Stage Curtain) where a colored-light show is projected. The show builds to a rousing climax, when an American flag is projected onto the Stage Curtain, while a scratchy recording of Kate Smith singing "God Bless America" is blared from loudspeakers.

For those who hate the thought of all that forced marching through the Stygian catacombs, two lazy-man's cave tours are recommended: **Fantastic Caverns,** Springfield, MO, "America's Only Ride-Thru Cave," and **Penns Cave,** Centre Hall, PA, "America's Only All-Water Cavern."

The guides of Fantastic Caverns carefully explain how the natural atmosphere of the cave is being preserved, as they drive their jeeps, with passenger trailers in tow, up and down the blasted-out paved passages. The jeeps run on propane so that accumulating fumes don't asphyxiate visitors. Fantastic's sordid history includes a period of ownership by the Ku Klux Klan, who conducted meetings and cross burnings in the grand ballroom in the 1920s. Today, the same room is rented out for opera performances.

Penns Cave is seen only by boat—a flat twenty-seater steered by a guide who also points the boat spotlight at whatever you're supposed to look at. The cave is composed of five massive chambers, which are fully illuminated at key dramatic moments in the tour. The guide is in an awful hurry to point out that every single rock, lump, and formation in the cave looks like some familiar image. As the boat moves and your shipmates follow the bouncing lightbeam, the guide rattles off his laundry list: "This is an Indian squaw with papoose and some say that looks like a kneeling camel and here's our Sphinx or Buddha, whichever you prefer, and you can see an upside-down farm valley here and that's a Lebanon bologna and over this way is a little boy pushing a cow across an iron suspension bridge . . ."

Howe Caverns, *Howes Cave, NY.*
The earmark of a beautiful cave is
a prominent sign that reads,
"Weddings Performed Here."

Cave matrimony seems to be the rage among some strange though prolific social set. **Bridal Cave,** Camdenton, MO, is America's premier high-volume wedding nexus, hosting over 900 since it opened in 1948. Before the practice was discontinued in 1977, Virginia's **Luray Caverns** had 208 weddings, accompanied by their huge "stalacpipe organ," which musically resonates through natural rock draperies.

One tour feature that seems to be universal is the Moment of Total Darkness, when the guide extinguishes all the lights in that section of the cave. "This is what it was like when the candle held by the first explorers went out," the guide asserts. Total darkness is an economical special effect for the cavern owners, and it also helps separate the mildly nervous from the truly claustrophobic. Most of these should know enough to avoid the tour in the first place, but we welcome any hysterical ravings or seizures as photo opportunities and a great story for the folks back home. It's the kind of thing people *expect* to see in a cave.

Secret Caverns

—Cobleskill, NY

While other caves boast of monstrous formations and passages, they lack what **Secret Caverns,** in Cobleskill, NY, has—an attitude.

Sure, next-door neighbor **Howe Caverns** has a cave elevator, hilltop chateau, restaurant, gift shops, and a reputation that draws over 100,000 visitors every year. So what? Secret Caverns can't tell us how many visitors *it* gets a year, "for tax reasons." Secret and Howe have spent decades as bitter, feuding rivals. But the latest advertising campaign by Secret Caverns may have its upscale competitor more annoyed than worried. Every Secret billboard for miles entices the unaimed traveler with cavemen riding dinosaurs, sea monsters, evil clowns, giant bats, and Grateful Dead skeletons, painted freehand by its guides. Secret Caverns gets the market segment it deserves—people like us.

A Secret Caverns tour is a personal experiment in luck and synchronicity. It's advertised at forty-five minutes, but sometimes, late in the day, your tour may move along a bit quicker. "The record time is eleven minutes from start to finish," says guide Kurt Piller.

"The first one hundred thirty-eight formations are known as 'steps,' "

Guides Kurt Piller and Tyrone Donnelly sweep up around the Frozen Niagara in Secret Caverns. All coins recovered from the Wishing Well go to the Secret Caverns' tour guide beer fund.

we're told as we descend to Secret's main passage. A broken wedge of rock juts from a low wall. "Some people think this looks like Jabba the Hutt—others say a hand with its fingers torn off," says guide Tyrone Donnelly to awed-but-accepting onlookers. Part of Secret's success formula is hiring experts like Kurt or Tyrone, crispy-edged rock philosophizers, intent on deconstructing every bulge and crack. They're also good at running the cash register and sweeping up.

"The Holy Family" formation is two rock chunks set on end and illuminated by an unshielded bulb—"Jesus." The brochure photo of "Wonderland" (also known as "The Yes Album Cover") is printed upside-down and lit to make the formations look forty feet tall. In real life, it spans about three feet on a ceiling overhang. "City of the Future"—formerly "Atomic City," formerly "City Hit by Atomic Bomb"—may undergo yet another name change. "We're thinking of calling it 'Baghdad,'" Kurt warns.

A large round thermometer hangs in the "Belfry" rock chimney, copped by a Secret commando from Howe years ago. Decades earlier, a large calcite heart was cut from Secret's "Frozen Niagara" (also called "Frozen Nicaragua" or "Frozen Margarita") to enhance the floor of Howe's bridal chamber. "We're proud to say that no one has been tacky enough to get married in *this* cave," our guide points out.

The tours ends as we revisit 138 formations and look for a memento in the denuded gift shop. The fluorescent orange T-shirt tops all souvenir wear, cave or otherwise, with art of a manly waterfall plunging excitedly into a cavern crevasse.

Secret Caverns seems eminently qualified to survive in the world of underground tourism, even if only as a necessary thorn in the side of its neighbor. It's a world where visitors ask questions like "How thick are the walls?" or "How much does this cave weigh?" The guides at Secret Caverns know the answer.

Irrational Geographics

Maps are key to any successful road trip, but are "map attractions"? The **Four Corners** is where Arizona, New Mexico, Colorado, and Utah meet— out in the middle of nowhere. The ceremonial slab is ringed by stalls of Navajos selling silver trinkets, T-shirts, and Pepsi at exorbitant prices. Tourists splay themselves on the slab for border comedy candids.

The U.S. Army Corps of Engineers prefers to map in 3-D, creating

Watch Army engineers change river channels with explosives and mud at the Waterways Experiment Station, Vicksburg, MS.

scale-model simulations of American waterways. The **Waterways Experiment Station** in Vicksburg, MS, tests channels and currents with miniature versions of New York City harbor, and Niagara Falls.

The **Mapparium,** Boston, MA, is a most impressive map attraction. Constructed in 1936 off the public lobby of the Christian Science Publishing building, the Mapparium is a hollow earth thirty feet in diameter. A bronze framework holds 608 concave colored-glass panels that brightly display territorial borders and country names circa 1935. Visitors enter through the Indian Ocean on an elevated crystal bridge and exit through the South Pacific. Acoustics are weird; people whispering privately over near Australia can be heard distinctly from Greenland.

U.S. Centers: Which One Is Right for You?

*G*eographic Center of
North America, Rugby, ND.

A wide swath down the middle of this country is loaded with centers. Tourism councils put up markers and invite vacationers to come see. The time-conscious traveler asks with good reason, "Which center is right for me?" After all, isn't there only one center to something, even something as big and bright as the United States? Let's examine the contenders.

The **geographical center of North America** is marked by a cairn in Rugby, ND. If you acknowledge this as *the* center, though, you give Canada and Mexico entirely too much credit. The **geodetic center of the forty-eight states,** near Osborne, KS, takes into account the curvature of the earth, and sounds much too four-eyed to possibly make for good tourism.

The **population center of the United States** is located ten miles southeast of Steelville, MO, as determined by the 1990 census. While ecstatic Steelville residents plot ways to exploit their statistical windfall, 1980's population center DeSoto, MO, has been defrocked and forgotten. This center has been moving southwest every decade since the first census in 1790, and is theoretically always shifting. Clearly a gamble.

Various limp centers confuse the issue. The **geographic center of Western Civilization** is in Dannebrog, NE, according to a plaque embedded in the floor of the Silver Dollar Saloon. Ripley, TN, is the wimpy **Center of Hands Across America,** marked by a stick in front of a roadside fruit stand.

From our view, only two centers are worthy of consideration—the **geographic center of the fifty states,** near Castle Rock, SD, and the **geographic center of the forty-eight states** in Lebanon, KS. It is hard to argue against Castle Rock. After all, there are fifty states in the Union, and there's a lot of firepower siloed nearby.

But consider this. A center is important because it is a place for our country to fall back to, and dig in to make a last stand if attacked on all sides by every other country in the world. If that happened, we'd have to forget Alaska and Hawaii. They'd be dead meat. No, we'd gather at the Lebanon center cairn—on a hill, giving us good lines of fire. No question: Bury the emergency food and ammo here.

Love Dem Big Trees

We have the biggest trees in the world—the giant redwoods of Northern California. U.S. 101 winds through these forest giants, and the fun begins in Leggett, CA, where you encounter the first of several drive-through trees open to the public. Drive-through trees are like a fine compromise between warring lumberjacks and Earth Firsters. The **Chandelier Drive-Thru Tree** is typical; you pay your money, drive over a mile on a bumpy, dusty road just to get to it, and then discover that your Winnebago is

Paul Bunyan, Babe the Blue Ox, and the six-foot-tall Hinged Man at Trees of Mystery, Klamath, CA.

too wide to go through anyway. All of this aggravation, just to drive through a hole cut in a tree. Don't you feel ridiculous?

In Piercy, CA, the **World Famous Tree House** is the rotted lower portion of a still-living giant redwood that also holds the title "the world's tallest single room." An appliance bulb suspended from a wire has glowed at the top of the rot—the "ceiling" of the room—for over thirty years, to the appreciative ooohs and aaahs of visitors.

Next stop, Phillipsville, CA, for a look at **Chimney Tree.** Chimney Tree is very similar to the World Famous Tree House, except it's missing the little appliance bulb. The owners have decided to pep up this attraction by adding **Hobbiton, USA,** to the neighboring property. Officially endorsed by the San Francisco Hobbit Club, Hobbiton, USA, is a nature walk that passes several concrete re-creations of scenes from Tolkien's *The Hobbit.* Prerecorded explanations of these scenes are narrated by an unidentified Hobbit fan, who sounds like he's spent the majority of his life playing Dungeons and Dragons and attending science fiction conventions.

Klamath, CA, is the upper end of Redwood Exploitation Territory, and also the site of its most stupendous attraction, **Trees of Mystery.** Two giant statues, one of Paul Bunyan and one of Babe, the blue ox, guard the entrance. Paul speaks, and his right hand gives a perpetual little wave as he greets all who enter in his cheeriest lumberjack style. "Well, hello, there, little girl . . . ever see a fellah as big as me?" A forest trail takes visitors through Trees of Mystery and begins at a giant, hollow redwood log, only this one is fake. Once inside, you'll make your way through a series of actual mystery trees, the ones shaped like pretzels and DNA strandoids. "Entirely by the forces of nature," we are reminded. At the Cathedral Tree, Nelson Eddy sings Joyce Kilmer's poem "Trees" from hidden loudspeakers.

Paul Bunyan: Friend or Foe?

Paul Bunyan's birthplace in **Bangor, ME,** is marked by a statue, but where you really fall all over monuments to the towering tree-biter are in the northern forests of Minnesota, Wisconsin, and Michigan. Minnesota offers big statues in **Brainerd** and **Bemidji,** which are also home to his axe, his phone, his pet dog, his pet squirrel, his toothpaste, razor, and

Sit in Mr. Bunyan's beefy hand in Akeley, MN.

Zippo lighter. In **Akeley,** a twenty-five-foot Bunyan bends down with hand outstretched, so that couples can sit in his palm for photos. Bunyan's girlfriend is in **Hackensack,** his anchor is in **Ortonville,** his rifle is in **Black Duck,** and he is buried (he died in 1899) in **Kelliher.** His epitaph: "Here Lies Paul, And That's All."

Michigan has erected the oddest tribute: A thirty-foot-tall statue made entirely of parts from old Kaiser automobiles watches over Business I-75 in **Grayling.** Other Michigan Bunyans include those in **Manistique** and **Oscoda.** The Castle Rock Lookout in **St. Ignace** has a seated Paul next to Babe, the blue Ox, while another Babe in **Ossineke** stands in front of a hairy-chested Bunyan that babbles prerecorded, long-winded yarns in a French accent. In the fifties, Ossineke Babe had his balls shot off by a handgun that was used to murder a man the next week. Out of respect, Ossineke Babe's balls have never been replaced.

Paul Bunyan never replanted, or worried about erosion or ecosystems. He probably took early naturalists by the head and used them to grease his mighty skillet. On the other hand, without Paul Bunyan statues and memorabilia pulling the tourists to these areas, they'd never get to see the trees that the ecologist works so hard to protect. Now that Paul is dead, and Saab-driving law-school naturalists have nothing to fear, don't be surprised if Paul Bunyan statues start coming under fire as teaching our children bad lessons.

Cypress Kneeland

—Palmdale, FL

Cypress Kneeland spreads itself across both sides of U.S. 27 like an overfertilized cabbage palm. It encompasses the Cypress Knee Museum, a three-quarter-mile swamp catwalk, and a gift shop, all single-mindedly devoted to the glorification of cypress knees.

Cypress knees are knobby growths that sprout from the roots of cypress trees. No one knows why they grow, and no one paid much attention to them until Tom Gaskins came along. Tom, a self-proclaimed Florida cracker, became obsessed with the knees in 1934. By 1939 he was exhibiting them at the New York World's Fair. Today, Tom is their chief cheerleader, authority, and spokesperson.

Tom Gaskins was awarded a Florida Folk Heritage Award by the Florida Secretary of State in 1988 for his work with knees.

The Cypress Knee Museum showcases the cream of Tom's vast cypress knee collection. Little signs in front of each knee offer suggestions as to what (or whom) each represents: Flipper, Joseph Stalin, or "Lady Hippo Wearing a Carmen Miranda Hat," which is the most spectacular knee in the world. The museum is built around the world's largest transplanted cypress tree; visitors are cautioned to watch for snakes that sometimes crawl through the hole in the floor.

Across the road from the museum lies the catwalk, a series of mossy, elevated two-by-fours. Tom estimates that over a hundred people have fallen off the catwalk into the swamp, mostly children. "Old people, they know better." The catwalk runs through Tom's "controlled knee growth" experiments, where he has attempted to alter the shapes of living knees. Tom has carved designs into some, shoved bottles (and, in one case, a phone receiver) into others, and flattened many with heavy weights. "When I control growth in knees, I brag about it," says Tom.

Tom is a devoted physical culturalist and, though well into his eighties, jogs five miles a day through the swamps. He bought his last pair of shoes in 1971 and rarely wears them.

"The knees have been good to me," Tom reflects, hopping across the highway asphalt toward the swamp. "By golly, I am the happiest man in the world!"

Water Worlds We Like

Water is a natural and inexpensive source of cheap dramatics. Clever real estate promoter Bob McCulloch (the same guy who brought the London Bridge to Arizona) outfitted a pond of recycled sewage treatment water to spray 560 feet in the air for fifteen minutes of every hour. It's the **World's Tallest Fountain,** in Fountain Hills, AZ.

Backyard geysers draw tourists as would any other "wonder of nature," and can be used for free home heating! If you don't already have a geyser, perhaps you'll get lucky like one man did in 1937 when drilling for water to fill a swimming pool. He struck both water and carbon dioxide gas, and today the **World's Only Man-Made Geyser** in Soda Springs, ID, still erupts every hour on the hour—although they turn it off when the wind shifts so it doesn't blow into the business district.

Fountain technology invented in Nazi Germany keeps water merrily squirting in attractions like **Waltzing Waters,** Fort Myers, FL. Every hour, six hundred patented hydraulic nozzles and 15,000 watts of multicolored lighting spring to life. The "liquid fireworks" are synchronized with music from *Switched-On Classics*. Onstage, plumes of water arc and rotate, while spotlights play on shimmering sprays and spritzes. There's the constant sound of water splashing back into the fountain in this mildewed theater, something akin to an overly dramatic car wash. At night, the show moves outside, spewing 7,000 gallons of water almost a hundred feet in the air.

Weeki Wachee, the City of Mermaids

—Weeki Wachee, FL

> *"We're not like other women*
> *We don't have to clean an oven*
> *And we nev-er will grow olllllllllld. . . .*
> *We've got the world by the tail!"*

—official Weeki Wachee mermaid anthem

The name "Weeki Wachee" conjures up as powerful an image as "Big Sur" or "Harlem." Visions of lovely mermaids performing graceful underwater ballet and sucking RC Cola bottles spring to the feverish fore-brain. Doomed dads have been steering their wood-paneled station wagons toward these mesmerizing maidens since 1947.

The enduring success of **Weeki Wachee** is built on a rigid mermaid code. "There's a lot more to being a mermaid than just knowing how to smile and wiggle your tail underwater," says Jana, who has been a mermaid for fifteen years.

The Rites of Mermaidhood are grueling, but necessary. "Our lives depend on each other; it's not your normal job." Half the trainees who make it through the formal interview and water auditions never achieve the rank of full mermaid; the year of on-the-job training and the final exam—holding your breath for two and a half minutes while changing out of costume in the mouth of the 72 degree spring—finishes many mermaid wannabes.

This exclusive sorority includes nineteen active performers. Mermaids who make it through tend to stay on the job for a number of years, then often move up to management positions. "It's not the kind of job you hold for six months and then quit," noted Jana.

The new show, written by Tamar, the mermaid supervisor, is an adaptation of Hans Christian Andersen's "The Little Mermaid." "It was always my dream to become a mermaid and 'The Little Mermaid' was always my favorite story, so writing this show was a dream come true."

Yup, the mermaid life ain't bad. They have only two natural enemies: thunderstorms, and the alligators that occasionally slip into the spring. Amorous dads 'n' grads are kept safely behind thick glass.

Aquatic lovelies flop onto the mossy rocks for a photo opportunity.

THE DOOM TOUR

The earth cracks! Waters rage! The hills burn! Forget that "I'm not evacuating" stuff. RUN! RUN! Take a tour of U.S. doom sites, and reconsider the wisdom in trying to take on a rabid, cleaver-wielding Mother Nature.

DAY 1: Just stand there as our sightseeing cyclone bears down and sweeps you off to the **1935 Hurricane Victims Monument** in Islamorada Key, FL. It's a bas relief of palm trees bending under tremendous wind, with a plaque that remembers those who died in the Great Storm of 1935. "Hurricane proof" houses in the Keys help new residents imagine safety.

DAY 2: Helltown, U.S.A., is **Centralia, PA.** A coal vein has been burning under it since 1961—*and there's no way to stop it!* Vent pipes poke from rocky nooks and hillsides; near some cracks, the ground is too hot to touch. Noxious gases leak to the surface and houses are condemned one-by-one, as Centralia is abandoned. All the shops along the main road have closed, and the only new building is the fire department. It may be too late for a planned 500-foot-deep trench to save surrounding communities!

Cool off in another Pennsylvania town, **Johnstown.** The killer flood of 1889 is chronicled in two separate attractions (see page 172).

DAY 3: Peshtigo, WI, is the site of "America's Most Disastrous Forest Fire," memorialized in the **Peshtigo Fire Museum.** Peshtigo was completely consumed in a fiery hell on October 8, 1871, the same night as the unrelated and overpublicized Great Chicago Fire. Peshtigo's fire destroyed every one of the town's 800 buildings and killed 1,200 people. Most fled toward the river, choking on gases or exploding into pyres. A painted triptych in the museum gives before-during-after snapshots of Peshtigo life- and death-styles. Surviving artifacts could fit into a lunchbox. Outside is the well-marked mass grave for 350 victims. A garden hose hangs coiled and ready.

Travel west to Hinckley, MN, known as "The Town Built of Wood," before a firestorm consumed it in 1884. Over 400 died in this conflagration. An old train station houses the **Hinckley Fire Museum,** which includes photos of the award-winning volunteer fire department of 1883, and the coroner's records. The stone monument and mass graves are on the other side of town.

DAY 4: Crosswinds of catastrophe carry you south to greet a group of tourists who have been trying to visit the U.S. since 1957—Killer Bees! The first crossing was at **Hidalgo, TX,** in 1990. The psychotic main swarm is punching through a trap line set up by the USDA, and dozens of counties are quarantined!

Meteors hurtle down from above! Hunker down or run, you may still be vaporized by a space boulder the size of Rhode Island. Peer into the **Meteor Crater** at Leeup, AZ, and you'll see how that would look. The hole is 570 feet deep, 4,100 wide, three miles in circumference. Where can you hide?

DAY 5: Earthquakes! At West Yellowstone, MT, see the world's most dramatic display of earthquake phenomena in the **Madison River Earthquake Area.** Earthquake Lake formed when the mountain fell in 1959, with a force equivalent to 2,500 detonating A-bombs. Abandoned homes and resorts still cling to the shores of Lake Hebgen, half-submerged, and old Highway 287 is cracked and visible. At the end of the drive is a visitors' center with a working seismograph.

Another earth-shaker hit **Mackay, ID,** in 1983, measuring 7.4 on the Richter scale and killing two people. The fault is visible on Double Springs Road off Highway 93, twenty miles north of town. No wonder hardly anyone lives around here.

DAY 6: Cave-ins and collapses! Man tries to control his environment, and is slapped down! The **Teton Dam** in Rexburg, ID, collapsed in 1976. Eleven were killed in the ensuing flood. Official state tourism guides urge, "Visit the dam site where you can see the disaster first-hand." A museum recaps the excitement; Teton Flood Mud sells in the gift shop for fifty cents a package. The **Sunshine Miners Memorial,** Kellogg, ID, commemorates ninety-one killed in a 1972 mine fire. A big miner, made entirely out of welding rods, defiantly clutches a rock drill.

DAY 7: The earth explodes! No time to run! The **Mount St. Helens National Volcanic Monument Visitors Center,** Spirit Lake, WA, chronicles the eruption, when fifty-seven people disappeared under black ash. Walk through a model of the volcano, and look into a simulated magma chamber. Climb to the top of the real volcano, if you dare.

A sign in the Forest of Nicene, near **Aptos, CA,** marks the epicenter of the 1989 San Francisco Earthquake and apologizes for the lack of noticeable devastation. Southern California's **Ripley's Believe It or Not Museum,** in Buena Park, displays the crushed Chevy of "Lucky Buck" Helm, who achieved immortality as the man who survived (at least for a little while) the Nimitz Freeway collapse. "Lucky" was pinned in his crushed Chevy for days until rescuers finally noticed and freed him. His license plate is at the **Fisherman's Wharf Ripley's** in San Francisco.

JOHNSTOWN FLOOD NATIONAL MONUMENT

—ST. MICHAEL, PA

•

JOHNSTOWN FLOOD MUSEUM

—JOHNSTOWN, PA

•

How do we spell disaster?

J-O-H-N-S-T-O-W-N.

In 1889, heavy rains caused a lake up the valley from Johnstown, PA, to crash through a neglected earthen dam. A forty-foot-high wave of water scooped up small towns and demolished the Gautier Wire Mill, adding miles of barbed wire to the wave. House debris, trees, and people were bound in a constricting knot. The surging death ball crashed into Johnstown, whisking most of the buildings down to a large stone bridge at the neck of the valley. Sixty acres of debris and people finally settled. Then it caught fire and burned for three days. Over 2,200 people died.

Now that's a disaster. Two attractions vividly chronicle the story in such a way that you're not always sure they're talking about the same flood.

The centerpiece at the **Johnstown Flood National Monument,** at the St. Michael, PA, dam site, is an artistic gray-toned film, *Black Friday*. At the rainy, mist-filled victims' mass grave, the narrator tells us, sadly, "they are the dead—victims of Black Friday. Armageddon—the last judgment . . . " The flood is blamed on fatcat industrialists—like Carnegie and Mellon—who were members of the South Fork Fishing and Hunting Club. They bought the lake and stocked it with fish, but did not maintain its poorly designed dam, jokingly referred to as the "Sword of Damocles." Edited scenes from old *Titanic* and Atlantis movies are combined with the destruction of models.

Water explodes everywhere on-screen. The veritable flume ride ends with a roll call of the dead, while ghostly images march across the cemetery. "Grave Number 45, Unknown, head burned off . . . " The doors open, and the numbed crowd races for the lavatories.

In Johnstown proper, the **Johnstown Flood Museum** is housed in the Carnegie Library. Its 1989 Oscar-winning film *The Flood* presents a markedly different view. While the rich people don't get off scot free in the documentary (the way they did in real life), their belated attempts to warn the town and raise the dam are given valuable screen minutes devoted in the other film to the screams of the undead. The lake is described as "a magic place to meet and picnic," where the privileged "could stroll and boat with those of their own kind."

And while *Black Friday* left its audience in a dark, wet cemetery, *The Flood* finishes with the triumph of the spirit. "Most were determined to stay and rebuild their town . . . the people themselves went back to work a few days later." A message that would warm the cockles of any industrialist's tiny black heart.

Mount St. Helens
Volcanic Ash
Salt and Pepper
Shakers

A popular souvenir in the years that followed the 1980 eruption of
Mount St. Helens, this shaker set is ingeniously crafted. Pepper
comes out the crater of the posteruption stump of the mountain;
salt is the mountaintop that blew off. Ceramics and "food-safe glaze"
are combined with actual volcanic ash from the eruption—perhaps
some of the very ash that buried feisty Harry Truman and his home!
Tour **Marti's Ash Creations** in Morton, WA, where volcanic spew
is fashioned into lovely souvenirs.

Made In America

High Point, NC, boasts the **World's Largest Chest of Drawers.**

A sure cure for *accidia*, that general sloth and paralysis of the will that affects us all during weak moments, is a vacation visit to those places Made In America. When product patriotism flags, stop by the factory that builds your favorite riding mower or salad spinner, and ask them to show you around. Many are happy to see you, the end-user, and make sure that the customer is always right at home.

Others offer us commercial food tours—extruded food spitting off an assembly line—with free samples for all at the end. Savvy vacationers need never spend for meals, if they don't mind a plastic bag of mini-marshmallows for dinner.

Industrial attractions are not without pitfalls. Some have fallen into the well-manicured hands of chain-smoking PR careerists, who don't really care about the athletic shoe of the twenty-first century, and who only want to trade out of their floor-level job into one doctoring spin for spill-prone chemical makers.

Finally, not enough of today's generation, protestant of the work ethic, visit our hydroelectric plants and assembly lines. But how else will they teach themselves the realities and dramas of success? Industrial sites seem most visited by golden-agers trying to remember America's golden age, or groups of young Japanese, here to learn our secrets.

So take our advice and catch up on your Made In America heritage, a heritage of invention, elbow grease, and spunk. And the next time some big-screen blow-dried cretin sadly shakes his talking head and bemoans our transformation from broadshouldered hog-butchers into telecommuting, decaffeinating, alpha-state, service-sector losers, you'll know better.

Hugh Lesley poses with a small fraction of his **World's Largest Collection of Edsels** *at "Lemon Grove," Oxford, PA.*

Industrial Magic

The days of industrial tours are numbered. Soaring liability insurance shut some. Trouble with protestors closed others. Spies caused Kellogg's to curtail its wonderful cereal factory tours. We applaud those who stay open, celebrating their gift to society, and steeling the bonds of brand loyalty. Your part? Visit, and if you like what you see, buy.

Stop at **Goodyear's World of Rubber** in Akron, OH. In its illuminated rotunda is a statue of that tragic genius, Charles Goodyear, with two slabs of his beloved rubber tightly clenched in his fists. A walk through a stand of simulated rubber trees leads to the main exhibit hall, displaying wonders like the 300 millionth tire made by Goodyear, a replica Apollo moon tire, and a collection of Charles Goodyear's personal rubber items.

Philip Morris Cigarette Tours are offered at its many plants, including the one in Richmond, VA. This great tour is seductively industrial. The plant is quiet, cool, efficient, beautiful. After beginning at a tobacco paraphernalia museum in the visitors' center, a forty-five-minute tram ride

Plant tours. Free beer. Most breweries have both. At **The Heileman Brewery** in La Crosse, WI, six storage tanks have been painted to resemble Heileman's Old Style beer cans, creating the World's Largest Six Pack. Inside, Heileman provides its tour goers with a little pub where they can drink free samples before the tour begins, while an instructional film shows the wonders of the Heileman beer group. Movie sound is thoughtfully piped into the rest rooms.

moves along shiny clean shop floors past huge cigarette machines, each invisibly fed tobacco from below. You're not in a factory, you're in an art gallery. The guide brags about the factory's ventilation system, but doesn't say why it needs to be so good. After the tour, Philip Morris supplies free souvenir postcards with free postage, and will mail them for you. Write your congressmen and tell them to lay off.

The keyhole-shaped entrance to the displays at the **Hallmark Visitors Center** in Kansas City, MO, announces a trip inside "the magical world of creativity." The keyhole shape reminds people that it is a door usually locked to them, and that they are not creative enough to make their own greeting cards. Visitors gasp with recognition at displays of best-sellers. "This was one of our Christmas cards. Now it's in a museum."

Hershey's Chocolate World in Hershey, PA, is so slick that you never enter the factory and don't even get any free chocolate. What you do get is an EPCOT-style ride through the romance of chocolate making. The tour starts in an African cocoa plantation, complete with safari sound effects. Little animated figures move crudely. Next, You Be the Cocoa Bean, as your car travels through a hot, red tunnel, roasting you. You're then reminded that Hershey's chocolate is part of a balanced diet for healthy, active families. Now, get out into that Hershey gift mall and buy some at retail prices.

Industrial tours remind us that innovation made us great. Our minds still lead the world in thinking up new stuff, and the fruits of this labor are all around us.

Hershey's Kiss Cap

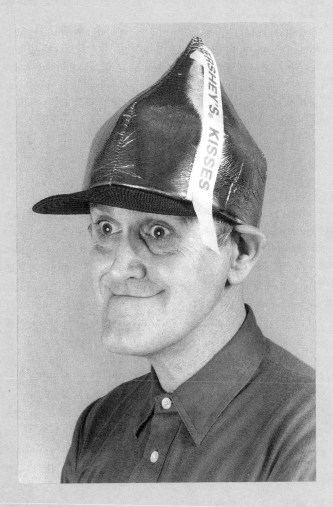

Is this really the most moronic souvenir cap that you can buy? We think so. It's not that the idea is stupid; the creative brains at Hershey's Chocolate World in Hershey, PA, really got it together on this one, opting for a custom-designed cap over a conventional generic model. But anyone who *wears* this silver boob risks being the cause of rubbernecking accidents, divorce, and involuntary commitment.

The **Tupperware Awareness Center** in Kissimmee, FL, is part of their World Headquarters building. We recommend stopping to see a series of rooms in a Tupperware Dream House. In the dream kitchen are side-by-side cabinets—one full of irrational rations, the other neat as a pin with all the snack foods sealed inside Tupperware "modular mates." "Presto, Chango!" says the happy sign. "Neatness, freshness, organization, courtesy of Tupperware brand products." The living and dining rooms feature elegant Tupperware displaying what might be called "Tupperfood."

In the showroom of **Hoegh Pet Casket Co.** in Gladstone, MI, the finished product awaits your perusal. One casket is presented as if at a viewing; a floral bouquet and candles add to the funeral ambiance. Above the casket are two black velvet paintings of sad, big-eyed dogs. Photo-metal headstones for the likes of Chuck the Lizard and Fruit Loops the Toucan are on display, and a video warns viewers that "burying pets in the backyard is against the law." Hoegh makes seven different sizes of caskets, including special pink and blue models in the smaller sizes (small pet owners tend to be fussier about such things). The tour through the factory concludes outside at a model pet cemetery, where a brass plaque on the crematorium informs tour goers, "If Christ had a dog, he would have followed Him to the cross."

Funeral finery for the most fastidious Fido at the Hoegh Pet Casket Co., Gladstone, MI.

The shoes of Emerson Mosler, who produced 1.4 billion crayons over a period of thirty-seven years. An inspiring tribute at the Crayola Hall of Fame, Easton, PA.

The Binney & Smith headquarters in Easton, PA, looks like any other nondescript suburban office complex. Ah, but here at the **Crayola Hall of Fame** you can touch the paraffin-spattered shoes of Emerson Mosler, who made an estimated 1.4 billion crayons during his thirty-seven years at the Crayola plant. Also here are four-foot-tall representations of the eight crayon colors retired by Crayola in 1990 (raw umber ditched for cerulean). A time line display shows the history of Crayola, from the first pocket box in 1903 to 1958's revolutionary, sixty-four-color vault with built-in sharpener. A separate display shows the evolution of Silly Putty, now also owned by Binney & Smith. The whole complex is permeated with the waxy, reassuring odor of warm crayons. Make sure you call ahead, tours are booked a *year* in advance.

Henry Ford Museum
—Dearborn, MI

The **Henry Ford Museum** and Greenfield Village is a 254-acre attraction in the process of metamorphosis. Once a vast humorless collection amassed by a vastly humorless man, it is being transformed slowly by the forces of coolness and light into an attraction well worth visiting. Much remains as Henry Ford originally planned. There are dull long lines of big steam engines dug into the floor so their flywheels will fit, a Fats and Resins display, the Lighting and Communications wing, a parade of office machines, and the Hall of Furniture.

But the automotive material, once an unorganized pile that battered you senseless with gray aggregation, is now an interesting homage to the automobile and its impact on America, using the museum's huge unair-conditioned spaces to full advantage. They have taken the resources only dreamed of by many curators and fashioned something impressive and inspiring.

Car Culture is fully exploited. They have full-sized billboards inside and a working drive-in (where Ford Motor's first production Edsel is displayed, hidden behind a speaker). A Holiday Inn hotel room, McDonald's and Howard Johnson's neon restaurant signs, and a Texaco gas station are here. High ceilings allow a whole roadside diner inside, complete with a live human waitress there to dispense museum information.

An Avanti. An Oscar Mayer Weinermobile. A 1971 Lunar Rover is parked next to an 1896 Ford Quadricycle. More and more around each corner.

You are shown how auto design happens, with scale models of the Lincoln Futura, the Packard Predictor, and the Ford Nucleon, powered by an atomic reactor. Full-sized dream cars include Ford's X-100 Fiftieth Anniversary model from 1953, with an electric shaver and Dictaphone as standard equipment.

Unfortunately, the "Path of Auto History" display ends not with a Ford or a Lincoln, but with a 1983 Honda Accord. Still, this is a small complaint.

Henry Ford proclaimed that his museum, which opened in 1929, would show how the inventions of a few (mainly Ford and his ubermensch industrialist buddies) had forever changed America. The artifacts of Harvey S. Firestone, Luther Burbank, and Thomas Edison (including his last breath, in a test tube) are sprinkled throughout. Their historic homes make up much of Greenfield Village.

But for all of the fascist scope and organization the museum once had, it never really made the connection with how American society benefitted from industrial progress. Now, finally, someone seems to be getting around to making Henry Ford cool.

One of the amazing similarities between Presidents Lincoln and Kennedy is that both of the objects they were sitting in when they were shot in the head are displayed at the Henry Ford Museum. Kennedy's death car, a 1961 Lincoln, is a short stroll from Lincoln's death chair (an 1861 Kennedy?), complete with bloodstained upholstery.

The World's Largest Tire,
Dearborn, MI. A car big
enough to use this could
have a Japanese import
as its hood ornament.

Harold Warp's Pioneer Village

—Minden, NE

Harold Warp's Pioneer Village cannot begin to equal the Henry Ford Museum in size or monetary investment, but it wins points for sincerity.

Warp is the president and founder of Warp Plastics, a Chicago-based manufacturer of window-screening material such as Flex-O-Glass, Glass-O-Net, and Red-O-Tex. If you haven't heard of any of these products then you're obviously not a midwestern chicken farmer, for it is these humble men who bought Warp's products and made him a millionaire. With his millions, he bought his hometown schoolhouse, his hometown church, an old depot, fort, and land office, and other places of no particular historical significance, and stuck them together in his Pioneer Village. Warp's collection now comprises over twenty buildings, including the oldest merry- go-round in the United States, which you can still ride for a nickel.

Harold Warp has dedicated his village to the period between the years 1830 and 1960—a period in which he believes America made its most important inventive strides. There are a couple of exceptions to this rule, like the 1974 Pinto once owned by Warp's son, but for the most part Warp remains true to his word. His exhibits include the world's second oldest Cadillac and a piece of the actual tin foil used on Edison's first phonograph. He also has a monkey-wrench exhibit in the agricultural building, the world's largest collection of restored farm tractors, and a living display of all seven native Nebraska grasses.

Boring? Former Secretary of the Interior Fred Seaton put it best: "What Warp has created probably isn't as greatly appreciated today as it will be in a few years."

Fun with Guns

One thing is obvious: Museums are not the place to fully enjoy guns. Like a beautiful sunset, or early Pink Floyd music, guns and ammunition just aren't the same when they're not live. A gun in a display case is denied its basic nature. Guns, as Aristotle might say, are only truly happy when they are being fired.

The line starts forming outside **FBI Headquarters** in Washington, DC, at 8 A.M.; lots of balding dads and tubby kids wearing neon surfing T-shirts wait for the famous tour. It is a disappointment. You're led around through some dull displays, including the FBI Firearms Reference Collection, then past a couple of windows where you can look in on bored lab technicians. Then into a little theater where you watch a couple of videos before the curtains sweep back to reveal a Special Agent standing behind thick glass. He fires about forty rounds from a Thompson into a paper target and that's it. No photos are allowed and there is no gift shop.

The FBI's Big Brother mentality is stressed throughout. "The FBI currently has 183,388,195 sets of fingerprints." "The FBI maintains a national shoe print and tire tread file." At the Serology lab, the tour guide tells you that "over eighty percent of the world's population are secretors," meaning that the FBI can trace you through your bodily fluids. If anything, you should be convinced that with a government this nosy, ordinary citizens need their guns.

At The Farm, outside Hot Springs, AR, owner Bob Warren waits behind his Browning for trespassing deer to clear.

Which is why you hope for a great **NRA National Firearms Museum,** also in Washington. But this, too, is a letdown. The exhibits are apolitical, historical in nature, and uninspiring throughout. "We don't want to give the anti-NRA people any ammunition," explained the gift shop operator. The only politicking that goes on here is at the free publications rack, where you can find "The Myth of the 'Saturday Night Special,' " and "Criminals Don't Wait—Why Should You?"

The Farm, outside Hot Springs, AR, is our favorite place to enjoy the real vacation fun of guns: shooting them. Opened in 1991 by dealer Robert L. Warren, The Farm is the place to shoot real guns—machine guns. Ten dollars gets you a spin on a Thompson submachine gun, and $20 a seat behind the tripod of a belt-fed Browning. Fifty dollars buys the top-of-the-line assortment: the Mac 11, the Uzi, the Thompson, the Browning, and finally, target pistol practice on a human silhouette.

The range backs up on many acres of land that Warren maintains as a wildlife sanctuary, which is not without its problems. "Sometimes we have to stop shooting to let deer cross," he says with a smile. Only about ten visitors a day make the five-mile trip from downtown Hot Springs to this secluded spot, but Warren seems happily content. "Some people ask, 'Why would you do this?' Well, why would you collect postage stamps?"

Next time you're in Vegas, pop a few at **The Survival Store.** This gun shop and indoor firing range is within an M-16 blast of downtown, and is always patrolled by Bo, a former Penthouse Pet, and survivalists' dream girl. Her posters, frontally nude holding different assault weapons, line the walls at The Survival Store, and are for sale at the counter. Bo loves cameras. Bring yours. And ask for her card.

Bo, the survivalist dream girl, offers up some points worth considering at The Survival Store, Las Vegas, NV.

THE WORLD OF COCA-COLA PAVILION
—ATLANTA, GA

The **World of Coca-Cola Pavilion** opened in 1990, a $15 million, 45,000-square-foot shrine to what Coca-Cola humbly calls "the most successful product in the history of commerce." It's an exhibit hall/ fun house that bombards you with superlatives until you are numb.

When you enter its lobby, happy, smiling hosts and hostesses in Coca-Cola red cardigans offer a cheery greeting and point in the direction of the giant glass elevators, which whisk you heavenward to where the exhibits begin. Here you'll see John Pemberton's original handwritten formula book (not open to the secret part, unfortunately) next to the original, prototype, six-and-a-half-ounce "hobbleskirt" Coke bottle, one of only two in existence.

The atrium bridge into the next gallery is blocked by giant Coke can video nooks. Inside, you touch a soft-drink "bubble" as it floats across a screen. This activates a videodisc that will show any one of several five-year synopses of world history, as seen through the eyes of Coca-Cola. The Spanish-American War is given equal billing with the opening of the first Coca-Cola bottling plant. Hitler's beer hall putsch is completely eclipsed by the introduction of the six-pack.

The "Every Day of Your Life" Theater experience is your next stop. Over its entrance, an electronic display chronicles the pace of Coca-Cola consumption around the world (it had reached 3,710,083,500,000 bottles when we visited). Beneath this, "Fabulous Facts" about Coca-Cola are continuously flashed on another electronic billboard. "A man large enough to consume a bottle filled with all the Coca-Cola ever produced would stand seventeen miles tall and weigh three hundred and twenty million tons." We watched this for over a half hour; the Fabulous Facts never repeated themselves.

A battery of doors slide silently open and another one of the ubiquitous, smiling Coca-Cola employees appears, directing you into

The "timeless symbol of quality refreshment" spins over the heads of dry-throated visitors eager to enter the World of Coca-Cola.

The towering "Bottling Fantasy" sets an appropriate tone at the World of Coca-Cola.

"America's first permanent, large-screen, HDTV cinema." Once inside, the Stereo-Surround Sound kicks in and you're yanked around the world on a thirteen-minute *ubercommercial* for Coke, propelling you at dizzying speeds from the Imperial Palace of Thailand to some godforsaken (but not Cokeforsaken) steppe in Africa. "Coca-Cola . . . every day of your liiiiiiife!!!!" wails the soundtrack over and over.

"Hey, mom . . . I'm thirsty!" cries one youngster as the video ends. The automatic doors on the far side of the theater swing silently open and the Coke goons are smiling. "There are thirty-eight flavors of soft drinks available in Club Coca-Cola," one responds. "Just go right this way."

But you're not to the watering hole just yet. First, you've got to survive a safari through The Real Thing gallery, chronicling the past forty years of Coke. Listen to the Moody Blues sing "Things Go Better with Coke" over a phone receiver, or simply stand in awe of the Coca-Cola Shooting for the Stars display, which showcases the unique Coca-Cola Space Can that gained Coke the coveted distinction of "first soft drink in space" in 1985. Hey . . . wasn't that also the year New Coke bombed? Where's the exhibit on that? The Coke guard only smiled and told us that this was a "selective" history.

Next in your path is Club Coca-Cola and its terrifying Spectacular Soda Fountain. This place is all black and spooky and ultra-hi-tech; neon flashes everywhere; synthesized thunder booms. As you nervously step up to the fountain and set down your cup, an infrared sensor automatically triggers overhead spotlights. You and your cup are illuminated in the darkness. The glass tubing and neon around you begin to pulsate. Frothing liquid rushes into a holding tank and gradually changes to the color of your chosen soft drink. Then blammo! Ejaculation! Soda arches twenty feet from some hidden high-pressure nozzle and makes a bull's-eye into your cup.

You stagger into the Tastes of the World display, where dozens of awful soft drink flavors from around the globe pour out of free fountain dispensers. Come on . . . you've gotta try at least one. Sip some tutti-frutti Fanta Kolita from Costa Rica, or try a mouthful of noncarbonated, sour cherry Cappy from Czechoslovakia. Gah! Mouth-befouled veterans encourage newcomers to sample Beverly—a quinine aperitif from Italy—then laugh hysterically as the victims bulge their eyes and spit it out. Survivors of the Tastes of the World display have no problem understanding why Coca-Cola is so popular overseas.

Want to sit down? Forget it. Your senses will be assaulted by a barrage of incomprehensible foreign Coke commercials blasting out of a video monitor suspended directly above your head. You get the message—Coke has had its way with you and wants you out, now. You're only so much gas to pass at this point.

Frank Aurelio hoists his soft drink of choice at tiny **Moxie Headquarters,** Lisbon Falls, ME.

You Can Do It!

Our problem is attitude. Think negative, and the mind is programmed for failure. If we're going to compete against the world and *win*, we have to believe in ourselves. If you need a shot in the arm, or a kick in the pants, may we suggest the following attractions.

The ten pillars of economic wisdom are chiseled on bronze tablets outside the **Amway Headquarters** in Ada, MI. In the center of the lobby is a sixteen-foot pyramid, "Building Together The American Way," showing how Amway works. To one side are statues of Amway's founders, Rich De Vos and Jay Van Andel. Bronze Van Andel sits pensively, while De Vos stands, fist on hip, revealing his bronze Sansabelt slacks. It was their "Let's just charge!" attitude that built Amway into the $3 billion supersuccess direct marketing business it is today.

After a film, the tour proceeds past Rich and Jay's office, and the tour guide points out that Amway's HQ is a self-contained city with its own water supply and fire department. Walls display the names of successful distributors from around the world. See the labs where new products are made, like bubble gum–flavored toothpaste for kids. Near the labs are plaques for each of the patents Amway has received. Here's one for a new drain cleaner. But it's not the product, it's people!

People make the difference at Wal-Mart, too. That's what you learn at the **Wal-Mart Visitors Center** in Bentonville, AR. Today, founder Sam Walton is one of the country's richest men, and Wal-Mart does more than $25 billion a year. Sam grew up in the Depression, and during this hard period forged his attitude of not "Can Do," but "Will Do."

The Visitors Center, at the site of Walton's first store, recalls an old five-and-dime store up front, while the back room is full of more modern displays. The 100 millionth square foot of Wal-Mart space is displayed. So are keys to many towns, as well as the hula skirt Walton wore down Wall Street after the company achieved 8 percent pretax profits in 1984. Videos explain the company's ascendance.

Wal-Mart's huge success in an understandable, low-tech business implies that anyone with the right attitude can win. So it is no surprise to see groups of men here, golf shirts, hairy forearms, and metal-band wristwatches, looking for that elusive spark.

Still don't get it? Try the shock therapy of a visit to **Enterprise Square, U.S.A.,** a $15 million glorification of the free-enterprise system on the campus of Oklahoma Christian College in Oklahoma City. Bob Hope greets you on videotape, then aliens crash-land and have to learn enough about free enterprise to repair their ship. This is what they (and you) encounter.

Enterprise Square, Oklahoma City, OK. Jefferson, Franklin, Washington, and Hamilton crack jokes, sing, and inspire youngsters to make as much money as they possibly can.

THE NEW ROADSIDE AMERICA

The Great American Marketplace, home of the World's Largest Functioning Cash Register. On a wall, big paper money replicas have animated president heads that talk and sing. In one passageway, disembodied voices argue the benefits of capitalism versus socialism. Guess who wins?

A visit before The Great Talking Face of Government—a giant head containing nine video screens—shows the problems arising when government oversteps its bounds. Though the curators suggest that to see everything at Enterprise Square, U.S.A. would take thirty years, after just a few hours you'll be ready to spend those thirty years borrowing money, hiring workers, and raising the standard of living for everybody. Because you can do it!

Babyland General Hospital
—Cleveland, GA

Now that communism is dying, wimpynism is the number one destroyer of youth. How do we fight back? We'd suggest an initial skirmish at one of the nation's prime sissy centers, **Babyland General Hospital.**

This is the spot where Cabbage Patch Kids are "born." Babyland is, in fact, located in an old doctor's clinic, but the fuchsia trim gives an early indication that something is wrong. The lot across the street is always full; expect to park several blocks away. Zombie couples pull their small children inside, like they're taking them to a rendezvous with a Seed Pod.

The place is jammed. The help are all dressed as "licensed Patch Doctors and Nurses." Local teenage girls serve as candystripers.

You first walk into the maternity ward, where dozens of Cabbage Patch dolls lie in incubators behind a glass wall, waiting for "adoption." Bunnybees, Cabbage Patch cousins, dangle on wires from the ceiling of every room.

Next is a small room devoted to the man who made all this possible, Xavier Roberts. Xavier began Babyland General in 1978; the Cabbage Patch craze hit the Christmas of '83; and by '87 more than 50 million had been "adopted" worldwide. Xavier's grinning mug is everywhere on Cabbage Patch literature and postcards, posing with all the earnest pleasure of a man who's fallen into very deep clover.

A series of rooms depict Cabbage Patch dolls in Home Ec class, riding on Santa's sleigh (special Christmas Edition dolls, $225), and ice-skating on a frozen pond (special Krystina Edition dolls, $250). More Bunnybees dangle above.

In the center of the final, great room stands the giant Magic Crystal Tree. Cabbage Patch doll heads poke out from cabbages underneath it. Suddenly the Babyland General intercom barks "Code Green! Cabbage dilation!" and a nurse emerges from a door in the trunk of the tree. Camera flashes pop, camcorders whirl. "The Mother Cabbage has dilated a full ten leaves," she explains through her face mask, poking the plastic plant with a dental tool. "Chlorophyll count is normal." IVs labeled "Imagicillin" and "TLC" drip. Suddenly, the nurse's voice grows serious. "Please . . . no children leaning against the rail," she scolds. The youngsters are yanked back. Yeah, get outta here, you real kids.

"We've never had to perform a C-Section—that is, a Cabbage Section— yet," she says as her hand darts down into the center of a plant. The crowd holds its breath for a long moment, then bursts into applause as the nurse yanks a doll out from the hole in the cabbage and wraps it in a blanket. "It's a girl!"

"Name it Melissa!" screams one adult. "No! Name it Melody!" cries another. "We'll name her Melissa, and her middle name will be Melody," says the nurse, used to dealing with such emotional outbursts. "Melissa will be up for adoption in the Babyland nursery," says the intercom as the nurse walks away. Her price—$195.

Under the Magic Crystal Tree at Babyland, another Cabbage Patch Kid is yanked into the world.

THE BORING TOUR

Have you ever felt a perverse desire to visit an attraction simply because you know it'll be boring? Don't worry, a lot of other people feel the same way. There is a certain sick thrill to be found in wasting time at some museum or display that seems purposefully designed to numb you. It's even more fun if you have a family.

As you may suspect, there are more than enough boring attractions to fill their own book—places that sound dull and do not disappoint. What follow are a few standouts, and God have mercy on you when you visit.

DAY 1: Dawn breaks over the foamy Atlantic and you find yourself in exciting Plymouth, MA, sipping a fresh cup of healthfulness at **Cranberry World!** Trace the history of the cranberry from colonial to modern times and visit a working bog!

Then head south to Camden, NJ, and their **Soup Tureen Museum.** Help yourself to free goldfish crackers and a Styrofoam cup of the soup du jour at the door, then go, go, go! *See* the tureens shaped like animal heads, *learn* about the legendary Red Anchor period of glazeware, and *remember* that soup is always served in an oval tureen.

DAY 2: Getting antsy? Don't worry, today will put you to sleep. Your first stop is the **Bethel Park Gas Meter Shop** in Bethel Park, PA. Here, guided tours explain the difference between gas and water meters, and allow you to follow an actual repair process! Next, head south to Thompson, GA, **Home of the Father of Rural Free Delivery.** It's not open for tours (that might have been too exciting) but you can drive by and touch the mailbox.

Budget your time wisely; your final stop of this day is the **Shuffleboard Hall of Fame** in St. Petersburg, FL! Learn the stats of such court legends as Mae Hall and Lucy Perkins and take in the

As this artist's rendering shows, the ***International Checkers Hall of Fame*** *in Petal, MS, is much too interesting to qualify for the Boring Tour.*

world's most complete collection of shuffleboard irons and history-making pucks. It's in a brand-new building ("solid concrete walls!" brags the excited curator) at the Mirror Lake courts.

DAY 3: Welcome to the Tedium Zone, the fertile bottom land of boredom that extends from central Ohio through western Minnesota. First stop: the **Illinois Historical Water Museum** in Peoria, where you can experience the history of water treatment from sedimentation to liquid chlorine.

Had enough? Your day's just begun! Head for the Buckeye State and the **Accounting Hall of Fame** on the Columbus campus of Ohio State University. You might want to spend the afternoon at OSU, which also boasts the **Insurance Hall of Fame** and the **Agricultural**

Drainage Hall of Fame. But don't stay too long; you have to drive west and buy some postcards in **Dull, OH,** before they roll up the sidewalks.

DAY 4: Hump day, but you've a long way to go. First you'll drive north to Ewen, MI, where the **World's Largest Replica Load of Logs** waits to entrance you. The original load was assembled for the 1893 Columbian Exposition; had it survived, it would still be the largest load of logs in recorded history. Happily, we have this replica load of logs to replace the real load of logs.

Then it's into the Badger State to the **International Credit Union Center** in Madison, WI. Trace the history of debt! You'll be overwhelmed by the center's dioramas and animated maps, but don't be too numb to take in *The Credit Union Legacy* in the ICUC's 175-seat theater.

DAY 5: Spend this entire day pondering the nuances of the **World's Oldest Rock** in Granite Falls, MN. It's a lump of Morton Gneiss, 3.6 billion years old, and it's on the property of the Yellow Medicine County Historical Museum. You don't want to rush this one.

DAY 6: The **Maytag Washer Exhibit** in Newton, IA, beckons. This dusty display of eight old washing machines occupies the second floor of the Jasper County Museum. Your photo album's not complete without a shot of its 1922 Model 80—the world's first Gyrofoam washer!

Next, it's on to Dodge City, KS, but keep away from any exciting wild West stuff! You're gunning for **The Kansas Teachers' Hall of Fame** to check out their display of antique textbooks! Tip your thinking cap to Herb Darby and Grace Casebolt, two of the many enshrined here.

DAY 7: The endless desert can't dull your enthusiasm for the **Gadsden Purchase Plaza** in Mesilla, NM. The bandstand occupies *the exact spot* where the Gadsden Purchase was signed in 1853, giving America the lower eighth of Arizona and New Mexico.

Quick, hop into your car, because your next stop is the not-very-near Pocatello, ID, where the **First Home in Idaho with Electric Lights** is open for tours. About to pass out? Hang on! You've only got to chase the sun to Port Angeles, WA, where Olympic National Park provides a fitting finale to your journey at their eternally tranquil **Hall of Mosses.** Now go home, you boring person.

Christianity

Christ of the Ozarks, *Eureka Springs, AR.*

*G*od is with us wherever we go—even when we're on vacation. The Omniscient One rides shotgun, gets us to the last tour of the day on time, finds an inn with HBO, and multiplies our travel dollars so that we don't have to go to the cash machine. But these assists aren't for free. This is one Supreme Being that doesn't mind a little adoration in return, and religious attractions help us fulfill our obligations.

Our nation is blessed with intricate shrines and ornate devotional grottoes. Giant crosses point heavenward. Da Vinci's *The Last Supper* provides inspiration for countless faithful artisans. God is everywhere—and he's definitely a Christian. It's enough to discourage even Satan.

Great fisticuffs of the Apocalypse! It's Satan and Jesus, duking it out in the heartland! The battle rages over thousands of square miles. In 1985, witnesses report a surprise appearance by the "image of the Shroud of Turin," on a hospital closet door in **Albany, NY!** But later, the shroud itself is proved a fake. It must be Satan! In 1986, Jesus appears on the side of a soybean oil tank in **Fostoria, OH.** The tank is soon painted over! In 1987, the face of Satan appears in the burn marks on a wrecked truck door in **O'Fallon, IL,** and draws the innocent to his circus tent for a peek. Within weeks, Jesus appears on a tablemat in an adjacent restaurant! Jesus rabbit-punches Mr. Bad News with successive cameos on a refrigerator in **Estill Springs, TN,** and on a woman's ceiling in **Taft, TX,** then his statue starts to blink and sweat in a church in **Ambridge, PA.** Jesus and Mary are spotted glowing and planning strategies in a firewood yard in **Barret Station, TX.** The Virgin appears to believers as a stain on a shower stall floor at Progreso Auto Parts, **Progreso, TX.** In 1991, a pizza-face Christ embellishes the toppings on a billboard in **Stone Mountain, GA.**

Who knows where the next photogenic blow will fall . . . ?

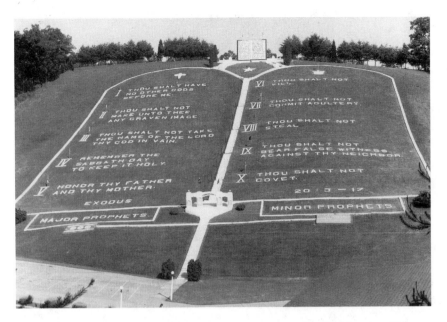

World's Largest Ten Commandments, *Fields of the Wood, Murphy, NC. With letters five feet high, these Ten C's rule.*

Of Crosses and Christs

During a summer night on Bald Knob Mountain in Alto Pass, IL, the light that can be seen from three states also draws bugs from three states. **Bald Knob Cross** is so bright that the caretaker can sneak up and stick a moth with a six-inch wingspan right in your face. "Look at *this*, fella."

The cross is 111 feet tall, with arms extending sixty-three feet. A steel framework is covered with white porcelain steel panels. It is engineered to withstand winds of up to 150 MPH (Satan take note). Completed in 1963 after smaller crosses had stood in the same spot, it was the idea of rural mail carrier Wayman Presley and the Reverend William H. Lirely. The cross was paid for entirely with donations. You can buy a copy of "PIGS!: A Story of Faith" in the welcome center. It tells about a woman who sold a miraculous number of pigs to raise money for cross construction.

Christ of the Ozarks stands along a ridge near the **Great Passion Play** amphitheater, **New Holy Land,** and the **Christ Only Art Gallery**

Cross in the Woods Catholic Shrine, Indian River, MI—Home of the Nun Doll Museum and the World's Second Largest Crucifix.

in Eureka Springs, AR. He is probably the World's Tallest Uncrucified Christ, standing seven stories and weighing two million pounds. According to "The Story of the Building of the Great Statue," as many as three automobiles could be hung on either wrist without damage. Visitors report that the eyes seem to move, but this is explained as the movement of the sun, not another incredible miracle. At night, attendees of the four-hour-long Passion Play walk off cramps around the eerie, illuminated Messiah. The whole cavalcade of Bible treats was founded by late radio racist Reverend Gerald L. K. Smith. More "Inspirational Sacred Projects" are under development.

The **Cross in the Woods,** Indian River, MI, is technically not a cross, but a crucifix—which means that you can see Jesus nailed to it. It is fifty-five feet high, twenty-two feet wide, weighs twenty-one tons, and claims to be the largest crucifix in the world, as long as Christ of the Ozarks doesn't get pinned to Bald Knob.

Cross in the Woods is impressive, but it is not the most grandiose devotion. That title belongs to the **World's Largest Crucifix,** at St. Thomas Church in Bardstown, KY. Built in 1986, it is sixty feet high, "Welded of stainless steel rods, garment of wire-cloth, hair of copper." It nails Indian River by a scant five feet.

Forest Lawn

—Glendale, CA

There are three links in the **Forest Lawn Cemetery** chain. The one in Glendale, across the street from the church of TV madman mystic Dr. Gene Scott, is the best—in fact, it's the best cemetery in the world. It is where history, art, and religion meet each other, decide they are in good moods, then do their best to see that that day's visitors have a fine time. Fun? How many graveyards have gift shops? Forest Lawn's map reads like an amusement park. "Lullabyeland," "Vesperland," and "Slumberland" are all special areas in which one can be interred. Literally tons of famous people like Clark Gable, Humphrey Bogart, Walt Disney, and Freddie Prinze are buried here. The speed limit is 30 MPH, great by cemetery standards. And there's more!

There are full-sized replicas of Michelangelo's *Pieta* sculpture, statues of George Washington and Christ, and bigger-than-life interpretations of the signing of the Declaration of Independence and the Crucifixion. Forest Lawn leaves you with the impression that the two best places to be are America and Heaven.

Itty-Bitty Churches

All measurements are for internal space.
Churches must be used for legitimate service or worship at least once a year.

1. World's Smallest Church (Elbe, WA)
The Evangelische Lutherische Kirche measures only eighteen by twenty-four feet.

2. World's Smallest Church (Davenport, IA)
"A Little Bit O Heaven," dedicated to the founder of chiropractic medicine, measures eight by ten feet.

3. World's Smallest Church (Festina, IA)
St. Anthony of Padua Chapel measures twelve by sixteen feet and seats eight.

4. World's Smallest Church (Plaquemine, LA)
Chapel of the Madonna is six by eight feet, and contains five chairs.

5. World's Smallest Church (Crestview Hills, KY)
The Monte Casino Church is seven by ten and a half feet and contains one pew.

6. World's Smallest Church (Wiscasset, ME)
This one is seven by four and a half feet, and sports a golf ball atop the steeple.

7. World's Smallest Church (Verona, NY)
Cross Island Chapel is an amazing three and a half by six feet, allowing only enough room for the minister to stand inside.

8. World's Smallest Church (Keystone, NE)
"The Little Church," at fifteen by thirty feet, is also the "only combined Catholic/Protestant church in world."

9. World's Smallest Church (San Antonio, TX)
Peaceful Valley chapel includes "an artist's conception of a great painting" and a black-light presentation of the Sermon on the Mount. It is eighteen by thirty feet.

10. World's Smallest Church (Horseshoe Run, WV)
Our Lady of the Pines is eight by twenty feet.

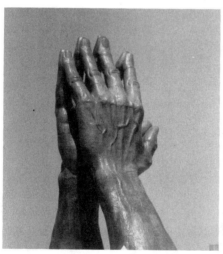

Healing Hands, Tulsa, OK, versus Praying Hands, Webb City, MO. Both statues are just plain scary, but for different reasons. The sixty-foot Healing Hands at the Oral Roberts City of Faith Hospital are so richly detailed with pores and blood vessels that they look like a medical model. The Praying Hands burst from the ground, unannounced and soul shaking, and grab the unsuspecting motorist turning the corner on Highway 71.

Catholicism Unleashed

Faithful followers fashion impromptu testaments of faith in secular neighborhoods across the nation. Sacred lawn statuary, Virgins in bathtubs, and Nativity scenes made from garbage remind us of the fragility and temporary nature of the real estate market.

But real grottoes and shrines are a decidedly Catholic thing, best executed by priests. Men of the cloth are often possessed of the proper mix of spiritual anguish, miraculous stamina, and free time to lug fifty-pound bags of cement up a ladder from dawn till dusk.

A Benedictine monk, Brother Joseph Zoettl, built Jerusalem in Miniature—the **Ave Maria Grotto,** in Cullman, AL. While the grotto itself is a rock and shell alcove, the 125 miniatures are neat replicas filling a hillside and a scenic walk through the three-acre Biblical fairyland. Brother Zoettl is long dead, but the structures are part of a college campus, and seem well maintained.

The **Grotto of the Redemption,** West Bend, IA, is a titanic landmark to the power of one's religious devotion. As a young seminarian, Father Paul Doberstein fell gravely ill and promised to build a shrine to the Virgin Mary if she interceded for him. She liked the idea, and the young priest started his payback in 1912. He continued building this greatest of American grottoes until the moment of his death in 1954.

Organ and church bell music boom out over nine grottoes that tell the story of Redemption through Christ. Every colorful mineral and crystal imaginable has been incorporated into this miraculous mound. Father Louis Greving was the creator's assistant for eight years. He continues to work toward the grotto's completion, though now he is old, has no young helper, and could be losing valuable time by giving hourly walkthrough tours to visitors. Father Greving loudly proclaims that the grotto has a geologic value of $2.5 million, which completely ignores its true value as a relic.

And Satan was at it again: "A tornado came by last week, took off the tops of trees and knocked off the cross, but didn't damage the grotto," Father Greving says, amazed. "It was coming right for the grotto, then jumped a hundred feet off the ground and missed it."

The **Shrine of the North American Martyrs,** Auriesville, NY, is dedicated to America's only three canonized martyrs, who "shed their blood for Christ" here in the 1640s spreading the doctrine of the Mother Church to unappreciative Native Americans. Father Isaac Jogues "died from the blow of a tomahawk," while Rene Goupil's and John Calande's fingernails were ripped out with teeth before they died. Details of the "barbaric torture" are provided in the Martyrs' Museum on the shrine grounds.

Grotto of the Redemption, West Bend, IA. America's Greatest!

Bottles of Ravine Water, drawn from the holy spot where Rene was buried, are only a dollar in the gift shop. Lots of statuary graces the property, which seems to be a favorite wandering spot for glassy-eyed ladies.

The altar in the center of the Coliseum Church is built to resemble a seventeenth-century frontier stockade, only this one has a giant crucifix ascending out of it. The altar is surrounded by over 1,500 novena candles that can be lit at the touch of a button.

The **Shrine of the Snowshoe Priest,** at the top of Michigan in L'Anse, is a sixty-foot-high bronze statue of Father Frederic Baraga, first Catholic bishop of the region. He stands on a cloud, supported by frozen beams of light streaming from five teepees. His snowshoes are twenty-six feet long.

The number one stateside healing shrine is **El Santuario de Chimayo,** Chimayo, NM, known as the "Lourdes of America." Around 1810, a friar was performing penance when he saw a light bursting from a hillside. Digging, he found a crucifix, quickly dubbed the "miraculous" crucifix of Our Lord of Esquipulas. After a small chapel was built on the site, miraculous healings began. The crucifix still resides on the chapel altar, but for some reason its curative powers have been overshadowed by *El Posito*, a "sacred sand pit" that sits behind the main altar. The Prayer Room is filled with discarded crutches and twisted, hand-made shrines that look like voodoo. Over 300,000 people visit this dustbin o' heaven every year, and go home either miraculously cured or miraculously burdened with T-shirts, caps, and refrigerator magnets.

In 1908, in the middle of a blinding snowstorm, Dr. John Espey saw a shimmering light on a hillside overlooking Trinidad, CO, followed it, and found a 250-pound statue of the Virgin Mary with a candle flickering

Ave Maria Shrine, Trinidad, CO.

at its base. Statutory rapture gripped the locals, who accepted this as a "divine sign" and began building the **Ave Maria Shrine** around the statue, which was eventually completed in 1961.

Since then, things haven't gone all that well for Ave Maria. The statue was destroyed by vandals in 1962, and papers discovered in its arm showed that it was manufactured in France, a somewhat less-than-divine origin. The little-used road leading up to the shrine is currently crumbling into nonexistence; the holy water fountain is bone dry; and the shrine itself (as well as its painstakingly restored statue) are locked behind a floor-to-ceiling metal grate. As a final blow, the hospital Dr. Espey was leaving that fateful night, and which the shrine still overlooks, is St. Vincent's of Trinidad, which has since become America's leading sex change center.

Saints Preserve Themselves

*Saint John Neumann—
in the chamber, safety off.
Philadelphia, PA.*

At the **National Shrine of St. John Neumann,** in Philadelphia, PA, one of America's few official saints is on public display. Zealot and apostate alike can view his sanctified visage through the church's glass altar. Eerie

fluorescence illuminates the wax facsimile molded around Saint John's skeleton; his high mass hat makes him look like a bullet.

The museum in the church has glass cases cluttered with mementos and personal relics, where the Ballistic Bishop's story is revealed. We see news accounts of his posthumous miracles (it takes an authenticated three for sainthood), and the instruments with which he practiced the spiritually cleansing act of mortification—his sharp-edged wire necklace, and his disciplina (for self-flagellation). Near the portal back into the church is the very stone step "On Which Bishop Neumann Rested Shortly Before He Died."

Dead saints are known for their powers of self-preservation—sporting moist tongues or giving off "supernatural perfume" when finally exhumed years later. Photos in the museum show the Holy Howitzer Shell's exhumation 100 years after his death in 1960; he wasn't moist, but shrine literature points out that it doesn't disqualify one from sainthood.

Shrewd visitors to his Philadelphia shrine can purchase an actual piece of the Canonized Cannonball for themselves! For $20, you can own a "first-class relic," in this case a Neumann leg bone chip (with Latin certificate of authenticity). "Third-class relics"—pieces of cloth rubbed on his bones—are available for those on a budget. Like potato chips, if one saint bone isn't enough, you can get more at the **Basilica of the National Shrine of St. Elisabeth Ann Seton,** Emmitsburg, MD. Rub friends with your new souvenirs, and turn everyone you love into third-class relics.

Saint Frances Xavier Cabrini, another American saint whose mummified remains are displayed, rests at the **Mother Cabrini National Shrine Chapel** on Manhattan's way–Upper West Side. She was dug up after fifteen years in the ground and discovered to be "in a remarkable state of preservation." No bones for sale here, but members of all faiths are invited to peek at the dead lady, and stop at the shrine museum, where you can see a check she wrote to the Seattle National Bank, a piece of dirt from her front yard, and a spring from her dentures.

Oral Roberts Prayer Tower

—*Tulsa, OK*

Part of the swollen membership of Oral's sects gathers at his Prayer Tower.

The **Oral Roberts Prayer Tower** is a powerful magnet for those seeking spiritual inspiration—or fundamentalist fun. Erected in 1967, this "20th Century Cross," with its stylized crown of thorns, commands a heavenly view of Oral Roberts University. A recording of Oral's son Richard in the observation deck says it best: "No second-class buildings for God."

In the top of the tower, visitors can see the special door to Oral's special prayer room. Oral scatters hundreds of prayer requests across the carpeting in there, and then waves his arms over them. The Prayer Tower's elevation combines with Oral's direct line to God to help those prayers get answered.

Two extravagant presentations reward pilgrims with startling visions. The first, "The Journey Through Faith," is six sound-and-light segments, each in its own soundproof room, each recreating a different phase in the life of Oral Roberts. The first segment puts the visitor on Oral's childhood front porch in Oklahoma, as Oral's father, himself a preacher, rants somewhere in the house. "Heal my neighbor's child," he intones, "and I will give you my own son!" The music swells: "Duh duh duh duh!!"

Next, schoolchildren taunt young Oral for his funny name. As if he wasn't having enough trouble, Oral collapses during a basketball game with tuberculosis! A doctor remarks that it doesn't look good. "All we can do is let the illness run its course," but God has other plans. A light begins to glow in Oral's bedroom. "God," Oral wheezes, "heal me . . . and I'll give my life to you!" Oral's brother and sister enter. "Oral, there's a healing service going on in town tonight . . . I've got thirty-five cents worth of gas—and we're goin'!" Minutes later, Oral is exclaiming, "I can *breathe!* I can feel the *illness* leaving my *body!*"

The "Journey Through The Bible" presentation has its own building, and its six rooms represent the first nine chapters of Genesis. You start in a spherical, pitch-black chamber. "And God said, let there be light!" Thousands of optic fibers embedded in the walls blaze. "The Way of Sin" is a harrowing hallway, which recreates Paradise Lost. Recorded moans and screams echo through the darkness. Pilgrims gladly flee to the swaying deck of Noah's Ark, where they are sheltered from simulated rain. "The Rainbow Covenant" room reveals the postdiluvian world of soggy and mildewy trees. In the final Prayer Room, a projected Oral harangues you for money.

Hey, *that's* not in Genesis!

Wendell Hansen's Bible Bird Show

—Noblesville, IN

Reverend Wendell Hansen has been presenting his **Bible Bird Show** since divine inspiration struck him over fifty years ago. Starting with a pair of Jacob's Ladder–climbing canaries, his bird-trick parables and mobile aviary grew to include macaws, doves, a toucan, a peacock, and other well-behaved birds in an hour-long extravaganza.

In its heyday, the Bible Bird Show ranged through surrounding states and the East, spreading The Word by bird in schools, churches, and auditoriums. Shows are now confined near his home, but the Reverend's Bird Van is always ready to roll and set souls aflight. His piano-playing

*T*he Reverend Wendell Hansen pauses between parables. "Let's play basketball!"

wife, Eunice, and grown son, Dean, assist the eighty-one-year-old Quaker minister at every performance.

The show starts when John the Macaw says "PreEEEE-Zen-TEEEENG . . . WennnnnDELLHan . . . Zennnnn . . ." The Reverend's patter starts, fast and furious. A macaw sings "Jesus Loves Me," accompanied by Eunice's piano and fine voice. Later, Eunice plays "Silent Night" for the virgin birth, when the Reverend cradles a bird, and "Low in the Grave," when the bird plays dead. Birds cry out "PRAISE THE LORD" at odd moments; one keeps saying "Water . . . Water . . ."

The Reverend draws on simple, resonant themes to motivate his audiences. "You know, there's good Christians . . . and there's bad Christians . . . But when Judgment Day comes, the Lord will separate those bad Christians and send them to Hell, just like Isaac is separating the blue and red rings!" Isaac uses his beak to separate the plastic rings, placing them correctly on the friendly blue post, or on the red spike of damnation.

Despite some brimstone shockers, the show is gentle; no crucifixion scenes or Old Testament pillars of salt. The Reverend does salt a bird's tail at one point, but the lessons are ambiguous. Should *we* wear little bibs and flip over backwards a dozen times? Did Jesus die so that someone would feed him a peanut?

Silently Dean sets the next prop in place—in this case, a church with a music machine inside it. "Put money in the church . . . that's where the money should go," reminds the Reverend, giving Jeremiah a dime. The bird tithes, and "Silent Night" plays from the music machine inside.

Two doves obediently sit in a small wooden chariot; they are pulled by a parrot, because "we should bear one another's burdens." Later the Reverend puts a bird's head in his mouth. The American flag is dutifully raised by one macaw as another poses, bald eagle–style, on the pole. God, Country, and Bird blend gloriously into one. The Bird Van heads off to another gig, pious squawks and screeches echoing in its wake.

"You are there!" This bas relief of The Last Supper *has a cut-out area behind Jesus and a walkway around to the back that allows for some dandy snapshots.* **Antone Martin Park,** *Yucca Valley, CA.*

Holylands

Sensible people have to wonder why nearly all of the stories in the Bible are about places far away from the U.S. The **Mormon Visitor's Center,** Salt Lake City, UT, copes, relying on Joseph Smith's update of the Good Book, which places "Jesus in America"—on a layover after his Resurrection, but before his Ascension. Your regular dresser-drawer Gideon conjures a dry, distant land, easier for a Scud missile to visit than a born-again family from the Sun Belt. Enterprising Christians have taken the golden calf by the ears and fashioned domestic versions of those same exalted sites.

Rub-a-Dub Dub . . . *it's Christ in a Tub! Save some soap for the Madonna.*

A *natural cross at **Black Hills Holyland,** Keystone, SD. If you found one in your backyard, people would pay to see it on their vacations.*

Velvet paintings of this thorny Savior are abundant enough to satisfy every art collector on a budget.

The **Holy Land of America,** Washington, DC, was built by the Franciscans to remind Americans of the Franciscan mission, which is to preserve Middle Eastern holy sites. The catacombs beneath the main church are reproductions of early Christian hideouts, constructed with poured concrete walls that have been airbrushed to make it appear as if they are made of mighty stone blocks. In the catacombs, Purgatory Chapel is composed of black-and-white tile frescoes of skeletons, including one that seems to be a tribute to the inner jacket of *Led Zeppelin IV*. The volunteer guides wear outfits that look like a combination of Good Humor Man and Banana Republic Dictator—spotless white jumpsuits, bedecked with medals and sashes—and white shoes with thick rubber soles.

Holy Land U.S.A., topping a hill above Waterbury, CT, is a postnuclear, *Road Warrior* vision of the Holy Land. Some two hundred miniature plaster and tin-foil buildings, shrines, and dioramas were assembled by a mysterious religious order, and were maintained by nuns. Satan attacks, evil and entropy take their toll. While Hollywood-style letters spelling "HOLYLAND USA" and a tall cross of steel and plastic still stand, the rest of the sculptures are being destroyed and carted off by vandals at an alarming rate. The main buildings are caving in and the catacombs look like a deathtrap.

Holy Land U.S.A., in Bedford, VA, occupies the entire four-hundred-acre farm of Bob Johnson, a retired supermarket owner. Every natural setting or farm outbuilding that can be related to the Bible has been. A group of three trees growing from the same root is "The Holy Trinity." A pond is "The Dead Sea"; a creek is "The River Jordan." Scattered across the property are over two dozen chronologically placed Biblical scenes, from manger to empty tomb. Along with these are two large outdoor amphitheaters, a huge Star of David, and an equally large cross. The "Joseph/Jesus Workshop" houses a gift shop where visitors can buy a crown of thorns or cut nails "similar to the ones used to crucify our Lord."

One of the Seven Wonders of The New Roadside America

PRECIOUS MOMENTS CHAPEL
—CARTHAGE, MO

Precious Moments figurines are the number one collectable in the country. These little porcelain bisque representations of teardrop-eyed cartoon children, many who have died and become angels (you can tell by their halos), are now sold by 10,000 retailers. More than 800 different figurines exist.

Creator Samuel J. Butcher's full-sized masterpiece is the stunning **Precious Moments Chapel.** Pastel billboards along I-44 in Southwest Missouri announce the impending exit. Once off the interstate, a growing caravan of fat lady Vanagons will let you know you are on the right track. Then, rising out of the surrounding farmland is a modern pastel brick complex. The parking lot is huge and crowded. Beautiful mood music is piped into the lot.

The visitors' center is full of gift, souvenir, and refreshment stores. It is supposed to look like an indoor European Village wonderland, with a twinkly starfield ceiling. Animated teardrop-eyed puppets are everywhere—hovering, waving, playing the violin. A strange aura is present. Aficionados have reached Mecca's anteroom, and are excitedly waiting for their guided tour of the chapel to begin.

The walkway through well-manicured grounds from the visitors' center to the chapel has rows of thigh-high painted bronze cartoon dead baby angel statues on either side. You get a creepy pang that recurs throughout your visit: My God! Cartoon dead babies! The panic subsides, and you join other tour goers at the chapel's entrance.

Before it begins, a well-rehearsed tour guide tells the Samuel J. Butcher story. We are told that Mr. Butcher's work is fine religious art, like that found in Europe. To either side of the chapel entrance are large bronze bas reliefs. The bronze on the left represents the Old Testament, with Jewish-looking baby angels clamoring amongst brambles and thorns. The New Testament is represented on the right, with Christian baby angels playing amongst flowers and trees.

Mahogany doors open onto a small room and a second set of doors.

The tension mounts. Then, the inner doors open and people gasp. "Hwwaaaaa." A whoof of air-conditioning rushes out, adding to the otherworldly atmosphere. "It's makin' me sick," wisps one overcome admirer. Visitors get as quiet as if they were in St. Peter's in Europe. But it's not St. Peter's! The chapel's interior is painted with cartoon characters! Dead babies!

The tour guide reminds visitors that they can speak and ask questions, because they are not in a church, it only looks that way. But most are simply at a loss for speech. On the walls are painted fifty-four murals mainly depicting scenes from the Bible. Two sweetly confused cartoon baby angels with flashlights illustrate "And God said, let there be light." And after God created the earth, several cartoon baby angels innocently play basketball with it.

The ceiling, thirty-five feet above you, is painted to look like the sky, with clouds along the edges and dead-baby *putti* floating and playing with stars. To paint the ceiling, Butcher had to lie on his back like a famous European artist.

The chapel's focal point, "Hallelujah Square," is a huge representation of a just-dead baby arriving at the gates of heaven (presumably to become a dead baby angel and pose for Precious Moments figurines). Already-admitted dead baby angels welcome the new addition. Dead children are everywhere in heaven, and in the mural's background, a grown-up Christ figure plays with some. He is the only adult painted in the chapel.

The guided tour ends, and the group is free to inspect the adjacent halls. Here, stained-glass dead-baby angels depict the Twenty-third Psalm and The Beatitudes.

Trams take you back to the visitors' center, for another look around the gift shop. Admission to the chapel is free, but as the dazed, touched visitors stumble back to their cars, many are holding gift-wrapped $60 bas tableau replicas of the chapel.

Precious Moments Chapel has only been open since 1989. Yet it already gets 500,000 visitors a year, 30 to 40 percent being collectors. Expansion is planned. A motel, waterpark, and other ways to create an entire vacation city are being considered.

What is to be made of Precious Moments Chapel? Is it an infomerical attraction built for the purpose of selling figurines? Though chapel literature says it was "not originally designed as a tourist attraction," why then did they build a five-hundred-person convention center adjacent to it? Is it really fine religious art, or is it spiritual artificial sweetners, not only fake, but containing something that when taken in large doses could make you retarded? You must decide for yourself.

The Hallelujah Square mural, centerpiece of The Precious Moments Chapel. A new cartoon dead baby is welcomed into heaven. "And God Said . . . 'I Wuv U This Much.' "

Meat and Nuts

World's Largest Mr. Peanut
in Fort Smith, AR.

The Nut Museum

—Old Lyme, CT

"Nuts are fresh tokens of primeval existence," explains The Nut Lady. "I mentioned that on my second appearance on David Letterman." Hidden behind a mask depicting the prickly burr of the sweet chestnut, she launches into an *a cappella* verse from her self-penned "Nut Anthem": "Oh nutttts, have a bee-you-tee-ful his-tory and lorrrre . . ."

The Nut Lady is Elizabeth Tashjian, an artist who has championed the aesthetic causes of Nutdom since 1973. Her antebellum mansion and tree-shrouded property make up **The Nut Museum,** an environmental gallery

The Nut Lady cradles her prize cocoa-de-mer at The Nut Museum, Old Lyme, CT.

of nut expression. "I'm trying to take the demerit marks off nuts with the power of art," she explains.

Nuts are everywhere, as are nutcrackers, nut sheet music, nut paintings, and the World's Largest Nut, a thirty-five-pound cocoa-de-mer from the Seychelles Islands. But the museum is under siege. The outdoor aluminum nut sculptures have been savaged by faceless vandals, and Ms. Tashjian inexplicably gets the civic cold shoulder from a town that prefers to be known only for its diseased deer ticks.

The Connecticut Department of Tourism has kept The Nut Museum out of its official guide since 1988, claiming that the house is infested with squirrels. "It was a fabrication," The Nut Lady says. "The state tourism bureau was bought out by some rich, local financiers who want my home. It's a plot." The latest indignity? Ripley's Museum offered to buy her cocoa-de-mer, but she refused. "They wanted to make it into a soup tureen," she scoffs.

The Nut Lady points to a painting of nutcrackers and nuts floating in what looks to be amniotic fluid. "In the outside world, nutcrackers are the nuts' mortal enemy," she explains. "Here, nuts and nutcrackers can be friends."

The Nut Museum is only the first of what Ms. Tashjian sees as an expanding series of shrines to her favorite seed. She fitfully dreams of a thirty-two-acre nut theme park overlooking Long Island Sound; a pier and line of shops would form a giant nutcracker, its hinge would be the "Nutcracker Suite" restaurant.

Ms. Tashjian dons the "Mask of the Unknown Nut" and peeks playfully through its eye holes, waving good-bye with an indelible image to match her philosophy.

Perry's Nut House

—Belfast, ME

You'd have to be crazy to go here. The only nuts on display are four cocoa-de-mers; the one still in its shell is labeled "world's largest," but that's cheating. Horribly decayed dead animals pack the second floor—some have their ears ripped off, others have patches of fur missing or faces that have been smashed and crudely reconstructed. Goats, bears, monkeys, seals, and lions stand cramped shoulder-to-shoulder. **Perry's** is a popular spot for Canadians who want to get out of the rain.

PEANUTS ENVY

The six-foot peanut in Pearsall, TX.

It began in 1954. **Blakely, GA,** boasting that it was "Peanut Capital of the World," mounted a thirty-inch-long cement peanut on top of what it called "the only known statue erected in honor of the peanut." For twenty years this goliath goober stood quietly, with dignity, in its sun-dappled courtyard.

Then the '70s arrived. **Durant, OK,** was the first to test the waters, building a thirty-six-inch peanut on top of its own granite marker and proclaiming it to be the world's largest. They should have left well enough alone because **Pearsall, TX,** quickly followed with its own world's largest peanut, this one a whopping six feet long. Texas had one too many boasts of this kind, cried the citizens of **Ashburn, GA.** They restored their state's honor by erecting a fifteen-foot-tall brick stack, capping it with a giant crown, and balancing on top a towering ten-foot-long peanut. "Georgia: 1st in Peanuts" is written on the crown, and so it will remain.

*The ten-foot peanut in Ashburn, GA. This gargantuan goober eclipses even the giant, smiling **Jimmy Carter Peanut** in nearby Plains.*

SQUIRREL WARS

Not one, but three towns use albino squirrels as their claims to fame, and none is particularly happy about the others.

Kenton, TN, has about 200 of the furry rodents. Residents insist that the squirrels "have been here the longest" and claim the squirrels were left by a "Gypsy caravan" in 1869. Is Kenton, we asked, where the other towns got their white squirrels? "Well, they had to come from *some*where."

Olney, IL, is the loudest boaster of all albino squirrel towns, titling itself "Home of the White Squirrels." They scoff at the other towns' albinos. "Most of theirs have dark eyes," they told us. Laws on the Olney books give the squirrels right-of-way on every street; residents are fined if they try to leave town with one. Local police patches bear an outline of a bushy-tailed albino. Big Squirrel is watching you.

Olney has overhyped themselves, according to a **Marionville, MO,** spokesperson. "They've got our backs up," Marionville told us, an opinion they've held ever since Olney appeared on the "Today Show" in 1965. Marionville believes that the squirrels arrived in town "just after the Civil War" and that they escaped from a traveling circus. "The squirrels in Olney were kidnapped from Marionville," they explain. Common gray squirrels found in Marionville are trapped and kicked out.

Black squirrel towns are downright cooperative, compared to the fracas between the albinos. **Council Bluffs, IA,** has had black squirrels since at least the 1840s, but lacks the fanatical eugenics policies of the white squirrel towns. As a consequence, Council Bluffs's nearly unique squirrel population is slowly disappearing through miscegenation. **Marysville, KS,** "Home of the Black Squirrels," holds an annual Black Squirrel Celebration and sings the "Black Squirrel Song" as its anthem; the black squirrels have been here since the late 1920s, when local historians say they escaped from a traveling circus. Or was it a Gypsy caravan?

Kenton, TN, is one of three towns that use albino squirrels as tourist bait.

Peekin' at Pecans

The 12,000-pound monster pecan in Brunswick, MO.

The giant pecan that sits in front of the **Seguin, TX,** city hall was the brainchild of a dentist who wanted to put his plastering skills to civic use. Erected in 1962, the pecan is five feet long and two and a half feet wide, and weighs approximately 1,000 pounds. It was dedicated to Cabeza de Vaca, a Spanish explorer who was held captive on the Guadalupe, "River of Nuts," for ten years. He thrived on a diet of local pecans. Seguin began billing itself as "Home of the World's Largest Pecan," a title it held for twenty years.

George and Elizabeth James have owned their pecan farm in **Brunswick, MO,** since before WW II. In 1982 they built a concrete replica of their patented Starking Hardy Giant pecan, discovered by George on their property in 1947. The pecan sits in front of their Nut Hut roadside stand—twelve feet long, seven feet wide, and 12,000 pounds. It beats Seguin by a mile.

Meat Map U.S.A.

We are a nation of meat. Blood and gristle forged a frontier; meat gave us courage. The American character is charcoal grilled, and dipped in Bar-B-Q sauce. Salad bar sissies can dive into our yards and weed the lawn for lunch. We'll have sirloin. While the vegeterrorists may have their moment, meat reigns supreme.

MEAT FIRSTS

1. Birthplace of the Hamburger—Hamburg, NY, or Seymour, WI, or New Haven, CT, or Athens, TX?: Hamburg strikes first with its claim that two Ohio brothers formulated a beef sandwich at the 1885 Erie County Fair and named it after their town. Seymour throws fat onto the fire in the form of "Hamburger Charlie" Nagreen—local inventor of the hamburger at the 1885 Seymour Fair. Louis' Lunch of New Haven (a still-standing brick beanery) sizzles as the first establishment to sell hamburgers as a menu item, in 1900. Athens grills the competition with an official plaque that says that "Uncle Fletch" Davis served 'em first in the late 1880s.

2. Birthplace of the Cheeseburger—Pasadena, CA, claims to have served one back in the 1920s, but the town has not supported its claim with anything physical, like a giant cheddar slab. Cheeseburger buffs should instead travel to **Louisville, KY,** where Kaelin's Restaurant still stands. It claims to have invented it in 1934.

3. The First McDonald's, Des Plaines, IL: See historic burger-abilia in the museum basement of Ray Kroc's restored 1955 golden arches; eat at a modern McD's across the street.

4. The First Wendy's, Columbus, OH: Noted with a plaque. Still open for business.

PROMINENT PIGS AND POULTRY

5. Colonel Sanders Museum, Corbin, KY: The colonel's original restaurant has been restored to its 1940 splendor. The colonel's talking pot tells his story. An official highway marker certifies the birthplace of KFC.

6. Grave of King Neptune the Pig, Mt. Pleasant, IL: This patriotic porker was "sold" countless times during WW II to raise funds to build the *U.S.S. Illinois* battleship. The King is buried in a roadside turnout off IL-146. The *Illinois* was never built.

225

7. Five-Story-Tall Chicken, Marietta, GA: Built in 1963 to advertise Johnny Reb's Chick, Chuck and Shake, this fifty-five-foot-tall sheet-metal monster was later acquired by Kentucky Fried Chicken.

8. World's Largest Prairie Chicken, Rothsay, MN: A 9,000-pound male fowl appears to be pecking tiny tourists to death. Rothsay built it for the bi-centennial in 1976.

9. World's Largest Turkey, Frazee, MN: The Thanksgiving Colossus.

10. Rhode Island Red, Adamsville, RI: A bas-relief marker commemorates the breed's establishment in 1854.

MEAT EATERS

11. Donner Party Museum, Truckee, CA, and Monument, Lake Tahoe, CA: Snowbound settlers-turned-cannibal.

12. Alferd Packer Sights in Colorado—Massacre Site and Museum (Lake City), Memorial Grill (Boulder), and Grave (Littleton): America's favorite cannibal!

13. Buffalo Jump State Historic Site, Three Forks, MT: Interpretive displays explain how hungry Indians stampeded large herds of bison over an eighty-foot-high cliff. Picnic area.

14. Coffeeburgers, Harrison, NE: At Sioux Sundries, try their famous twenty-eight-ounce hamburger, named after the first person who ate one. Eat two, get a third free.

15. Big Texan Steak Ranch, Amarillo, TX: A roadside institution, featuring a seventy-two-ounce steak. Eat it all, get it free.

16. Tail O' the Pup, Los Angeles, CA: Trendy hot dog–shaped hot dog stand.

17. Reelfoot Meats, Union City, TN: Their mascot is a cartoon Indian with a hatchet. They don't give tours and they don't like photographers.

MYSTERY MEAT

18. Spam Museum, Austin, MN: Hormel maintains an exhibit of meat history at the local mall. See old copies of *Squeal,* the Hormel company magazine, the first canned ham, and "Slammin' Spammy," the bomb-throwing pig symbol from WW II.

19. Meat and Blood Shower, San Francisco, CA: Forteana! On July 20, 1851, this stuff fell from the sky on an unsuspecting populace. Apparently beef.

20. Flesh and Blood Shower, Los Nietos, CA: On August 1, 1869, flesh and blood rained down on two acres of Mr. J. Hudson's farm in particles and strips one to six inches long. Also, short hairs!

21. Meat Shower, Olympian Springs, KY: From a cloudless sky on March 3, 1876, one- to four-inch-square chunks of meat fell on an area 100 yards long by fifty yards wide. Witnesses said it looked like fresh beef, but tasted like mutton or venison.

22. Frozen Hamburger Shower, Syracuse NY: In February, 1957. Air-line mishap, or manna supporting near-by Hamburg's hamburger birthplace claims?

23. The Beaver Feed, Laurel, MT: Little Big Men Pizza and Curt's Saloon hold the annual Beaver Feed, where participants enjoy a smorgasbord of wild beaver meat, venison, and moose sirloins.

24. Testicle Festival, Clinton, MT: Since 1985, a yearly celebratory chow-down of Rocky Mountain Oysters at the Rock Creek Lodge.

*Albert, the world's largest bull,
Audubon, IA. His framework was
built with steel salvaged from
abandoned Iowa windmills.*

25. Gatorland Zoo, Kissimmee, FL:
Sells line of gator meat treats and
sauces as souvenirs.

**26. U.S. Meat Animal Research, Clay
Center, NE:** Government-funded meat
manipulation and experimentation. What
will the veal of tomorrow look like? Tours
by advance appointment.

27. Possum Monument, Wausau, FL:
This bas-relief granite slab stands
across from the Wausau gas station.
"Erected in grateful recognition of the
possum . . . Their presence has provided a source of nutritious and flavorful
food."

CONDIMENTS

**28. World's Largest Catsup Bottle,
Collinsville, IL:** It towers above the
Brooks Food factory; Collinsville is also
"Horseradish Capital of the World."

**29. Tabasco Sauce Visitor's Center,
Avery Island, LA:** Tour the pepper
sauce factory, view a film about the
origins of Tabasco, and gaze at a
facsimile of the capsicum pepper plant.

**30. Lawry's Seasoned Salt Factory
Tour, Los Angeles, CA:** Multimedia
theater presentation, then a walking tour
through the test kitchens, labs, and
production facilities. Dine at on-site
restaurant; seasoned salt always tastes
better fresh from the factory.

BIG BOVINES

**31. Albert, World's Largest Bull,
Audubon, IA:** Forty-five tons, thirty feet
tall, fifteen feet from horn to horn. Giant
concrete gonads. Push a button and
Albert will tell you in his own voice that
he was built in 1964 as a replica of the
perfect Hereford bull. Buy a ceramic
replica in town.

**32. World's Largest Buffalo,
Jamestown, ND:** Sixty tons of steel and
concrete.

**33. World's Largest Holstein Cow,
New Salem, ND:** 12,000 pounds of
fiberglass.

**34. Big Ben, World's Largest Steer,
Kokomo, IN:** 4,720 pounds, six feet four
in height, sixteen feet, two inches in
length. He fell on ice and broke a leg in
1910. The doctor who was called shot
him. Big Ben was stuffed and paraded
around the county before coming to rest
in a glass-enclosed shed in Highland
Park.

35. Big Red, Bozeman, MT: "The last
ox to pull freight over the Bozeman
Pass." On display at the Powderhorn
Sporting Goods Shop. Purchased from
a museum in Helena that went broke.

36. "Steer Montana," Baker, MT: 2,980
pounds. Dead—and on display in the
O'Fallon Museum. Raised by a former
jockey east of town, used to tour local
stock shows and circuses. When they
found him dead, they "strung him up on
a windmill," stripped the carcass, and
preserved the hide in a tank of brine.
Steer Montana disappeared for many
years, but was finally rediscovered in a
storage facility in Billings. The bill came
to $5,000.

37. "New Faithful," Three Forks, MT:
One of two cement oxen statues that
stand outside the Prairie Schooner
Restaurant, apparently pulling it. The
cashier asks newcomers, "Have you
seen Old Faithful?" No matter what they
answer, the cashier replies "Well, take
a look at *New Faithful!*" then hits a secret
button. New Faithful *pees!* Prairie
Schooner regulars often run in and
demand that the cashier "turn him on!"
to impress friends.

Cannibalism: Where Nuts and Meat Meet

One sure way to gain immortality—no matter how hopeless your social and monetary position—is to eat somebody else. The man who did this best was Colorado's Alferd Packer, and the Centennial State has accordingly embraced Alferd to its bosom. California lobbyists howl that they, too, had a cannibal—several, in fact—but a quick visit to the **Donner Party Museum** in Truckee will show you that these starving pioneers only ate people who were already dead. Alferd, on the other hand, was far from famished and preferred a hot lunch.

Colorado shows its appreciation of its favorite son at the **Alferd Packer Memorial Grill,** in Boulder at the University of Colorado Medical Center. A small, marble bust of Packer, unveiled by Colorado governor Roy Romer, sits on a pedestal at the hub of the grill.

The **Alferd Packer Massacre Site,** once a remote wilderness, is now only five minutes south of the Lake City miniature golf course. A big sign shows cartoon caricatures of two mountain men, mouths agape in horror or pain as (we are left to imagine) an axe is driven into their skulls. A small rock marks *the* spot, and a plaque lists the victims. Five white crosses are arrayed in front. Free brochures fill a metal box adjacent to the site, chock full of juicy tidbits about Alferd's ghastly doings.

In downtown Lake City the **Hinsdale County Museum** displays a skull fragment from a victim, a pair of shackles used on Alferd when he was in the Lake City jail, and a number of buttons from the clothes of the five men he ate.

After he was released from prison—on a technicality—Alferd became a vegetarian, made a modest living selling autographed photos of himself, and died. You can visit **Alferd Packer's Grave,** in the Littleton Cemetery. The gravestone cutter—obviously not a Packer fan—spelled Alferd's name wrong.

A piece of Frank Miller that Alferd Packer forgot to eat. Hinsdale County Museum, Lake City, CO.

Dreamers

*The angry rabbit and his giant carrot disturb children of all ages at **Santa's Land,** Cherokee, NC.*

Everyone tells us to dream. Weekend seminarists tell us we must dare to dream. Infomercials tell us we must dream of greatness. Junk mail says we must live our dreams—just check the middle box. Why do people have to tell us that?

Because most of us are somnambulent automatons. The only spark of inspiration we ever volunteer to our van pools is a review of the great R-rated feature on last night's Showtime. We're spiritual cocooners, the full range of life pinioned by a gooey blanket of routine we secrete around ourselves.

But there are those who are not like us. Men and women of vision, with the courage to act, damn the court of public opinion. Those who are not afraid to go it alone. They are true dreamers, the ones who are truly awake.

Dreamer attractions awaken us all to the possibility of possibilities. You may redesign yourself with new doors of perception after visiting a house made of doors in Half Moon Bay, CA, or salt in Grand Saline, TX, or formaldehyde bottles collected from mortuary parlors in Buford, WY. A one-woman opera house in the middle of the desert in Death Valley Junction, CA, and a 600-pound solid ball of postage stamps in Omaha, NE, are sure cures for the waking sleep of daily existence.

Some dreamers build structures of illusion and trickery, fever dreams from their slumber in the arms of Mobius. Other creations are towering tributes to the insignificant, from true genii of the specious. Whichever you visit, scales will fall from your eyes, and you'll finally have something to talk about.

Watts Towers, Los Angeles, CA, *faced the bulldozers and won. These soaring, speckled towers of concrete and garbage rise above the Watts ghetto and are perhaps the country's most famous eccentric busy-bee assemblage. They were condemned, but admirers managed to get them registered as a National Landmark. The site has been restored and brought into compliance with building codes, although some of the old junk has been removed and replaced by a new shell of pop opulence.*

Dementia Concretia

There's a bug some old people get. They work hard all their lives, and when retirement finally arrives, instead of quietly going into that dark night, a strange earwig burrows into their brain and forces them to build, build, build! Taking whatever is handy—usually concrete, bottles, and household junk—they fashion icons and structures until they are exhausted.

At **Fred Smith's Concrete Park,** in Phillips, WI, a jumbled crowd of some two hundred folk-art figurines clog the landscape. In 1950, at age sixty-five, this northwoods lumberjack and tavern owner began crafting his conclave of concrete cowboys, coolies, Indians, and soldiers. Broad shouldered and blocky, some ride horses or drive teams of oxen. Others stand in long rows, the sun glinting off their glassy armor. Ben Hur and a distorted angel loom among their followers. Two concrete wedding parties wonder who invited the coolies.

*F*red Smith's Concrete Park, Phillips, WI. Tavern owner Smith used beer bottles to decorate his life-sized horde.

*N*aked concrete man greets the day at Thunder Mountain, Imlay, NV.

In Forest City, NC, stand **Charlie Yelton's Bottle Houses.** Charlie was a retired lumber mill worker, who recently died at the age of eighty-four. The first house took four years and 12,000 bottles to complete. In one room, the floor is studded with his granddaughter's baby food jars. There is a spooky altar room done in red, containing a throne. "This is where Charlie would pray," says the wife who survives him. Before he was done, Charlie had built two smaller bottle houses, a bottle wishing well, and a bottle flower garden. Sitting on the porch next to rotting cardboard boxes filled with dusty bottles, Mrs. Yelton muses, "We don't get as many visitors as we used to."

Henry Luehr has turned an eight-story-high condemned grain elevator in Pettibone, ND, into a thing of beauty. The shiny **Pettibone Pagoda** is filled with discarded junk from his family, and is covered in old aluminum offset printing plates. Henry, seventy, started working on it in 1981 because he "needed something to do." Phase one took him 10,000 hours. Elaine, Henry's wife, hates the thing. Henry is now building a thirty-foot-long Hereford bull, inspired by the giant fiberglass cow in nearby New Salem. "Henry doesn't like to do anything small," Elaine explained. "He wants to be noticed."

Chief Rolling Mountain Thunder was sixty-two when he began **Thunder**

Mrs. *Pope's Museum, Cairo, GA. Mrs. Pope is long gone, but you can still tell that townsfolk were scared of her. Her concrete sculptures, including those of Dwight Eisenhower and WW II heroes, are visible for all to see.*

Mountain near Imlay, NV. Numerous flumes of concrete snake up and around his house. Its top floor is made of bottles. Car windshields serve as windows. In the back, a sign stuck into the ground lets visitors know that beneath them an underground house was built "to demonstrate the all-round feasibility and the economy of underground living." Live animals run free amid numerous concrete sculptures. A single-engine concrete plane rests on pylons set onto the hood of an old car below it. A nude female, "Bearer of Life," leans back against a rock, arms waving above her head. Other nudes dance throughout the concrete web that surrounds the house.

Grandma Prisbey was probably the best known demented concretian. In 1955, when she was sixty-two, Grandma started **Prisbey's Bottle Village** as a single bottle house to hold her 17,000 pencils. Before she was finished, the village had thirteen bottle houses and nine other sculptures. Her village has become the proof rock by which other concrete concoctions should be measured. The street through the middle of the village is paved with license plates, toys, and hubcaps. An exterior wall is made from television picture tubes. Outside is a display of baby doll heads on sticks. Burgeoning Los Angeles County has pushed its population into the once-remote Simi Valley, and today Prisbey's Bottle Village shares a fence with a generic prefab condo complex. Bets are being taken on which will last longer.

Finally, lest you think Dementia Concretia strikes only individuals, we direct your attention to the remains of the **S.S. Atlantus,** visible as a lump in the ocean from Cape May Point, NJ. A marker on shore reads, "Remains of experimental concrete ship built during World War I. Proven impractical because of weight."

The Garden of Eden

—Lucas, KS

On a quiet residential street in Lucas, KS, a sudden profusion of ivy-covered concrete and sculpture emerges from the yard of one home: **The Garden of Eden.** A concrete Adam and Eve greet you; Eve offers an Apple of Friendship. Above them on tall concrete pillars are the devil, frolicking concrete children, and two love storks. To the left, high in the air, an all-seeing concrete eye watches over the garden.

Biblical scenes are interspersed with political messages. In the back-yard, Labor is crucified while a banker, lawyer, preacher, and doctor nod approvingly. On one pillar, an octopus representing monopolies and trusts grabs at the world. A soldier and a child are trapped in two of its tentacles. Fear not. On the Goddess of Liberty tree, Ms. Liberty drives a spear through the head of another trust octopus, as free citizens cut off the limb that it rests upon.

The creator of this concrete and limestone paradise was pioneer show-man Samuel Dinsmoor. Dinsmoor was an extremely patriotic American, lover of freedom, and hater of the conspiratorial trusts. Gripped by severe dementia concretia, he started building The Garden as a residence in 1905 at the age of sixty-four. Having that knack for popular eccentricity (he married his first wife on horseback decades before such stunts swept the nation), he opened his home as a tourist attraction in 1908, even as his vision of Biblical and Modern man was being molded out of 113 tons of concrete. He continued building and displaying up until his death in 1933, taking time out to marry a twenty-year-old in 1924.

Dinsmoor had prepared for the day of his demise, building a forty-foot-high limestone pyramid mausoleum in one corner of his garden. When he died, he was specially embalmed and put on display. Even after sixty years you can look through his glass-sided coffin and see the moldering creator of this splendor.

Labor crucified in the backyard of the Garden of Eden. The "Motivated Japanese Worker" bust must've blown down.

TWINE BALL BATTLE

In **Darwin, MN,** sits the world's largest twine ball. It weighs 21,140 pounds, is twelve feet in circumference, and was the creation of Francis A. Johnson. After Johnson's death, the city moved the ball and the silo that sheltered it into a special city lot across from the park. Unfortunately, it has put a big Plexiglas shield over the entranceway, making photos and true communion difficult.

Frank Stoeber of **Cawker City, KS,** saw Johnson's twine ball as a challenge. He started amassing his own ball, and soon had over 1,600,000 feet of twine rolled into a sphere eleven feet in circumference—only a foot shy of the Darwin champion. Success seemed inevitable. Then, Frank Stoeber died. Cawker City, in a touching tribute, built an open-air gazebo over his ball and set it up on Main Street, where it can still be smelled and admired by travelers.

Hole 'N' the Rock, *Moab, UT, was the home/cavern of Albert Christensen, who blasted and drilled for twelve years, then moved in with his wife, Gladys, in 1952. Albert died in 1957, but Gladys lived seventeen more years, operating a café and gift shop. Forty thousand visitors annually visit The Hole's fourteen rooms, including a cavernous bathroom known as "a toilet in a tomb."*

Collections of Number

The best collections are those whose *only* value lies in number. Collect pencils, and you better have a bunch in the drawer before you get the nerve to charge admission. Tourism's Law of Large Numbers clearly states: The more you have, the more interesting it is.

The Fossil Bowl in Clarkia, ID, is a motocross track where priceless prehistoric treasures were found in one of the embankments. Paleontologists dig during the week, motocross cyclists roar over the site on the weekends. But Fossil Bowl is most special because of its collection of 185 FIRE HOSE NOZZLES! All different! And who can pass up an audience with 500 VENTRILOQUISM DUMMIES!? You can't. And that's why there's a **Vent Haven Ventriloquism Museum** in Fort Mitchell, KY.

Of course, less than a thousand of anything is ho-hum. So, why not look at 1,000 TELEPHONES! Where else than at the **House of Telephones** in Coffeyville, KS, where Mr. and Mrs. Oral Watts will also be happy to show you thousands of spare parts. Or check out **Mom-Pop's Cap Museum** in Marietta, OK, for a gander at 2,400 BASEBALL CAPS! Many are autographed by celebrities.

Like the sound of 5,000 SOUVENIR SPOONS!? Then the Keompel collection of souvenir spoons, displayed at **Lambert Castle Museum** in Paterson, NJ, is just for you. Spoons are for goons? Well, then visit **Mr. Ed's Elephant Museum** in Mt. Union, PA, and pore over 7,000 ELEPHANTS! Don't miss "Ellie," Mr. Ed's life-sized talking pachyderm.

Of course, less than 10,000 of anything isn't really exciting. That's why you're after 25,000 BEVERAGE CANS! Where? **The Museum of Beverage Containers** in Millersville, TN, that's where. But for our money, the nonpareil stop for collections of number is John Schmit's **Fantastic Museum** in Redmond, OR. In addition to showing off Liz Taylor's motor home, and a pair of Bing Crosby's fishing boots, still caked with mud, Schmit proudly presents 7,000 matchbooks and 1,000,000 BUTTONS! Oh, my!

Evidence of Genius

The mysterious **Coral Castle** in Homestead, FL, was built over a period of twenty years by Edward Leedskalnin. Ed was a native of Latvia who emigrated to the United States when his sixteen-year-old fiancée, Agnes Scuffs, broke their engagement on the eve of their wedding. Once settled, he began laboriously carving his memorial to Agnes, whom he called "Sweet Sixteen."

Ed worked in secret, usually at night, never allowing anyone to see how he carved the hard coral rock into the various chairs, tables, and monuments that fill the Castle. Ed, who weighed only 100 pounds, also never revealed how he managed to raise and position the massive coral blocks that make up the Castle's battlements. Some of these blocks weigh over twenty-five tons. All in all, Ed quarried and sculptured over 1,100

Coral Castle, Homestead, FL, was once known as Rock Gate.

tons of coral rock for his Castle, using mostly tools that he fashioned from junkyard auto parts.

The Castle today exists pretty much as it did in 1951, when Ed died of stomach cancer. It is an impressive display of obsessive, unrequited love. The only one unimpressed by Coral Castle is "Sweet Sixteen" herself, still alive, who has known of the Castle's existence for years but has never visited.

The Orange Show is a colorful cacophony of sculpture and junk set in a residential Houston neighborhood. It appears as some recently crash-landed alien carnival. Multihued metal juts from a jumble of balconies and buildings. American and Texas flags flutter in the breeze.

Jeff McKissack originally planned to build a beauty parlor on the site, but the idea of an artistic tribute to the orange took hold of him. Over the next twenty-five years, McKissack transformed tons of masonry block, tiles, and throw-aways into whimsical sculptures, doorways, gates, and displays, all based on his personal philosophy that oranges were "the perfect food."

Fred Ehn was a self-taught seventh-grade dropout whose concrete sculptures once graced his **Trapper's Lodge Motel** in Burbank, CA. He fashioned scenes from the old West out of concrete and painted them in

Geronimo's father makes off with the body of a white leader to store at his fraternity's secret initiation teepee, or so it appears. Fred Ehn's sculptures, Pierce College, Woodland Hills, CA.

bright colors, including a Mormon doing bloody hand-to-hand battle with one Indian, while his scantily clad woman friend is carried away by another. Fred died in 1981, and his work was moved to a quiet, park-like area at Pierce College, in Woodland Hills, CA. There is a big Bar-B-Q grill in the center, a fine place for cookouts and ghost stories.

Roadside America's vague billboards ("You Have To See It!") have been luring travelers since 1941. It is not until after you arrive that you know this Shartlesville, PA, attraction is a miniature village representing small-town Pennsylvania life at various stages in history. The late Laurence T. Gieringer spent his entire life crafting this tiny town. As a lad, he thought that far-off structures were actually small and not just distant, a misconception that left a lasting scar, and led to the creation of Roadside America.

This well-named attraction is laid out in one big room with walkways around the perimeter. There are lots of buttons to push to get mechanical things to work, trains to move, or lights to come on. Every half hour, the town goes dark as projectors illuminate one long wall with faded slides of, among other things, the Statue of Liberty, and a boy steering a ship's wheel with Jesus at his shoulder. A plane on a stick circles over the village while "God Bless America" plays.

There's not much room for expansion at Roadside America; no space to add a nuclear power plant or a rocket station. The fact is that since

Jeff McKissack's tribute to the perfect food: oranges.

Gieringer died nothing has been added and the march of history comes to parade rest, circa 1960.

Tinkertown, of Sandia Park, NM, is the creation of Ross Ward. For more than thirty years, he has carved and collected material for his attraction. Over 12,000 objects are displayed, including a miniature, animated, hand-carved wooden Western town and circus. Walls are made of glass bottles. His motto: "I did this while you were watching TV."

A Crazy Man's Home Is His Castle

Bishop's Castle—Beulah, CO,
and Soloman's Castle—Ona, FL

We like Jim Bishop.

Jim Bishop has been building a castle at the crest of a mountain out in the middle of central Colorado since 1969. "Did it all myself, don't want any help," he says mechanically, unloading a pile of rocks at the seventy-foot level of one tower. To Bishop, the castle will be "a monument to

Jim Bishop's Castle, Beulah, CO.

hard-working poor people" and "a fight for freedom to keep the government under control."

At the moment, the castle is a soaring, if hollow, shell of cemented rocks and ornamental ironwork. Plans include three 100-foot towers (the tallest capped by an observatory and solar furnace), underground torture chambers, and a forty-foot-high castle wall protecting the two-and-a-half-acre property. The fire-breathing dragon chimney, already in place, belches flames out of its hinged mouth with the help of a propane tank.

Like many a visionary, Bishop constantly battles the government. The Colorado Tourism Bureau refuses to list **Bishop's Castle** as an official attraction in its guides and the feds want to charge Bishop for the rocks he uses in construction, which he gathers from San Isabel National Forest. He feels they are his for the taking; the government wants to gouge him $16 a ton.

Bishop realizes that he may need assistance if he wants to live to see the Castle's completion. He may, he concedes, let other people help with the wall "if I don't have to be a boss or a supervisor." Otherwise, Bishop shrugs, "I can do it myself."

We like Howard Soloman.

"I hated school. My teachers told my parents I was borderline retarded," says Soloman. One day when he was seventeen and his folks were at work, he ripped the back wall off their new suburban home and began adding a porch. "I found that I really enjoyed building things on a grand scale." Now Soloman's parents live in a back room of their son's home, a castle in a Central Florida swamp.

Soloman's Castle covers 8,000 square feet and stands three stories high. The exterior is covered with discarded aluminum printing plates, blinding in the Florida sun. To one side is a thirty-five-foot bell tower.

Once inside, Soloman shows you some of his many sculptures, the only grueling aspect of an otherwise enjoyable visit. A turtle with hair is called "The Tortoise and the Hair." A gun that shoots toilet plungers is "for flushing out perpetrators." We won't spoil "Gnome on the Range" and "Holy Mackerel." Tourists wishing to stay overnight can book the Honeymoon Suite with "a wonderful view of the moat."

The soft-spoken Soloman began in 1972. When he discovered the swampland he bought wouldn't suit horizontal building, he built vertical instead. "I never was a very good planner," he admits. "But when people in town found out what I was doing, they wanted to see it. I ended up making a tourist attraction out of my seclusion. It's serendipity."

Soloman's newest project, the Boat in the Moat, is a sixty-foot replica galleon that will serve as the Castle's restaurant. His ultimate goal? "To get out," he says. "I want to find a rich Japanese or Arabian investor and sell the place. It's gotten too big."

Howard Soloman opens a trap door in front of his TV. It reveals a dungeon, complete with shackled torture victim!

Men at Work

⭐ **Great Statues of Auburn**
—Auburn, CA

Ken Fox, sixty-four, did not start sculpting until he was forty. Today, in the parking lot of his dental practice, stands an eclectic mix of huge concrete statues. His two Amazons are most impressive. One thrusts a spear skyward, poised on one knee. The second, forty-two feet high and weighing 120 tons, aims a bow and arrow.

Why Amazons? "I just got to thinking about them one day, and I have always liked the female figure. Real Amazons cut off one breast so they could shoot their bows. But I just couldn't do that to a woman." A taller, eighty-foot caveman was planned. "I had it checked by engineers, but I couldn't get final approval. That's the thing about art. You have to be able to take disappointments."

⭐ **The Gourd Museum**
—Angier, NC

"I've made lots of friends through gourds," says Marvin Johnson, eighty-seven. Johnson's **Gourd Museum** is nestled in the woods behind his home. Inside is lots of musty gourdalia, including a Last Supper made of gourd seeds, a gourd xylophone, and an old Timex display case filled with pseudo-Fabergé eggs—made of gourds. The place is illuminated with gourd lamps.

Johnson and his late wife, Mary, started the museum in 1965 because they had too many gourds lying around the house. Mary is gone, and the Johnson house is again filled with gourds, along with every other kind of debris you can imagine, piled high on every surface. "I'm gonna build another building, next to the museum," he declares. "I need more room for the gourds."

 **Tower of Pallets
—Sherman Oaks, CA**

Dan Van Meter lives quietly in a tree- and scrap-metal-lined retreat below eight lanes of Los Angeles freeway overpass. Out back is Dan's **Tower of Pallets.** A plumb line hangs from the top of the twenty-five-foot structure to the center of its dark interior. "I did it when they were having A-bomb tests in Nevada," says Van Meter, seventy-nine. "I'd bring a radio in, and sure enough, four to five minutes after the explosion, it'd start rocking back and forth."

Jailed by Chief Justice-to-be Earl Warren during World War II as a "dirty America Firster" subversive, Dan believes that Warren is responsible for the sad state of Constitutional jurisprudence. "George Washington worked for my family as a surveyor. Earl Warren's father was a mulatto."

One of the Seven Wonders of The New Roadside America

HOUSE ON THE ROCK

—SPRING GREEN, WI

Alex Jordan, Jr., wanted to show Frank Lloyd Wright a thing or two about architecture. The lesson started years ago.

Jordan's dad, a budding architect, had been dismissed at Wright's Taliesin home, near Spring Green, with the declaration, "I wouldn't hire you to design a cheese crate or a chicken coop." Soon after, the senior Jordan chose a pinnacle rock south of Taliesin to build a parody of Wright's fancy-pants architecture, the **House on the Rock.**

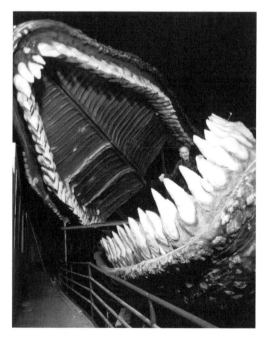

Alex Jordan, Jr., plays peek-a-boo in the mouth of a 200-foot-long sea monster. It was his final creation.

*T*he House on the Rock's Infinity Room was originally designed to be all glass, but the Wisconsin Building Commission demanded a wood floor.

HoR opened to the public in 1961. Today, it is only a small portion of the magical collection that spits in the dead eye of Mr. Big Deal Architect. When Alex Jordan, Jr., took over the project from his dad in the 1940s, he never dreamed where it would end; but with a half million visitors a year at $14 a head, it probably won't end anytime soon.

Big pseudo-oriental serpent planters greet you at the entrance and line the drive. Fake palm fronds lend shade to areas around the house. At the ticket window, cautious old people ask, "How many rest stops again?" The tour is self-guided, rumored to take four hours, and not air-conditioned. No amount of mall-walking prepares you for the strenuous, humid HoR tour.

The house itself is multitiered, a low-ceilinged, claustrophobic shamble through darkened dens and hallways lit by Tiffany lamps. An automated band plays *Bolero*, the first of some thirty-five music machines on the route. There's carpeting on everything, oriental art, low ceilings, and big fireplaces—was this place designed to be the ultimate bachelor's love nest?

Climb to the top of the house. Waddling camcorderists clog the many choke points on landings and corners. Children are getting antsy; older people stand in the darkness and wheeze. The music machines in the house play incessant make-out music: "Harbor

Lights," Liszt's Hungarian Rhapsodies, and "Love Theme from *The Godfather*."

Once you get out of the house the fun really begins, as you enter a series of eight interconnected buildings that house Jordan's startling collection.

The Streets of Yesterday building is an indoor re-creation of some murky Victorian era. Here, coin-operated music machines abound. Robotic fingers and invisible lips start at the drop of a token. We wonder—Are those magnificent instruments really being played, or is this a tape?

Next is a new section, Heritage of the Sea. This three-level blimp-hangar-of-a-room is dominated by a 200-foot-long sea monster battling a giant squid. Ship replicas and other flotsam line the ramp that climbs to the top of the chamber. People grip the railing, fixing their sights on the exit, far above. The next room has a display of Santa Claus items. And there's a rest area! Old people buttonhole employees and ask over and over, "When is the next stop?" Then they start trying to get out. "When is the next exit?"

Jordan's creations rivet visitors. "It must've cost him a million dollars." "No, no, he was a genius, an eccentric genius." "And they keep saying he was a poor man." "Well, he never had any in his pocket since he was always buying things."

The Carousel Room wakes you up with a cacophony of music. The 239 carousel beasts, collected from around the world, are half-human and demonic looking—a runaway circus from Hell. Hundreds of topless mannequin angels hang from the walls and rotate overhead. The room contains 182 chandeliers. Exit via an open dragon mouth, and walk down its red shag-carpeted throat. More music machines suck tokens from the surviving oldsters, giving them an excuse to stop.

Next is the Organ Room, crisscrossed by catwalks and affording all possible camcorder angles of the huge theater organs, giant copper vats, and an immense red glass chandelier. After this, another exit point/grill/gift store/arts village store, with another hour advertised ahead of you. People may have been here for days. Some are dizzy. "Haven't we seen this before?" "Your grandma's gotta sit down."

We stagger to the Cannon Room. Camcorders have exhausted their batteries. Too bad, because this complex is dominated by the world's largest cannon, a weapon so absurdly large that the room

Winged nymphets float above the Carousel Room for dad's perusal.

had to be constructed around it. The Doll Room and Circus Room are a weary blur; we finally hobble to the welcoming glow of the gift shop.

A recent addition is the Alex Jordan Experience Tour II across the road, which is a look at the old HoR workshop and the genius of Alex Jordan. Despite the globe-trotting aura of the collection, Jordan (who died in 1989) hated to travel, and never left the country. He liked the coziness of the House on the Rock. It *had* to be a bachelor's make-out pad.

Fantasy Worlds

The world of Mother Goose and the rest of the Fairy Tale Kingdom is an odd and bloody one. Mice get their tails hacked off, grandmothers are eaten by wolves. This mayhem is apparent when you visit a fantasy or a storybook land, where the climactic moment from each tale is re-created, larger than life.

You have to wonder about the intentions of some of the builders of these attractions as well. Are they doing it out of a love for children, or is it a gingerbread house–style ruse to get kids into their clutches, so they can scare the bejesus out of them?

Take **The Enchanted Forest** in Turner, OR, for instance. Walk inside a witch's opened mouth and crawl around inside her head. You can hear her maniacal laughter, and see out of her eyes. Neat! But tunnels in other parts of the park suddenly become claustrophobic nightmares, or endless mazes. The Mrs. Peter Peter Pumpkin Eater begs to be released from her orange Alcatraz, but it's no use. The children can't save her.

The walk-through witch's head at The Enchanted Forest, Turner, OR.

Scariest are those mixing the fantasy horror of Mother Goose with the real horror of modern life. Our two favorites in this regard are **Fairy Tale Forest** in Oak Ridge, NJ, and **Fairyland,** in Oakland, CA.

Fairy Tale Forest is the closest such attraction to Manhattan, and children of the wretched refuse yearning to breath free compete with you for space in front of Humpty Dumpty. It's in a real forest, making this decaying place of half-light and shadow all the more disturbing. At Rabbit School, stuffed dead bunnies in children's clothes rot behind wire mesh and glass that hasn't been cleaned in years. Dioramas are in musty little houses equipped with audio tape loops, which battered speakers render unintelligible.

Adults without children are not allowed at Oakland's Fairyland, and a cyclone fence topped with barbed wire protects the land of make-believe from unescorted grown-ups. It hasn't kept brightly colored wonderland figures from receiving cigarette burns, however.

Ellicott City, MD's **Enchanted Forest** features the delightful shenanigans of The Chicken Little Trio, furry animated endomorphs that play musical instruments. In between songs about sunshine and happiness they try to get the children in the audience to bug their parents into buying more tickets and refreshments. **Storyland,** in Glen, NH, has a fake fiberglass cow that gives a real white liquid when the boys and girls yank on its teats.

The Old Woman Who Lives in the Shoe sneaks over for a pull at the sword in the stone at Storybook Forest, Ligonier, PA.

The nicest fantasy park is **Storybook Forest** in Ligonier, PA. It is very clean and attractive, with the right mix of live fairy tale characters and fiberglass models. It does not dwell on the gruesome and its lake has no scum. It also gains points for largely staying away from petting zoo displays, with their emaciated "Bambis" and vicious "Goosey-goosey Ganders" that you would have to be nuts to pet. The land of make-believe is macabre, but it should not be dangerous.

"Look On My Shoe, Ye Mighty, And Despair." **The Shoe House** of Hellam, PA, was built in 1947 by "Shoe Wizard" Colonel Haines for advertising purposes. He walked up to an architect, handed him an old shoe, and said, "Build me a house like this." Haines owned fifty shoe stores, was a millionaire and an honorary Indian chief, and knew the value of self-promotion. He would stand up at baseball games and offer $20 to anybody who knew who he was. Today, the flamboyant Haines is long gone, and the house, cramped and aging, is for sale.

Rock City

—Lookout Mountain, GA

Garnet Carter invented miniature golf. This would be enough for most people. Instead, in 1932, he and his wife decided to risk all and open Frieda's Rock City Gardens to the public. It paid off. By 1940, **Rock City** was a roadside institution. Its inviting slogan, "See Rock City," was painted on barns and birdhouses throughout the Southeast. It still beckons today.

Everything in Rock City is conveniently located along its narrow "Enchanted Flagstone Trail" and there's only one way you can go—forward. At first, Rock City may bore you. A rock. A tree. Another rock. The trail winds its way through grottoes and glens while it crosses and recrosses itself at varying elevations. This enables you to drop things on other tourists.

Finally, you reach the entrance to Fairyland Caverns. This is where it gets good.

Fairyland Caverns is a most magnificent showplace of ultraviolet sculpture. Demonically grinning and glowing elves perched on simulated rock shelves greet you as you descend a long series of underground rooms.

The walls, floors, and ceilings are completely covered with fake crystals, stalagmites and stalactites, all painstakingly glued in place.

In little manufactured grottoes are a succession of hand-painted dolls depicting children's fables. Overhead float fluorescent Barbie Dolls wearing wings and glowing tutus, while "Dance of the Sugar Plum Fairies" echoes faintly over the speaker system. Dolls and models look as if Rock City put distorted old people's heads on healthy children's bodies. Giant eyes. Bloated lips. Exaggerated lines and creases on every face and, of course, all are aglow in the "groovy" colors only blacklight can produce.

Fairyland Caverns climaxes at Mother Goose Village, inside a dark room the size of a small auditorium. It stretches before you into the darkness—an alien ultraviolet landscape of dozens of intermingled nursery rhymes, topped by a ten-foot-tall castle. Families shuffle like zombies around the village, barely illuminated by the glowing dioramas. No children cry. All are in awe. Hushed voices of parents and children mingle with unrecognizable music echoing from above. There's Jack Spratt. And Little Bo Peep. And a dish running away with a spoon. Who needs drugs? Life doesn't get any freakier than Mother Goose Village.

And then, you're out in the sunlight. Back in the real world. A giant, animatronic elf named Rocky, the Rock City mascot, nods reassuringly. Out the front gate, back in your car, driving down Lookout Mountain toward Chattanooga you wonder, "Where *was* I? What *was* that?"

Rock City, brother. See it.

Children drugged with PhenoBarbiedoll sleep it off in Rock City's incredible Fairyland Caverns.

Wade's Page

Wade Petrilak is *Roadside America*'s #1 fan! He made it his mission to visit every one of the more than 600 sites mentioned in our first edition.

We were always excited to get another postcard from Wade. To be sure, we were taken to task on more than one occasion, as Wade would find an error in our index, or a closed attraction. He developed his own numbering system for the attractions, and after his name he would always sign the number he had visited to that point.

Wade's breakthrough came when he located the misplaced Fountain of Youth in Delaware. We couldn't find it for *RA* #1, but Wade did.

We dedicate this page to Wade Petrilak. Below are excerpts from recent letters. He's #1!

9/6/88—Love *Roadside America!* But I CANNOT find Wescoat's Corner, Delaware [elusive home of the Fountain of Youth] and no one I've asked in Delaware knows where it is, either. I'd appreciate it if you could give me any kind of help to locate it.

Undated—I've located (but not actually *visited*, natch) all the rocks on page 125, except Eagle Rock in AZ. But here's a thought: Could Eagle Rock be "Eagle Mesa" in Monument Valley, just across the line in UTAH?

8/30/89—If I could only find Wescoat's Corner, life would be perfect.

1/9/90—[hand-made postcard featuring photo of Wade at the Fountain of Youth] The Fountain of Youth, Lewes, Delaware. Discovered by Wade Petrilak in September, 1989, it eluded the authors of *Roadside America* completely. I'd hoped that I would have heard from you by now.

6/12/90—Since you are obviously uninterested in correspondence with arguably your most faithful disciple, this will be the last time I write. I have found over 135 targets in *Roadside America* that are NOT in the index. I am now at work on a complete index, to make the *RA* searches of myself and others much easier. Goodbye. Thanks for nothing.

9/1/90—[after hearing that we were all very sick] Get well soon. Meanwhile, I'm laboring mightily to reach my 100th *RA* target. Jack's *American Quest* is funny, but too shallow.

12/30/90—[after receiving our Christmas card proclaiming him #1 fan] God bless you, every one! I've been telling people for years that I was the #1 *RA* fan and now I've got proof! P.S. Where the hell in New York is Alligator Rock?

1/5/91—No luck locating the 5-legged dog along the TN/GA border. Rumor has it that Rover + 1 no longer exists.

8/9/91—My sources inform me that we can look forward to an updated *RA* next year. I will begin compiling a list of the many textual and factual errors in Vol I to make Vol II more accurate.

Wade Petrilak at The Fountain of Youth, Andover, DE.

Santa's Villages

Santa's Villages are an incongruous part of a summer vacation, that's for sure. A stint on St. Nick's lap is a hairy, sweaty thrill on a hot July day.

Many Santa Lands have interesting, magical histories. **North Pole, NY,** was born in the '40s, when a clairvoyant eight-year-old girl described her dreams of Santa's home to a Walt Disney artist. He translated them into blueprints, and soon her dream was reality. Fortunately, her dream was mundane enough that the place looks exactly like every other Santa Land. You will not see any Salvador Dali-esque reindeers diving upside-down into pools of burning Christmas tree lights here. **North Pole, CO,** was a second Santa home based on that same dream.

Both places display an actual frozen North Pole, which never melts. Overly talkative youngsters can be dared into licking them. In New York, spiritual and material sides of the holiday coexist. Take in the inspiring Nativity Pageant and the nutty Christmas Capers show the same afternoon! Colorado's Pole is watched over by a mesmerized waving Santa on top of a three-story peppermint stick slide.

Santa at Colorado's North Pole.

Santa Claus, IN, was in business even before the invention of the car and paid vacations. In 1850, a group of town elders spent months trying to come up with a name for their town. On Christmas Eve, they heard a young child yell, "It's Santa Claus," and they decided that indeed it was. The entrance to this quiet town is marked by a giant Santa statue surrounded by corn fields. The streets have names like Three Kings and Noel.

Unfortunately the town's Santa's Village attraction is now part of a bigger theme park, Holiday World. Christmas shares billing with "4th of July" and "Halloween." Even the town's new housing developments seem intent on diluting the mystique of a town named Santa Claus, building new streets named Good Friday Boulevard and Easter Circle. Santa deserves better.

Santa Claus, CA, was named because the original owner was amused by all of the Santa Barbara's, Santa Maria's, and Santa So-on's in California. It is on the coast, near Carpenteria, and is more a roadside strip of buildings than a village. A large Santa defines the horizon, the vast Pacific behind him. While the kids are shopping for gifts or the famous quarter-pound date shakes, drop in for a cool one at The Reindeer Room, or pick up some "Vixen's Patty" burgers for the road.

At **Santa's Land** in Cherokee, NC, kids get to see Santa and Indians in one place! Climb on giant rabbits and kangaroos. An oversized tomato plays guitar in a garden. There is a genuine moonshine still on the premises. And the nativity scene is just minutes from The Haunted Tree!

"How come there are so many gravestones? I thought you said there was only one Santa Claus." **Santa Claus Cemetery,** *Santa Claus, IN.*

Dopey Utopias

Cy Teed was visited by the Mother of the Universe in the 1870s. She told him that the earth was hollow, and that mankind lived inside it. Teed became Koresh, and while converting the world to a new way of life, he found a natural magnetic center on which to build his New Jerusalem at Estero, FL, just south of Fort Myers.

Some 200 followers arrived from the north and, with a nervous industry born of group celibacy, created a successful community. Large streets and buildings were built, all in harmony with first principles.

After Koresh died, the community started to disband. Just when all looked lost, a new batch of hollow earthers escaping Hitler's Germany moved in, and rebuilt the place. New Jerusalem became **Koreshan State Park** in the 1960s. Florida keeps the site in good order, and relics and charts explaining it all are on display.

Soul City, NC, was built with tax dollars in the early '70s when Floyd McKissick, a local civil rights lawyer, received lots of federal money to create a model black community that would provide decent housing and employment. It opened in 1974, and quickly became a mismanaged nightmare.

Only thirty houses were built, and less than 125 people moved in. In 1979, after pumping in $52 million, or half-a-mil per resident, HUD finally pulled the plug on McKissick's boondoggle.

All this helps you appreciate what's left of Soul City, which is very little. Some houses still remain, but Soul City consists mainly of miles of paved, still-virgin streets winding nowhere. Liberation Road and Freedom Drive lead past dozens of useless fire hydrants and street lamps until they suddenly end. Soul City is a near-ghost town that you might as well visit—*you paid for it.*

Paolo Soleri's lifetime project is the construction of **Arcosanti,** in Mayer, AZ, habitat of the future. Arcosanti is the prototype "arcology." Arcologies are designed to hold hundreds of thousands of people in densely packed city units that look like big space stations.

Yet spacemen don't inhabit Arcosanti, hippies do. They sell their handcrafted bells and wind chimes to busloads of bewildered retirees shipped up I-17 from Phoenix. Visitors tour the grounds, eat at the organic Cafe and Bakery, use the rest rooms, and get back on the bus.

Arcosanti looks like a peacenik wonderland, baby-block constructions with moon-shaped windows, glass domes, flags. It also has that unfinished, "hippie" look and smell. It's hard to imagine natty futurepeople living here. One day, Arcosanti will house 5,000, but today only about fifty call it home. The place has been under construction since 1965, and with little momentum is only 3 percent complete. This means they'll be cutting the ribbon in the year 2525.

The latest utopia opening its doors for tourism is **Biosphere II,** also in Arizona, near Oracle. Fifty million dollars have been spent by the likes of modern billionaire free-thinker Edward Bass on this hopefully self-contained ecosystem in which four men and four women will be living for the next two years. Only sunlight and information are allowed into the biosphere. Everything else must be produced inside this three-acre steel and glass terrarium.

Tourists are invited to buy tickets and observe the experiment, but as often as the guides divert your attention to the pipes and recycling systems, the question everyone wants answered is "Who is doinking who?" Which is perhaps why the Mother of the Universe told Cy Teed to keep it celibate.

Meccas

*These two country cuties in **Eureka Springs**, AR,
are both under six feet tall.*

*W*hat is a mecca?

A mecca is a "vacation destination." A place that has it all. Fun for the whole family. Fun for all ages. From six to sixty. Not just a plaque and a post office. Not just a marker and a mini-mart. Meccas provide everything: food and rest, excitement and relaxation, film and souvenirs.

Thousands of people walk ahead of and behind us from the Dinosaur Park to the Bible Land to the Mother Goose Forest. Time stands still. All is as it should be.

A mecca's pilotfish, the **Ripley's Believe It or Nots, Guinness World Record Museums, Wax Worlds,** and **Waterslides** gently scrape the last scraps of green from our billfold. All meccas share certain bony protuberances, Old Tyme Photo Booths and go-karts, funnel cakes and fudge, arcades and Goofy Golfs. Yet each mecca is different, individual as children's fingerprints on your sunglasses.

A typical summer afternoon in GATLINBURG, TN, finds traffic at a standstill. Its one main street is overwhelmed by guests. In addition to all the standard accoutrements, Gatlinburg features **Christus Gardens,** with a Jesus-head sculpture whose eyes follow you, the **Mysterious Mansion** haunted house, and an observation tower and ski lift.

*SOMETIMES A POSTCARD IS WORTH THE TRIP: Harrisburg, PA, may not be anyone's first choice as a tourist destination, but we think a stop at **The Inn at Blue Mountain** is justified.*

At night, Gatlinburg becomes the biggest cruise strip east of Reno. Porkettes in "Button Your Fly" sweatshirts roam the sidewalks. Legions of old people creak back and forth in the countless rocking chairs that crowd the porches of downtown motels.

Adjacent PIGEON FORGE, TN, is further out of the mountains, and has wider roads and more breathing space than Gatlinburg—more room for tourist attractions. It is Water Slide Central, but also offers the **Flyaway Freefall** simulated sky dive experience, **Hee Haw Village,** and a stray **World's Largest Cuckoo Clock** to amuse and delight. But don't say we didn't warn you about **Dollywood,** Dolly Parton's rancid theme park.

CHEROKEE, NC, a throwback to the vacationscape of your parents' time, is only hours from Gatlinburg. Sheltered by the Smoky Mountains on all sides, and part of an Indian reservation, Cherokee is the land that progress forgot, and as such is an entertainment feast. Two long rows of gift shops stretch to the vanishing point. But save some wampum to buy a photo of you next to a real Indian! An Indian hangs out at every

"Hey, mister, have you seen Geronimo's head flying around?" this Cherokee bear seems to be saying.

...near as I can tell, we're somewhere behind Mt. Rushmore

Variations of this popular Black Hills graphic are available on everything from sweatshirts to golf towels. For your information, it's (left to right) Lincoln, T. Roosevelt, Jefferson, and Washington.

The double-decker outhouse at Booger Hollow, AR, is familiar to all those who stop in for a Boogerburger.

corner in Cherokee, in full costume and headdress. Chief Henry, **"The World's Most Photographed Indian,"** is best, head and shoulders above the generic Geronimos.

The World's Largest Bingo Game is here, as are bear pits! Baby bears are in display pits downtown, and **Saunooke's Bear Land** has big grown-up bears in pits outside. Visitors hurl stale pieces of bread into them, hollering "Hey, bear!" at the dour captives.

The BLACK HILLS of South Dakota are not really black, they just look that way from a distance. But visitors don't come to look at black hills anyway, they want to see **Mount Rushmore**, which is not always possible. Many a tourist dad has been known to blow his top after driving umpteen miles from the motel only to find that thick fog has obscured those giant faces, goddammit.

In the latest skirmish between presidents and Indians, on a nearby mountain, a still-under-construction **giant sculpture of Chief Crazy Horse** grows. When complete, it will be bigger than the Sphinx! The head of his horse alone will be bigger than all of the white men on Rushmore. Completion due date? The middle of the twenty-third century.

EUREKA SPRINGS, AR, and BRANSON, MO, are two Ozark hot spots that pull them in from all over. The Eureka Springs area contains a geographically diffuse group of attractions, with **Christ of the Ozarks** here, **Dogpatch, USA** there, and **Dinosaur World** way over yonder. If you want to grab a Boogerburger at Booger Hollow, it's an hour's drive from Dogpatch.

Branson concentrates its punch along one long strip. Branson is the headquarters for Ozark Country Music, and live music theaters are the main attractions here. An **Ozark Music Hall of Fame** displays the clothes of David Struble ("The Singing Dentist") and a Baldknobber Dobro. Observing these exhibits, one gains a greater understanding of the relativity of fame. But change is coming, with Big Names settling in the area. Roy Clark, Johnny Cash, and Mel Tillis are elbowing in, threatening Dr. Struble and the rest of the anonymous hillbilly jamboreers.

For our money, the WISCONSIN DELLS area is one of the best pure tourism plays there is. During the day, the humid white sky wraps around you like a reassuring blanket, and a walk down Highway 12 gets you a headful of memories in a single afternoon. **The Wonder Spot, Biblical Gardens, Storybook Gardens,** and **Tommy Bartlett's "Ski Trek" Waterski Show** are what it's all about. We also revel in the nearby climate-controlled pari-mutuel dog track, **Wisconsin Dells Greyhound Park.**

But stay clear of the awful All U Can Eat **Paul Bunyan Cook Shanty** restaurant. All U Can Eat—bread, water, pot roast, chicken, and beans! Busboys leave untouched pot roast next to the tip. Waitresses take it back to the kitchen. Put a note between your roast coasters: Warn the next people. Free hot tea or coffee, but iced tea is extra!

Photo Opportunities

The value of photo opportunities rarely escapes even the most brick-headed shutterbug or camcorderist. Posing situations can be found in many places—a chance to appear with a hoop-skirted **Cypress Gardens** southern belle before she passes out from the heat, for example. There are plywood facades with head holes, life-sized celebrity cutouts, even electric chairs and gallows.

Kodak sponsors some of these areas, and usually indicates where the photographer should stand. We consider these a vital facet of any tourism experience, especially those that allow for no freedom on the part of the photographer.

Eventually, everyone will possess exactly the same vacation shots and will subject all their friends to viewings, until a collective photo unconscious develops—a primal memory of parrots on people's shoulders and rocket sleds with waving old ladies.

Dinosaur World in Beaver, AR.

Gift Shops with Something Extra

Sitting by themselves in the middle of nowhere, daring you not to stop, are the gift shops with something extra. Those deserving special mention include the two **Little Americas** (the "World's Largest Gas Stations") that straddle Wyoming; **White's City, NM,** and its blistering billboard barrage; and **Fort Cody** in North Platte, NE. The names **Fun-Land** in Panama City Beach, FL, and **Boomland,** in Charleston, MO, say it all.

Where I-40 crosses the New Mexico–Arizona border, the **Tomahawk Indian Store** offers a fifty-foot teepee, and will ice your jugs free. And the finest collection of shrunken heads outside of Ecuador is on display at **Ye Olde Curiosity Shoppe** in Seattle, WA.

Sylvia (left) & Sylvester Mummy at Ye Olde Curiosity Shoppe in Seattle, WA.

America's Most Rewarding Wishing Well, **Tomahawk Trading Post,** White's City, NM. If you get your coin through the hole in the saucer, you stand a good chance of hitting a rattlesnake on the head.

*GET GAS: The World's Biggest Badger, fifty feet tall, fearsome and multiclawed, wants you to gas up at his big hollow log in Birnamwood, WI. If you hit "E" further west, attendants at **The World's Largest Covered Wagon,** in Milford, NE, will gladly fill your tank.*

One of the Seven Wonders of The New Roadside America

WALL DRUG

—WALL, SD

The name **Wall Drug** strikes a familiar note of horror with anyone who's driven the interstate system west of the Appalachians or east of the Rockies with a back seat full of screaming children. "Mommy, Daddy, lookit the funny signs! Can we stop huh please huh can we just for a minute puh-leeeeeze?" Those who have been denied this pleasure may still have heard of Wall Drug if they've visited the North or South Pole, for even at the ends of the earth, Wall Drug has posted signs advertising the mileage to itself.

Wall Drug is much more than a drug store. It's a sprawling tourist mall that rakes in millions of dollars every year, which is not bad for a place that sits in the middle of the South Dakota prairie. It occupies the majority of downtown Wall, which used to be known by locals as "the geographical center of nowhere." That was before Ted Hustead came along. Ted was a Nebraska native who moved to Wall and opened a tiny drug store in 1931. Five years later, it was still a tiny drug store. Dorothy, Ted's wife, thought that the travelers driving past their store must be thirsty, and suggested that Ted put up a sign outside of town advertising free ice water at Wall Drug. Ted thought it was a silly idea, but he was desperate

*T*ed and Bill Hustead pose with the ice water that made Wall Drug a Wonder.

Don't miss Wall Drug's Mount Rushmore photo opportunity.

and put up the sign. By the time he got back, thirsty tourists were already lining up for their free ice water. They've been stopping ever since.

Over a million people currently visit Wall Drug every year. These adventurers are lured by the tantalizing Wall Drug billboards, thousands of which once beckoned from roadsides coast to coast and from Canada to Mexico. Once Ted got it into his head that signs could draw customers, he went billboard crazy. Painted wood signs proclaiming "Have You Dug Wall Drug?" and "Wall I'll Be Drugged" appeared in every state in the union.

Those glory days ended in 1965, when Lady Bird Johnson bulldozed her nationwide Highway Beautification Act through Congress. Fortunately, Bill Hustead, Ted's son, got himself appointed Chairman of the South Dakota Transportation Commission and waged a personal battle to protect his signage. The results are mixed; today, you'll still see Wall Drug signs along South Dakota's highways and in numerous countries overseas, but almost nowhere else.

Wall Drug is now managed by Bill Hustead, and under his guiding hand it has grown considerably. "I was embarrassed when I was in high school," Bill remembers. "All those signs, and when you arrived it was just an ordinary small town store. It was my crusade to develop the store into something special." He has. Wall Drug still has a tiny pharmacy (the only one within 500 square miles) but its peripheral amusements have taken over and now extend across several blocks.

Wall Drug's famous free ice-water well now pumps several thousand gallons of water cooled by one and one-half tons of man-made ice on a good summer's day. In its "backyard" stands a giant, fiberglass jackalope, a six-foot-tall rabbit on wheels, a replica Indian village that comes to life (sort of) at the drop of a quarter, and a miniature Mount Rushmore photo opportunity. A sign next to the miniature cautions, "Please do not climb on faces."

Many animatic creations inhabit the nooks and crannies that surround the shops inside Wall Drug. Gyrating bears overhang a doorway leading to a boutique that sells snake ashtrays and stuffed jackalopes. Above the bears, a lively Spirit of '76 trio comes to life every fifteen minutes. The famous Wall Drug Chuck Wagon Four—a band of cowboys the Husteads smuggled out of a Mays Department Store window in Denver—performs regularly. It's just down the hall from the Traveller's Chapel, a replica of an 1850 Trappist monastery in Dubuque, IA, which is right next to Wall Drug's immense postcard store, which specializes in Wall Drug postcards too numerous to count. Across from this stands the Pharmacy Museum—a replica of the original Wall Drug—displaying the machine Bill Hustead's grandfather used to make suppositories. And across from this is an indoor cafeteria, built around the first tree planted in Wall, which continues to grow through a hole in the roof.

The line between success and failure on the prairie is thin, but the Husteads aren't worried that anyone will shut down their drug store any time soon. Over fifty Minuteman missile silos surround Wall, making Wall Drug the best-defended tourist attraction in the world. Bill Hustead's shrewd policy of giving all missile crews (and newlyweds) free coffee and donuts guarantees that it will remain that way.

Eating and Sleeping

The solace offered by Motel 6s and McDonalds is a two-edged sword. They offer safety in the wilderness, welcome sights like the old cavalry forts.

But their commendable devotion to uniformity means you know what you're missing if you pass their exit. Who knows what you miss when you pass the café where they throw rolls at you (**Lambert's Cafe,** Sikeston, MO). The steak house where they'll cut off your tie and pin it to the ceiling (**Pinnacle Peak,** Scottsdale, AZ). The motel where you watch drive-in movies from your bed, the speaker in your room (**Best Western Movie Manor,** Monte Vista, CO). The hotel where you can fish from your window (**The Edgewater Inn,** Seattle, WA).

What do tourists like to sleep in most? Cabooses and teepees, if popularity is any indication. Don Delinger started the caboose trend with his **Red Caboose Motel** in Strasburg, PA. In addition to sleeping in one, you can eat in a rail car that shakes and moves during your meal. **The Caboose Motel** in Dunsmuir, CA, **The Union Pacific Caboose Park** in Waterloo, NE, and the **Goodrich Motel** in Avoca, NY, all offer similar accommodations.

Noah's Ark Restaurant *in St. Charles, MO. Originally built as a steamship, it became an ark when its owners moved its vandal-prone fiberglass animals to the roof.*

If you don't trust your papoose in a caboose, three **Wigwam Villages** are open to serve your needs. Individual teepee units ring a larger structure serving as the office. The one in Cave City, KY, is in good shape, the one in Rialto, CA (its sign reads "Water Beds," and "Do It in a Wigwam"), is not. Happily, the one in Holbrook, AZ, once closed and abandoned, has been renovated and reopened. We think you should stop.

The Wigwam Village in Cave City, KY, has been in business for over fifty years. If you make a "reservation" joke when you call, you will not be the first.

Buckhorn Baths, *Mesa, AZ: This classic roadside motel is unaffected by Mesa's modern sprawl. Natural hot springs bubble out back, rooms are individual bungalows, walkway walls are made with Indian grinding stones, and a wildlife museum in the lobby features a stuffed Javelina Wall. Alice Sliger and her late husband started it in the '30s. Alice still has the welcome mat out.*

Medieval Times

—Kissimmee, FL

How would you like to spend an evening in a large indoor stadium watching knights joust to the death while you chomp chicken and ribs? Zounds!

Medieval Times re-creates a typical evening repast at an "eleventh-century" Spanish castle. MT has been franchised in places like Secaucus, NJ, and Buena Park, CA, but the theater in Kissimmee is the original. "Fifty wenches and servants prepare the lavish four-course banquet, which is served concurrently with the big event," they explain if you call.

"Hi! My name is Lynn, and I'll be your wench for the evening," a young lady announces, serving whole chickens that you rip apart by hand (no utensils in the eleventh century). Cocktail and camera wenches assist, tending to your various needs.

A thousand diners wearing Burger King-esque crowns are seated around the dirt-and-sawdust-floored arena, where the jousting and sword fights take place. The crowns are color coded to match the colors of six competing knights. After a couple of glasses of beer or sangria, the rabble gets in a bloody mood. "Kill him! Go Green . . . Kill that Blue Knight!" screams one section. "Black and White! Black and White!" yells another, stamping their feet rhythmically.

Prerecorded fanfares and marches blast over the PA system as the pageantry progresses. Sword-fight choreography may remind you of a professional wrestling match, but overall the fantasy works. As host Lord Raposom del Fife says at the close of the festivities, "Got bless Ameh-reeca!"

"Kill! Kill! Kill!" chant Disney World families at Medieval Times Dinner Theater in Kissimmee, FL.

Casa Bonita

—Denver, CO

Casa Bonita's strolling mariachi band will perform for just about anybody.

The weirdest thing about **Casa Bonita** is that it does much better what so many tourist attractions attempt to do, but it's not a tourist attraction. Casa Bonita is a Mexican restaurant. In a shopping center. In Denver.

Casa Bonita has three floors and seats 2,000. Everyone over two years old must purchase a dinner before entering, but the all-you-can-eat Mexican platter is cheap. Dress is highly casual.

When you first enter Casa Bonita you cross a small bridge that affords you a view of a twenty-five-foot waterfall and sea-monster-infested lagoon, into which plunge Casa Bonita's cliff divers, as well as the losers in the wild West gun battles that are staged on rock cliffs atop the falls. Would you like a cliffside table? No trouble at all!

While you're waiting for your meal, why not stroll over to the old-tyme photo booth and suit up in authentic Mexican garb? Watch out for the strolling mariachi band, and don't trip over the little robot with the pencil-thin moustache that scoots around saying, "Buenos dias!" and "Caramba!" Send the kids off to Black Bart's hideout-funhouse, or the puppet theater that projects Three Stooges shorts between shows. Say, aren't those jugglers and monkeys in costume over by the Casa Bonita jail?

Is your food ready yet? Maybe you should explore the rooftop garden; it's not really on the roof, but it does look out over authentic Mexican tiles. Or how about the Gold and Silver Mines? The Mayan Room? The Governor's Mansion? Here comes your entree, but a furry orange creature blocks the waiter's path!

FantaSuite Motel

—Muscatine, IA

The Royale Hospitality Group hit upon a great idea. Take generic motel properties in out-of-the-way locations, redo some of the rooms into whimsical theme chambers, and stand out from the crowd. Currently, eight **FantaSuite** Motels exist in six states, and we recommend a visit.

The Canterbury Inn Royale in Muscatine is typical of a FantaSuite property. There are twenty-one different FantaSuites, but the rest of the motel's rooms are standard. In the Sherwood Forest Suite, the bed is nestled in the branches of a concrete tree. The Riverboat Gambler Suite has working one-armed bandits, with crushed velour and a red color scheme. Northern Lights has two rooms, the bed is inside an igloo, with the aurora borealis painted on the wall opposite the entrance. In Arabian Nights, camels are painted on the walls, and the bed exists in a tent-like atmosphere. Each FantaSuite has its own private whirlpool.

All FantaSuite properties have rooms unique to that location. Mus-

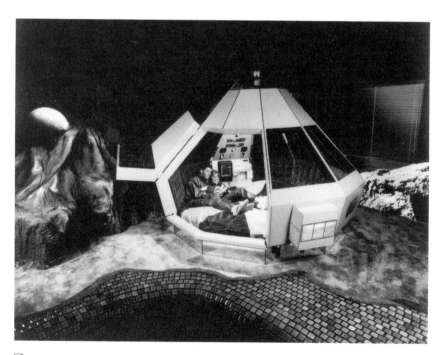

The Space Odyssey Room. Champagne is left in the rooms, and as a result FantaSuites are not rented to minors. Many a prom night reservation gets bumped.

catine's is the Henry the VIII Suite, with numerous animal heads on the walls. The flagship **Don Q Inn** in Dodgeville, WI, has a medieval room complete with manacles.

But don't let manacles give you the wrong impression. FantaSuites go out of their way to present an image of wholesome, safe excitement. Most of the customers are local couples out for a honeymoon, anniversary, or night on the North Pole. Some come in once a month trying a new room each time, or stay several nights and move to a new room each night.

"Our motels are quieter than you might expect," said Muscatine night manager John Carlson. "Couples smile at you when they check in, disappear into their rooms, and are gone the next day. We're not adventuresome. We're just a little livelier than their lives."

The Madonna Inn
—San Luis Obispo, CA

This is the best place to spend a vacation night in America. Located in San Luis Obispo, CA, **The Madonna Inn** represents the best things about a democracy. First, it offers up an incredible choice of hundreds of radically different rooms. Second, everyone is welcome, and you see them all, from cowboy to corporate, pulling up to this pinkish castle set off on a hillside. Third, its fun is in its excesses. Pink is everywhere—trash cans, pay phones, and Coke machines are all pink. The restaurant serves pink toast.

How different can two rooms be in the same hotel? The Madonna Inn's gift shop has postcards of each room. Each has its own name (painted on the door), color scheme, and meaning. There is, for example, the Safari Room, with jungle-green walls and carpet, and upholstery made of zebra, leopard, and tiger skin. Popular honeymoon spots include the Love Nest and Just Heaven suites.

Golden cherubs float from the walls and ceiling of Cloud 9. The Pony Room is supposed to remind one of a barn, and the popular Caveman Room, with a stained-glass window of a Neanderthal, of a cavelike stone grotto. It connects, via a secret crawl-space tunnel, to the Daisy Mae Room.

There is liberal use of exposed rock as decorative material. The rooms are color coded. If you want a room that says lime green, electric blue, or neon pink, you'll get it.

Even if you can't stay overnight, we recommend a stop here, if only to go to their famous bathrooms. The men's room urinal at first looks like a mere tile floor with a drain. "Am I supposed to go here, on the floor?" you wonder. Since there is nowhere else that looks right in the room, certainly not in the clam-shell sinks, you finally guess you should. Miracle of miracles, your urine breaks a photoelectric beam, which activates a cascade of water from the rock wall in front of you. Wait till they hear about that at home!

Pushing the Envelope: Attraction of Tomorrow

Battletech, in Chicago's North Pier Mall, is the first in a wave of "virtual worlds," where the electronically addicted may spend the rest of their lives. It's a sci-fi battle simulator, using NASA technology to put players in control of thirty-foot-tall human-shaped tanks—"Battle Mechs"—on 100 miles of terrain. "The year is 3028. The Fourth Succession War has begun."

But you're not up against some smug, easily outwitted computer, like in most video games. Your enemies, other Mechs, are controlled by real humans.

The Battletech Center is a slick future environment a la *Aliens*. On the mall's floor below, the Baja Beach Club pulses to disco music, while upstairs pumped technonerds in XL T-shirts get psyched for their next deadly engagement.

"Lord Rat," one of the black-jumpsuited Tech staffers, gives us our mission briefing and assigns our Mechs Loki and Thor configurations. He inputs our battle names—"Merman" and "Geronimo." We'll be up against novices "Killer" and "Dog."

Our training film features pathetic bungler "Wilson" crashing his Mech into rocks while a tough female commander emasculates him via radio. A "Wilson" is what a "Herbert" was a generation ago. "He's *such* a Wilson," laughs a wizened Cyberpunk, watching.

Rows of combat pods are arrayed in a black-lit tactical chamber. After the film, each player is led to a different pod. The pod's lid is lowered. This is where "100 tons of walking, hulking armored destruction" is controlled.

The control pods have dual foot and hand controls, radio links, radar, and too many options to even notice, let alone use, during your first fifty missions. More advanced players, like the inscrutable "Hitman" or the merciless "Poet," have developed their own language, and battle each other in the dark using infrared.

Our match with Killer and Dog is a fast-paced ten minutes of drunk drive and cybernightmare. Enemies race past our view screen toward the hills. Things are exploding, the radio is crackling with incoherent shouts and commands. We fire missiles across the desert, accidentally blasting each other.

Merman's Loki destroys Dog's Thor at 1:25 on the mission clock . . . Killer shoots reconstituted teammate Dog . . . Someone is stuck on the rocks . . . Geronimo sends Dog up in flames at 5:05 . . . at 5:09, Geronimo crashes and destroys himself . . . Units overheat . . . Merman liquidates Killer's Weapons Pod . . . at 10:00, mission completed. Whew. Let's do that again!

Battletech, the nightmare world of the thirty-first century, available today in Chicago's North Pier Mall, just above the Baja Beach Club.

A Curator Alone

Max Nordeen's Wheels Museum

—Woodhull, IL

Without the ring of billboards in our nose, we wander off the beaten path into the farmland of Woodhull, IL. We pull up at the aluminum building with the big metal flywheel out front, and Max Nordeen strides over from his farmhouse. We are alone with him, and, though we don't know it yet, will be for the next several hours. Max Nordeen is a man of knowledge, a strong man who is determined to make his **Wheels Museum** work.

"I've been a collector all my life," says Max with humble pride. "I'm gonna give you the whole guided tour." We walk into the building, and Max shuts the door.

Last year, Max's admission revenues totaled $208. "People are so tight. I had no idea it would be like this." Even neighbors neglect his wonders. "They'll get in their cars, drive several hundred miles, and pay ten times as much money to see something half as good."

Max is an open fire hydrant of facts as he points out every odd collectible displayed in glass cases ringing the first half of the building. "That was sold at the Ringling Brothers circus as a souvenir years ago. That was Tom Thumb and his band of midgets playing, they're all dead now. I have one of the largest World's Fair collections in the world . . ."

We methodically move on to his spark plug collection and his gear shift knob collection. Max's fast patter is well rehearsed, but on whom? When you start drifting off, Max sounds a Klaxon horn. He is shocked, he says, that some would-be tourists see that he charges $2.50, and leave without staying. "How can people say it's not worth it if they haven't seen it?"

He points toward his naughty key chain collection. "You look through the peephole and you see naked ladies on the inside—those are all World War I souvenirs from Paris, France. And as you can see, some of these women are *completely nude*."

We see Sally Rand photos. "People came from hundreds of miles to watch Sally Rand dance nude . . . I had the privilege of seeing Sally dance twice . . . a very gorgeous-looking woman. If you don't believe me, take a look through this telescope . . . she was gorgeous."

On to war collectibles—a case of WW II regalia and Wehrmacht novelty items. "Hitler loved nudity . . . he had a lot of pictures of nude women. Oh yeah, Hitler loved nudity, a lot of people do. People won't admit it— I'll admit it . . . Here's a picture of Hitler when he was a baby—and that little baby cost the lives of *seven million German people!*"

The pride of Max's collection is what he believes to be the world's only surviving original announcement of John Deere's death. "The John Deere company didn't even know when the hundredth anniversary of his death was. I did. I called the TV news, and they came out to interview me. But nobody who watched it ever came by."

He holds up a big meat cleaver. We back away. "Later on, I'll show you one twice this size . . . I like things exceptionally big, and exceptionally small . . . I'm fascinated by little tiny women. Sally Rand was very petite, very petite."

We try to skip ahead, but Max pulls us back. "Hey! Come back! This next piece is real interesting."

Max's very rare and unusual items are saved for the last case. He holds up a giant petrified leech. "Look at it. Perfect. You can still tell what sex it is."

Max adds stuff weekly, despite the lack of tourist interest. He is well known at local flea markets and gun shows. "I use a hearse at auctions— it's handy to haul stuff in."

This ends the first half of the tour. A load of vintage cars is arrayed in the back half of the building. So that Max doesn't accuse us of giving it all away, see these for yourself.

See them you should. Max is a hero. He builds his museum because of his restless spirit, the spirit of roadside tourism. Sure it bugs him that no one visits, and that his edifying materials lay fallow like his fields. But he doesn't quit. It would be easy. Who would know? Who would care? Max would. Max does.

Is the Wheels Museum worth $2.50? At least. Maybe ten times as much. But it goes beyond that. When you visit Max, or Tom Gaskins, or The Nut Lady, or any of those welcoming purveyors of amazement and wonder, you vote "Yes" to the continuing lure of the road.

As Max says, "You're going to see some things in here you've never seen before in your whole life and you'll never see again—unless you come back."

Index

(Bold page number indicates photo)

Note to the reader: Those places only mentioned in the "Why Leave America" map (pp. 101–102), the "Rockside Rock Garden," (p. 153) and the "500 Places Not Mentioned In New Roadside America" map (p. 288) are not listed in the index.

(Photo credits continued from copyright page)

500 Places Not Mentioned in the New Roadside America

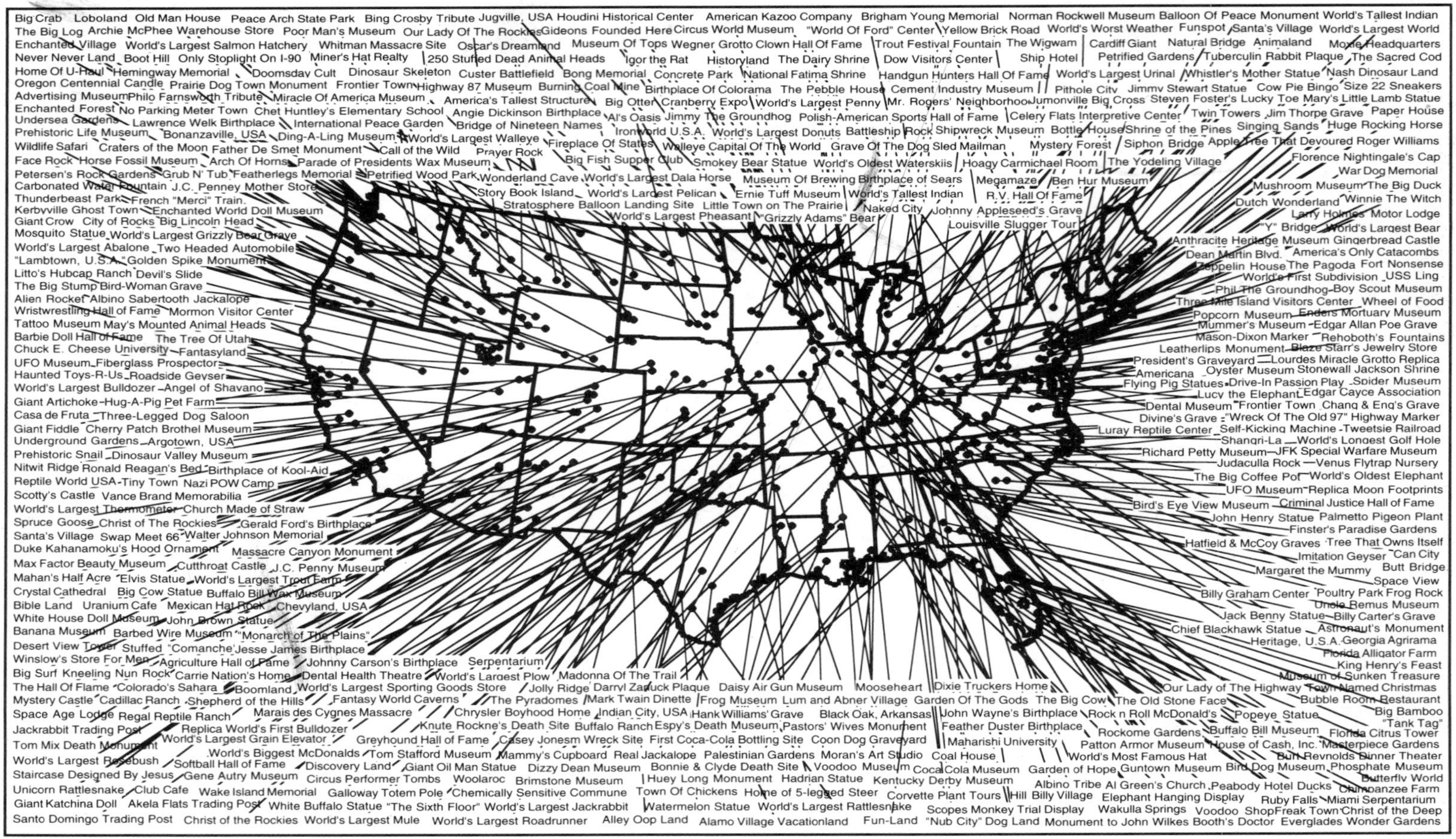